CW00831951

Microsoft®

ACCESS FOR WINDOWS® 95

Step by Step

Other titles in the Step by Step series:

For Microsoft Windows 95

(available in Fall 1995)

Microsoft Access/Visual Basic for Windows 95 Step by Step

Microsoft Excel for Windows 95 Step by Step

Microsoft Excel/Visual Basic for Windows 95 Step by Step

Microsoft Office 95 Integration Step by Step

Microsoft PowerPoint for Windows 95 Step by Step

Microsoft Project for Windows 95 Step by Step

Microsoft Visual Basic 4 for Windows 95 Step by Step

Microsoft Windows 95 Step by Step

Microsoft Word for Windows 95 Step by Step

Microsoft Works for Windows 95 Step by Step

More Microsoft Windows 95 Step by Step

Upgrading to Microsoft Windows 95 Step by Step

For Microsoft Windows 3.1

(available now)

Microsoft Access 2 for Windows Step by Step

Microsoft Excel 5 for Windows Step by Step

Microsoft Excel 5 Visual Basic for Applications Step by Step, for Windows

Microsoft Visual FoxPro 3 for Windows Step by Step

Microsoft Mail for Windows Step by Step, versions 3.0b and later

Microsoft Office for Windows Step by Step, version 4

Microsoft PowerPoint 4 for Windows Step by Step

Microsoft Project 4 for Windows Step by Step

Microsoft Word 6 for Windows Step by Step

Microsoft Works 3 for Windows Step by Step

Microsoft®

ACCESS FOR WINDOWS® 95

Step by Step

Microsoft Press

PUBLISHED BY
Microsoft Press
A Division of Microsoft Corporation
One Microsoft Way
Redmond, Washington 98052-6399

Copyright © 1995 by Catapult, Inc., and Microsoft Corporation

All rights reserved. No part of the contents of this book may be reproduced or transmitted in any form or by any means without the written permission of the publisher.

Library of Congress Cataloging-in-Publication Data
Microsoft Access for Windows 95 step by step / Catapult, Inc.
     p.   cm.
   Includes index.
   ISBN 1-55615-876-9
   1. Microsoft Access.   2. Database management.   3. Microsoft
Windows 95.   I. Catapult, Inc.
QA76.9.D3M557 1995
005.75'6 5--dc20   95-38722
                                                         CIP

Printed and bound in the United States of America.

1 2 3 4 5 6 7 8 9 QMQM 0 9 8 7 6 5

Distributed to the book trade in Canada by Macmillan of Canada, a division of Canada Publishing Corporation.

A CIP catalogue record for this book is available from the British Library.

Microsoft Press books are available through booksellers and distributors worldwide. For further information about international editions, contact your local Microsoft Corporation office. Or contact Microsoft Press International directly at fax (206) 936-7329.

Macintosh is a registered trademark of Apple Computer, Inc. Avery is a registered trademark of Avery Dennison Corporation. Paradox is a registered trademark of Ansa Software, a Borland Company. dBASE, dBASE III, and dBASE IV are registered trademarks of Borland International, Inc. 1-2-3 and Lotus are registered trademarks of Lotus Development Corporation. FoxPro, Microsoft, Microsoft Access, Microsoft Press, and MS-DOS are registered trademarks and Windows is a trademark of Microsoft Corporation. Btrieve and Xtrieve are registered trademarks of Novell, Inc.

Companies, names, and/or data used in screens and sample output are fictitious unless otherwise noted.

For Catapult, Inc.
Managing Editor: Donald Elman
Writer: Julia Kelly
Project Editor: Ann T. Rosenthal
Production/Layout: Jeanne K. Hunt, Editor; Dale M. Nelson
Technical Editor: Brett R. Davidson
Indexer: Julie Kawabata

For Microsoft Press
Acquisitions Editor: Casey D. Doyle
Project Editor: Brenda L. Matteson

Catapult, Inc. & Microsoft Press

Microsoft Access for Windows 95 Step by Step has been created by the professional trainers and writers at Catapult, Inc., to the exacting standards you've come to expect from Microsoft Press. Together, we are pleased to present this self-paced training guide, which you can use individually or as part of a class.

Catapult, Inc. is a software training company with years of experience in PC and Macintosh instruction. Catapult's exclusive Performance-Based Training system is available in Catapult training centers across North America and at customer sites. Based on the principles of adult learning, Performance-Based Training ensures that students leave the classroom with confidence and the ability to apply skills to real-world scenarios. *Microsoft Access for Windows 95 Step by Step* incorporates Catapult's training expertise to ensure that you'll receive the maximum return on your training time. You'll focus on the skills that increase productivity the most while working at your own pace and convenience.

Microsoft Press is the independent—and independent-minded—book publishing division of Microsoft Corporation. The leading publisher of information on Microsoft software, Microsoft Press is dedicated to providing the highest quality end-user training, reference, and technical books that make using Microsoft software easier, more enjoyable, and more productive.

Contents at a Glance

Table of Contents

Table of Contents

Table of Contents

Part 3   Asking Questions and Getting Answers

Lesson 9   Selecting the Records You Want   125

Lesson 10 Creating User-Friendly Queries   147

Part 4   Customizing Your Forms

Lesson 11 Using Controls to Show Text and Data   169

Table of Contents

QuickLook Guide

Opening a table, see Lesson 1, page 12

Viewing and creating relationships, see Lesson 8, page 107

Relating tables, see Lesson 8, page 111

Linking to external databases, see Lesson 7, page 92

Basing a form on a table, see Lesson 7, page 99

Creating a new table, see Lesson 6, page 79

Creating a new database, see Getting Ready, page xliii

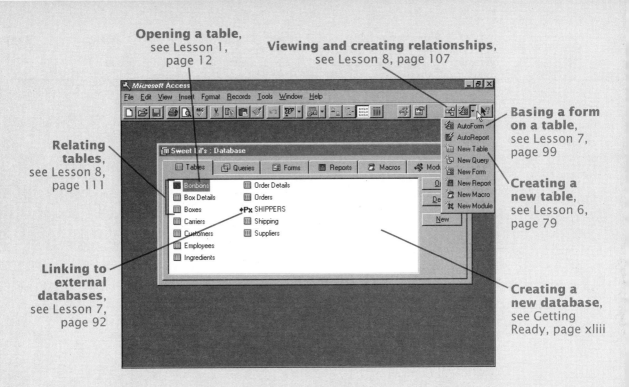

Sorting in Datasheet view, see Lesson 4, page 53

Filtering by selection, see Lesson 4, page 50

Setting and changing field properties, see Lesson 6, page 85

Moving to different records, see Lesson 1, page 9

Creating a new table by adding data to a blank datasheet, see Lesson 6, page 82

Adding new records, see Lesson 2, page 29

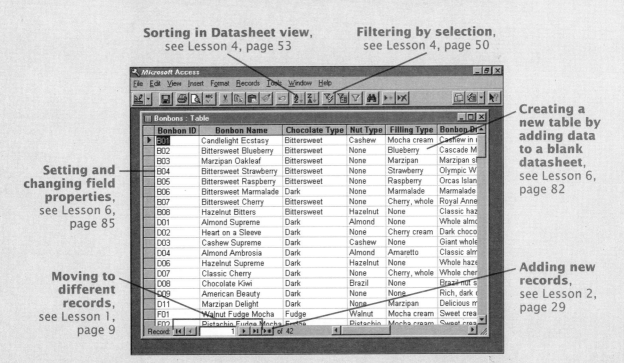

QuickLook Guide

Sorting a query in Datasheet view, see Lesson 9, page 131

Finding specific records, see Lesson 4, page 47

Switching views with the new View button, see Lesson 2, page 19

Changing field names in a query, see Lesson 9, page 142

Basing a report on a parameter query, see Lesson 10, page 153

Creating parameter queries that prompt for criteria, see Lesson 10, page 149

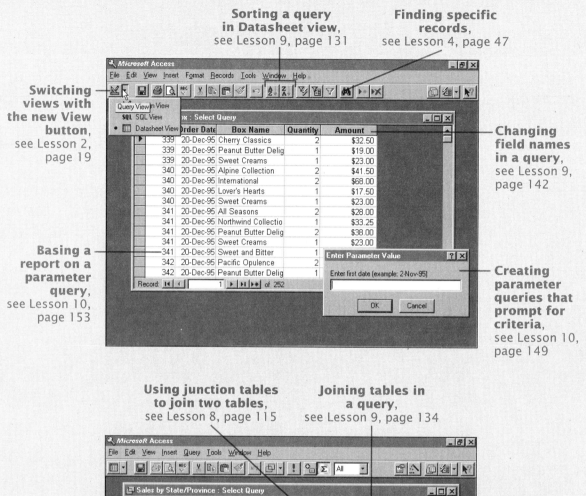

Using junction tables to join two tables, see Lesson 8, page 115

Joining tables in a query, see Lesson 9, page 134

Calculating totals in a query, see Lesson 9, page 136

Building expressions, see the Appendix, page 269

Creating calculated fields, see Lesson 9, page 140

Setting query criteria, see Lesson 9, page 129

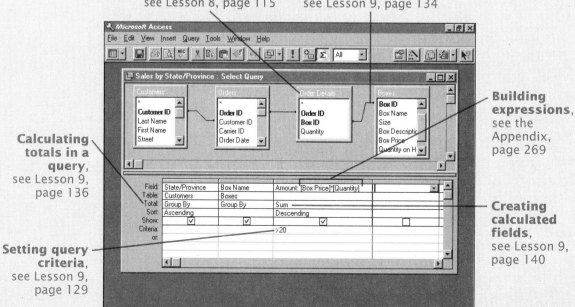

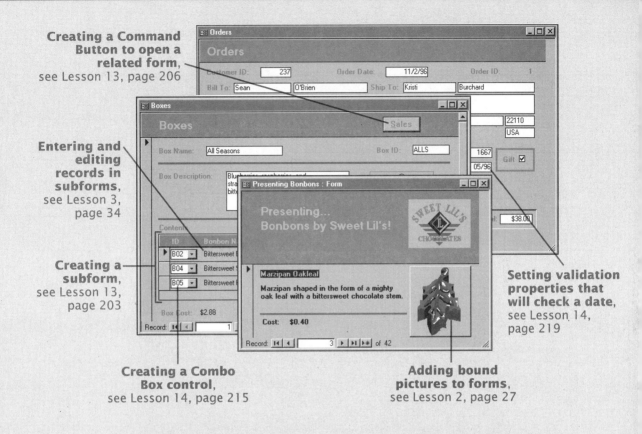

Creating a Command Button to open a related form, see Lesson 13, page 206

Entering and editing records in subforms, see Lesson 3, page 34

Creating a subform, see Lesson 13, page 203

Setting validation properties that will check a date, see Lesson 14, page 219

Creating a Combo Box control, see Lesson 14, page 215

Adding bound pictures to forms, see Lesson 2, page 27

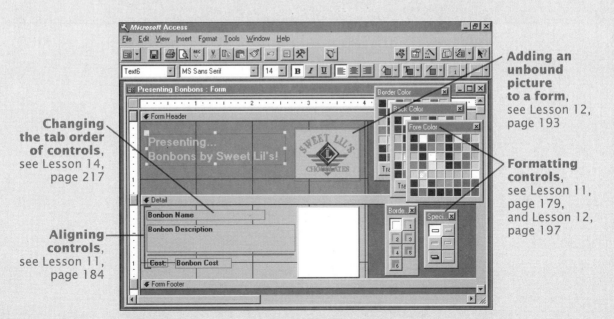

Changing the tab order of controls, see Lesson 14, page 217

Adding an unbound picture to a form, see Lesson 12, page 193

Formatting controls, see Lesson 11, page 179, and Lesson 12, page 197

Aligning controls, see Lesson 11, page 184

XV

Using the new Report Wizard to create a report and add an automatic print date, see Lesson 15, page 234

Grouping similar records under a single heading, see Lesson 16, page 253

Setting or changing the sort order, see Lesson 16, page 253

Previewing a report, see Lesson 5, page 61

Printing a report, see Lesson 5, page 63

Keeping groups of values together on one page, see Lesson 16, page 255

Adding custom page numbering to a report footer, see Lesson 16, page 256

Bonbons by Box
April 4, 1996

Box Name	Bonbon Name	Cost of Bonbons
All Seasons		
	Bittersweet Blueberry	$0.50
	Bittersweet Raspberry	$0.50
	Bittersweet Strawberry	$0.46
	Sweet Blueberry	$0.50
	Sweet Raspberry	$0.52
	Sweet Strawberry	$0.40
		$2.88
Alpine Collection		
	Bittersweet Blueberry	$1.00
	Bittersweet Strawberry	$1.15
	Sweet Blueberry	$1.00
	Sweet Strawberry	$1.00
		$4.15
Autumn Collection		
	Marzipan Finch	$1.92
	Marzipan Maple	$2.22
	Marzipan Oakleaf	$2.40
	Marzipan Swallow	$2.04
		$8.58
Bittersweets		
	Bittersweet Blueberry	$1.25
	Bittersweet Cherry	$1.04
	Bittersweet Marmalade	$0.85
	Bittersweet Raspberry	$1.25
	Bittersweet Strawberry	$1.15
		$5.54

Page 1of 5

About This Book

In "About This Book" you will learn:

- How to find your best starting point in this book based on your level of experience.
- What the conventions in this book mean.
- Where to get additional information about Microsoft Windows 95.

Microsoft Access for Windows 95 is a powerful data management program that you can use for sorting, organizing, and reporting the important information you need every day. *Microsoft Access for Windows 95 Step by Step* shows you how to use Microsoft Access to simplify your work and increase your productivity. With this book, you can learn Microsoft Access at your own pace and at your own convenience, or you can use it in a classroom setting.

IMPORTANT This book is for use with Microsoft Access for the Windows 95 operating system. To determine what software you are running, you can check either the software documentation, the installation disk labels, or the exterior product packaging.

You get hands-on practice by using the practice database and files on the disk located in the back of this book. Each lesson explains when and how to use the appropriate practice files. Instructions for copying the practice files to your computer hard disk are in "Getting Ready," the next chapter in this book.

Finding the Best Starting Point for You

This book is designed for new users learning Microsoft Access for the first time and for experienced users who want to learn and use the new features in Microsoft Access for Windows 95. Either way, *Microsoft Access for Windows 95 Step by Step* will help you get the most out of Microsoft Access.

This book is divided into five major parts, each containing several related lessons. Each lesson takes approximately 20 to 45 minutes, with an optional practice exercise at the end of each lesson. At the end of each part is a Review & Practice section that gives you the opportunity to practice the skills you learned in that part. Each Review & Practice section allows you to test your knowledge and prepare for your own work.

Use the following table to determine your best path through the book.

If you are	Follow these steps
New to a computer or graphical environment, such as Microsoft Windows 95	Read "Getting Ready," the next chapter in this book, and follow the instructions to install the practice files. Carefully read the sections on "If You Are New to Microsoft Windows 95." Next, work through Lessons 1 through 5 for a basic introduction to Microsoft Access. Work through Lessons 6 through 16 in any order.
Familiar with the Microsoft Windows 95 graphical computer environment, but new to using Microsoft Access	Follow the instructions for installing the practice files in "Getting Ready," the next chapter in this book. Next, work through Lessons 1 through 5 for a basic introduction to Microsoft Access. Then work through Lessons 6 through 8, 9 through 14, and 15 through 16, in any order.
Experienced with Microsoft Access	Follow the instructions for installing the practice files in the "Getting Ready," the next chapter in this book. Next, read through "New Features in Access for Windows 95," which follows "Getting Ready," for an introduction to the new features in this version. Complete the lessons that best fit your needs.

Using This Book As a Classroom Aid

If you're an instructor, you can use *Microsoft Access for Windows 95 Step by Step* for teaching computer users. You might want to select certain lessons that meet your students' particular needs and incorporate your own demonstrations into the lessons.

If you plan to teach the entire contents of this book, you should probably set aside up to three days of classroom time to allow for discussion, questions, and any customized practice you might create.

Conventions Used in This Book

Before you start any of the lessons, it's important that you understand the terms and notational conventions used in this book.

Procedural Conventions

- Hands-on exercises that you are to follow are given in numbered lists of steps (1, 2, and so on). An arrowhead bullet ( ) indicates an exercise with only one step.
- Characters or commands that you type appear in **bold lowercase** type.

Print

- You can carry out many commands by clicking a button at the top of the program window. If a procedure instructs you to click a button, a picture of the button appears in the left margin, as the Print button does here.

Mouse Conventions

- If you have a multiple-button mouse, it is assumed that you have configured the left mouse button as the primary mouse button. Any procedure that requires you to click the secondary mouse button will refer to it as the right mouse button.
- *Click* means to point to an object, and then press and release the mouse button. For example, "Click the Cut button on the Standard toolbar." *Use the right mouse button to click* means to point to an object, and then press and release the right mouse button.
- *Drag* means to point to an object, and then press and hold down the mouse button while you move the mouse. For example, "Drag the window edge downward to enlarge the window."
- *Double-click* means to rapidly press and release the mouse button twice. For example, "Double-click the Microsoft Access icon to start Microsoft Access."

Keyboard Conventions

- Names of keyboard keys that you are instructed to press are in small capital letters, for example, TAB and SHIFT.
- A plus sign (+) between two key names means that you must press those keys at the same time. For example, "Press ALT+TAB" means that you hold down the ALT key while you press TAB.
- Procedures generally emphasize use of the mouse, rather than the keyboard. However, you can choose menu commands with the keyboard by pressing the ALT key to activate the menu bar, and then sequentially pressing the keys that correspond to the highlighted or underlined letter of the menu name and command name. For some commands, you can also press a key combination listed in the menu.

Notes

- Notes or Tips that appear either in the text or in the left margin provide additional information or alternative methods for a procedure.

- Notes labeled "Important" alert you to essential information that you should check before continuing with the lesson.

- Notes labeled "Warning" alert you to possible data loss and tell you how to proceed safely.

Other Features of This Book

- The "One Step Further" exercise at the end of each lesson introduces new options or techniques that build on the commands and skills you used in the lesson.

- Each lesson concludes with a Lesson Summary, which lists the skills you have learned in the lesson and briefly reviews how to accomplish particular tasks.

- References to Microsoft Access online Help at the end of each lesson direct you to Help topics for additional information. The Help system provides a complete online reference to Microsoft Access. You'll learn more about Help in "Getting Ready," the next chapter in this book.

- The "Review & Practice" activity at the end of each part provides an opportunity to use the major skills presented in the lessons for that part. These activities present problems that reinforce what you have learned and demonstrate new ways you can use Microsoft Access.

- In the Appendix, "Using Expressions," you'll find guidelines for writing expressions and examples of common expressions, as well as an introduction to the Expression Builder.

Getting Ready

In "Getting Ready" you will learn how to:

■ Copy the practice files to your computer hard disk.

■ Start Microsoft Windows 95 and use the mouse.

■ Use basic Windows 95 features such as windows, menus, dialog boxes, and Help.

■ Start Microsoft Access and get acquainted with some of its tools.

This chapter of the book prepares you for your first steps into the Microsoft Access for Windows 95 environment. You will learn how to install the practice files that come with this book and how to start both Microsoft Windows 95 and Microsoft Access. You will also get an overview of some useful Windows 95 techniques, and you'll get an introduction to some terms and concepts that are important to understand as you learn Microsoft Access.

If you have not yet installed Windows 95 or Microsoft Access, you'll need to do that before you start the lessons. For instructions on installing Windows 95, see your Windows 95 documentation. For instructions on installing Microsoft Access for Windows 95, see your Microsoft Access documentation.

IMPORTANT Before you break the seal on the practice disk in the back of this book, be sure that you have the correct version of the software. This book is designed for use with Microsoft Access, an application that runs on the Windows 95 operating system. To determine what software you are running, you can check either the software documentation, the setup disk labels, or the exterior product packaging.

Installing the Step by Step Practice Files

The disk attached to the inside back cover of this book contains practice files that you'll use as you work through this book. You'll use the practice files in many of the lessons to perform the exercises. For example, the lesson that teaches you how to find documents stored on your computer instructs you to find and open one of the practice files. Because the practice files simulate tasks you'll encounter in a typical business setting, you can easily transfer what you learn from this book to your own work.

NOTE If you would like an introduction to using the mouse before you set up your Step by Step practice files, refer to the section "If You Are New to Microsoft Windows 95" later in this chapter. When you are finished practicing with the mouse, return to this section and copy the practice files to your hard disk.

Copy the practice files to your hard disk

You must have Microsoft Windows 95 installed on your computer in addition to Microsoft Access for Windows 95 to use the practice files. Follow these steps to copy the practice files to your computer hard disk so that you can use them with the lessons.

IMPORTANT Do not attempt to use the practice files directly from the floppy disk. Some or all of the practice files might be in a compressed format and will not work properly unless you install them onto your hard disk by using the setup program. Follow the steps below to install the practice files.

If you do not know your user name or password, contact your system administrator for further help.

1 If your computer isn't already on, turn it on now. Windows 95 starts automatically when you turn on your computer. If you see a dialog box asking for your user name and password, type them in the appropriate boxes, and then click OK. If you see the Welcome dialog box, click the Close button.

My Computer icon

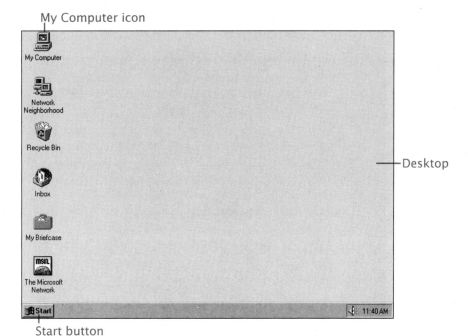

Desktop

Start button

2   Remove the disk from the package on the inside back cover of this book.

3   Put the disk in drive A or drive B of your computer.

4   On the taskbar at the bottom of your screen, click the Start button.

5   On the Start menu, click Run.

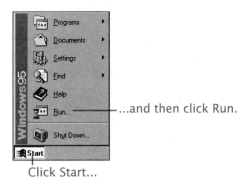

...and then click Run.

Click Start...

6   In the Run dialog box, type **a:setup** (or **b:setup** if the disk is in drive B), and then click the OK button. Do not type a space anywhere in the command.

7   Follow the directions on the screen.

The setup program window appears with recommended options preselected for you. For best results in using the practice files with this book, accept the recommendations made by the program.

8   After the files are copied, remove the disk from your computer, and replace it in the envelope on the inside back cover of the book.

The Step by Step setup program copies the practice files from the floppy disk onto the hard disk into a subfolder called Access SBS Practice. The setup program makes use of the Windows 95 Favorites folder. Follow the steps presented in each lesson to open or save your practice files.

Using the Practice Files

The text in each lesson in this book explains when and how to use the database in that lesson. The installation doesn't create any icons on the desktop—when it's time to use the database or a practice file in a lesson, the book will list instructions for how to open the file.

Lesson Background

The Sweet Lil's database is a collection of data used to manage a fictitious company named Sweet Lil's Chocolates. Sweet Lil's Chocolates sells boxes of gourmet chocolates by phone and mail order. For these lessons, imagine that you are in charge of the database that handles all the operations information for Sweet Lil's. As the company's business increases, more and more requests for specific information comes to you. You use Microsoft Access to manage the data and to provide answers to the various departments at Sweet Lil's.

If You Are New to Microsoft Windows 95

Microsoft Windows 95 is an easy-to-use work environment that helps you handle the daily work that you perform with your computer. Microsoft Windows 95 also provides a common look and functionality among the many different programs you might use—both in the way they share data and in the way you use the programs. This makes it easy for you to learn and use different programs in Windows 95. In this section, you'll get an introduction to Windows 95. If you are already familiar with Windows 95, you can skip to the section "Working with Microsoft Access," near the end of this chapter.

Start Windows 95

Starting Windows 95 is as easy as turning on your computer.

If you do not know your user name or password, contact your system administrator for further help.

> If your computer isn't already on, turn it on now. If you see a dialog box asking for your user name and password, type them in the appropriate boxes, and then click OK. If you see the Welcome dialog box, click the Close button or press ENTER.

Windows 95 starts automatically when you turn on your computer. Your screen looks similar to the following illustration.

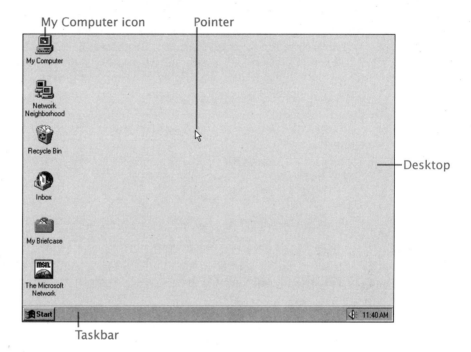

Using the Mouse

Windows 95 is designed for use with a mouse. Although you can use the keyboard for most actions in Windows 95, many of these actions are easier to do with a mouse.

The mouse controls a pointer on the screen, as shown in the preceding illustration. You move the pointer by sliding the mouse over a flat surface in the direction you want the pointer to move. If you run out of room to move the mouse, lift it up and then put it down in a more comfortable location. The pointer moves only when the mouse is touching a flat surface.

Moving the mouse pointer across the screen does not affect the information that you see; the pointer simply indicates a location on the screen. When you press the mouse button, an action occurs at the location of the pointer.

You will use four basic mouse actions throughout the lessons in this book.

Pointing   Moving the mouse to place the pointer on an item is called *pointing*.

Clicking   Pointing to an item on your screen, and then quickly pressing and releasing the mouse button is called *clicking*. You select items on the screen by clicking. Occasionally there are operations you perform by pressing the right mouse button, but unless you are instructed otherwise, use the left mouse button.

Double-clicking   Pointing to an item, and then quickly pressing and releasing the mouse button twice is called *double-clicking*. This is a convenient shortcut for many tasks. Whenever you are unsure of the command to use for an operation, try double-clicking the item you want to affect. This often displays a dialog box in which you can make changes to the item you double-clicked.

Dragging   Pointing to an item, and then holding down the mouse button as you move the pointer is called *dragging*. You can use this action to select data and to move and copy text or objects.

Try the mouse

Take a moment to test-drive the mouse.

1   Slide the mouse pointer over the Windows 95 Desktop.

The pointer is a left-pointing arrow.

2   Move the mouse pointer on top of the Start button at the bottom of the screen, and then press the left mouse button.

The Start menu opens.

3   Move the mouse pointer outside the Start menu, and click the Desktop.

The Start menu closes.

My Computer

4 Point to the My Computer icon, and then double-click it by using the left mouse button.

The My Computer window opens, where you can view the disk drives and folders stored there.

5 Move the mouse pointer over the bottom edge of the My Computer window until the pointer changes to a double-headed arrow.

When you move the mouse pointer over different parts of the Windows 95 Desktop or different areas in a program window, the pointer can change shape to indicate what action is available at that point.

6 Hold down the left mouse button, and move (drag) the mouse pointer downward.

7 Release the mouse button.

The My Computer window is resized.

Using Windows-Based Programs

After you become familiar with the basic operation of Windows 95, you can apply these skills to learn and use Windows-based programs—programs that are designed for use with Windows 95.

All Windows-based programs have similar characteristics as to how they appear on the screen and how you use them. All the windows in Windows-based programs have common controls that you use to scroll, size, move, and close a window.

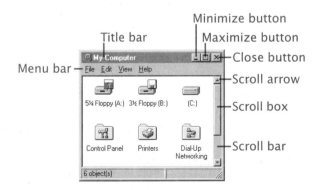

To	Do this	Button
Scroll through a window	Click a scroll bar or scroll arrow, or drag the scroll box.	
Enlarge a window to fill the screen	Double-click the title bar, or click the Maximize screen button.	
Restore a window to its previous size and position	Double-click the title bar, or click the Restore button. When a window is maximized, the Maximize button changes to the Restore button.	
Reduce a window to a button on the taskbar	Click the Minimize button. To display a minimized window, click its button on the taskbar.	
Move a window	Drag the title bar.	
Close a window	Click the Close button.	

You'll try out these Windows techniques and learn more about them in the following sections.

Using Menus

To choose a command on a menu, you click the menu name to open the menu, and then you click the command name on the menu. When a command name appears dimmed, either it doesn't apply to your current situation or it is unavailable. For example, the Paste command on the Edit menu appears dimmed if the Copy or Cut command has not been used first.

Some commands have a *shortcut key* combination shown to the right of the command name. Once you are familiar with the menus and commands, you might prefer to use these shortcut keys to save time if your hands are already at the keyboard.

To close a menu without choosing a command, you can click the menu name again or click anywhere outside of the menu. You can also press ESC to close a menu.

Open the Edit menu

To make menu selections with the keyboard, press ALT, and then type the underlined character in the menu or command name.

1   In the My Computer window, click Edit in the menu bar.

The Edit menu appears. Notice which commands are dimmed and which have shortcut key combinations listed.

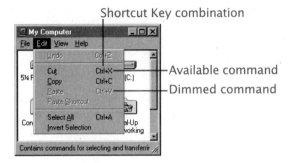

Shortcut Key combination

Available command

Dimmed command

2   Click the Edit menu name to close the menu.

The menu closes.

Make menu selections

Commands on a menu are grouped by common functions. Commands that are in effect are indicated by a check mark or a bullet mark to the left of the command name. A check mark indicates that multiple items in this group of commands can be in effect at the same time. A bullet mark indicates that only one item in this group can be in effect at the same time.

1   On the menu bar, click View.

The View menu looks like the following illustration.

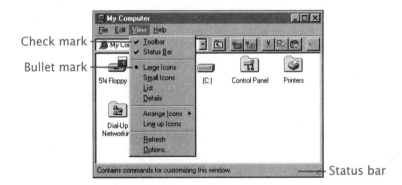

Check mark

Bullet mark

Status bar

2   On the View menu, click Toolbar.

The View menu closes, and a toolbar appears below the menu bar.

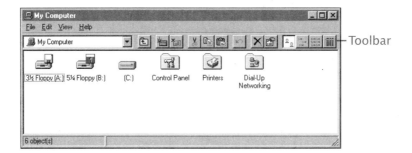
Toolbar

3 On the View menu, click List.

The items in the My Computer window are now displayed in a list.

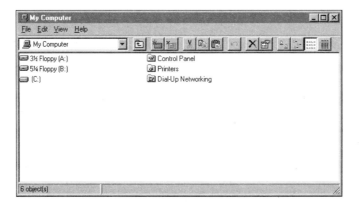

Large Icons

4 On the toolbar, click the Large Icons button.

If you do not see the button, drag a corner of the window to enlarge it until you see the button. Clicking a button on a toolbar is a quick way to select a command.

5 On the View menu, point to Arrange Icons.

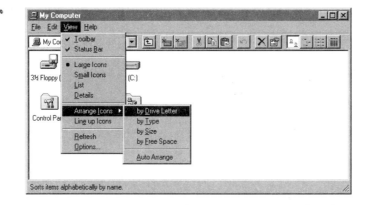

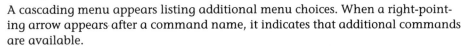

A cascading menu appears listing additional menu choices. When a right-point-ing arrow appears after a command name, it indicates that additional commands are available.

6 Click the menu name or anywhere outside the menu to close the menu.

7 On the menu bar, click View, and then click Toolbar again.

The View menu closes, and the toolbar is now hidden.

Close

8 Click the Close button in the upper-right corner of the My Computer window to close the window.

Using Dialog Boxes

When you choose a command name that is followed by an ellipsis (...), Windows-based programs display a dialog box in which you can provide more information about how the command should be carried out. Dialog boxes consist of a number of standard features as shown in the following illustration.

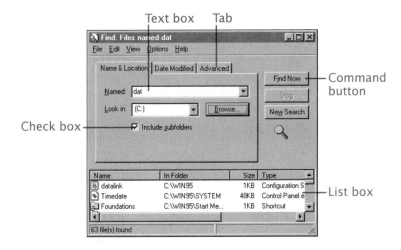

To move around in a dialog box, you click the item you want. You can also hold down ALT as you press the underlined letter. Or, you can press TAB to move between items.

After you enter information or make selections in a dialog box, you either choose the OK button in the dialog box or press the ENTER key on the keyboard to carry out the command. Click the Cancel button, or press ESC, to close a dialog box and cancel the command.

Display the Taskbar dialog box

Some dialog boxes provide several categories of options displayed on separate tabs. You click the top of an obscured tab to bring it forward and display additional options.

1 On the taskbar, click the Start button. On the Start menu, point to Settings, and then click Taskbar.

2   Click the Start Menu Programs tab.

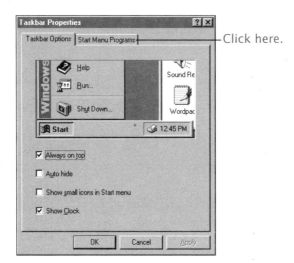

Click here.

On this tab, you can customize the list of programs that appears on your Start menu.

3   Click the Taskbar Options tab, and then click Show Small Icons In Start Menu.

Clicking a check box that is selected (that displays a check mark) turns the option off.

4   Click the check box a couple of times, and observe how the display in the dialog box changes.

Clicking any check box or option button will turn the option off or on.

5   In the dialog box, click the Cancel button.

This closes the dialog box without changing any settings.

Getting Help with Windows 95

When you need information about a procedure or how to use a particular feature on your computer, the online Help system is one of the most efficient ways to learn. The online Help system for Windows 95 is available from the Start menu, and you choose the type of help you want from the Help dialog box.

For instructions on broad categories, you can look at the Help contents. Or, you can search the Help index for information on specific topics. The Help information is short and concise, so you can get the exact information you need quickly. There are also shortcut buttons in many Help topics that you can use to switch directly to the task you want to perform.

Viewing Help Contents

The Help Contents tab is organized like a book's table of contents. As you choose top-level topics, or "chapters," you see a list of more detailed topics from which to choose. Many of these chapters have special "Tips and Tricks" subsections that can help you work more efficiently.

If you are new to Windows 95, you might be interested in the Help topic under "Introducing Windows 95" named "Ten minutes to using Windows."

Find Help on general categories

In this exercise, you'll look up information in the online Help system.

1　Click Start. On the Start menu, click Help.

　　The Help dialog box appears.

2　If necessary, click the Contents tab to make it active.

3　Double-click "Introducing Windows."

　　The book icon opens to display a set of subtopics.

4　Double-click "Using Windows Accessories."

5　Double-click "For General Use."

6　Double-click "Calculator: for making calculations."

　　A Help topic window appears.

Maximize

7　On the Help window, click the Maximize button.

　　The Help topic window fills the entire screen.

Minimize

8   Click the Minimize button to reduce the Help window to a button on the taskbar.

Whenever you minimize a window, its button appears on the taskbar.

Finding Help on Specific Topics

There are two methods for finding specific Help topics: the Index tab and the Find tab. The Index tab is organized like a book's index. Keywords for topics are organized alphabetically. You can either scroll through the list of keywords or type the keyword that you want to find. One or more topic choices are then presented.

With the Find tab, you can also enter a keyword. The main difference is that you get a list of all Help topics in which that keyword appears, not just the topics that begin with that word.

Find Help on specific topics using the Help index

In this exercise, you'll use the Help index to learn how to change the background pattern of your Desktop.

1   On the Taskbar, click the Windows Help button.

The Help dialog box appears as you left it.

Restore

2   Click the Restore button so that you can see both the Help window and the Desktop.

3   Click the Help Topics button at the top of the Help dialog box, and then click the Index tab.

The Help index appears.

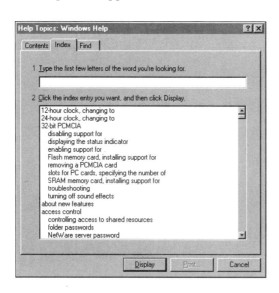

4   In the text box, type **display**

A list of display-related topics appears.

5   Double-click the topic named "background pictures or patterns, changing."

The Topics Found window appears.

6   Double-click the topic named "Changing the background of your Desktop."

7   Read the Help topic.

8   Click the jump button in Step 1 of the Help topic.

The Properties For Display dialog box appears. If you want, you can immediately perform the task you were looking up in Help.

9   On the Display Properties dialog box, click the Close button.

10   On the Windows Help window, click the Close button.

Jump

Close

> **NOTE**   You can print any Help topic. Click the Options button in the upper-left corner of any Help topic window, click Print Topic, and then click OK. To continue searching for additional topics, you can click the Help Topics button in any open Help topic window.

Find Help on specific topics using the Find tab

In this exercise, you'll use the Find tab to learn how to change your printer's settings.

1   Click Start. On the Start menu, click Help.

The Help dialog box appears.

2   Click the Find tab to make it active.

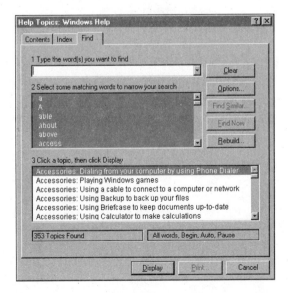

3 If you see a wizard, select the best option for your system, and then click Next. Click Finish to complete and close the wizard.

The wizard creates a search index for your Help files. This might take a few minutes. The next time you use Find, you won't have to wait for Windows 95 to create a topic list.

4 In the text box under step 1, type **print**

All topics that have to do with printing appear in the list box at the bottom of the tab.

5 In the list box under step 3, click the topic "Changing printer settings," and then click Display.

The Help topic appears.

6 Read the Help topic, using the scroll bar as necessary.

7 On the Windows Help window, click the Close button.

Close

 NOTE You can also get help about the controls in a dialog box by clicking the question mark button in the upper-right corner of the dialog box. When you click this button and then click any dialog box control, a Help window pops up that explains what the control is and how to use it.

Working with Microsoft Access

Now that you are familiar with the Windows 95 operating environment, you can start Microsoft Access. The easiest way to start Microsoft Access is from the Programs menu, but you can also use My Computer.

Start Microsoft Access from the Programs menu

 NOTE If you do not see Microsoft Access listed on the Programs menu when you do step 1 below, skip to the exercise, "Start Microsoft Access from My Computer" to start Microsoft Access.

➤ Click Start. On the Start menu, point to Programs, and then click Microsoft Access.

Microsoft Access opens, and the Microsoft Access dialog box appears. From this dialog box, you can create a new database or open an existing database.

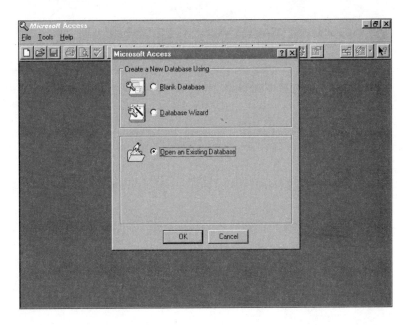

Start Microsoft Access from My Computer

If Microsoft Access is not listed on the Windows 95 Programs menu, you can start the program from My Computer.

1 Double-click the My Computer icon.

2 In the My Computer window, double-click the Drive C icon to display the files and folders stored there, and then double-click the MSOffice folder to open it.

3 Find and then double-click the Microsoft Access folder to open it.

You might have to scroll downward in the list to find the folder.

4 Double-click the Microsoft Access program file called MSaccess.exe to start the program.

NOTE If you want your screen to match the following illustration, perform the steps in the "Open a database" exercise in Lesson 1.

Exploring the Database Window

The Database window shows the tables that store data about Sweet Lil's business. From the Database window, you can open and work with any object in the database. To work with a table, you double-click the name of the table you want. To work with another type of object, you click the tab for the type of object you want. For example, to work with a form, you click the Forms tab. Microsoft Access displays a list of forms in the database. Then you can double-click the name of the form that you want to use.

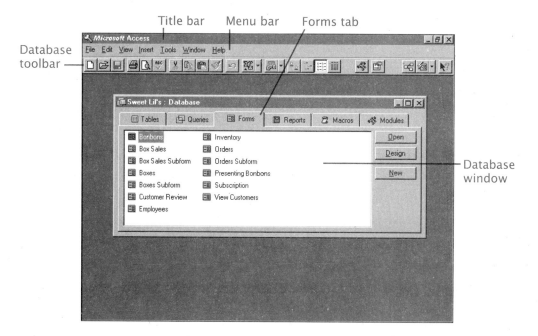

Using Toolbars

The first row of buttons below the menu bar is the *Database toolbar*. This toolbar contains buttons for performing basic operations for working with the program, such as opening another database and printing a table or report. The following illustration identifies the buttons on the Database toolbar.

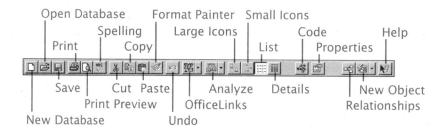

There are several toolbars in Microsoft Access that are displayed depending on the object you have open. Each toolbar is composed of buttons that perform related tasks. For example, you'll use the Form Design toolbar to control the appearance of your forms, including the color of the form's background and the style and size of your text. It is generally much faster to click a button on a toolbar than to select a command from a menu.

When you click certain buttons on a toolbar, such as the Print button, Microsoft Access carries out the corresponding command using the command's default options. If you want to specify different options for carrying out a command, use the command from the menu. Other buttons, such as the Open Database button, perform in the same way as the corresponding command. The instructions in this book emphasize using the toolbar for almost all Microsoft Access operations.

Take a quick tour of the Database toolbar

Take a moment to get acquainted with the buttons on the Database toolbar. If you accidentally click a button, you can press the ESC key or click the Undo button on the Standard toolbar.

If you do not see the button name, from the View menu, choose Toolbars. Click the Show Tool-Tips check box.

➤ Move the pointer over a button, and wait.

After a moment, the name of the button appears.

ToolTip

To get more information about a button, you can use the ScreenTips described in the following exercise.

Using Tips and Wizards

Wizards are intelligent assistants that guide you through the steps of performing specific tasks, such as creating a new form or table. When you run a wizard, it asks you for preferences that will be incorporated into your database element. In addition, there are ScreenTips that provide brief descriptions of buttons and options in dialog boxes.

The Answer Wizard, available from the Microsoft Access Help menu, can assist you with a topic of your choice. In this wizard, you type a topic or question, and then the wizard presents you with a list of related topics from which you can choose. After you choose a topic, the wizard displays additional information for completing the task or provides a demonstration of the steps.

Use a ScreenTip

Help

1   On the toolbar, click the Help button.

2   On the toolbar, click any button.

A brief description of the button appears below the button.

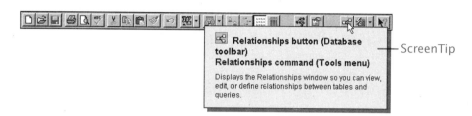

ScreenTip

3   Click anywhere on the screen to hide the ScreenTip.

Use the Answer Wizard

Depending on the kind of information you wish to focus on, you can view your data in several different ways. You can use the Answer Wizard to learn more about the different views available in Microsoft Access.

1   On the Help menu, click Answer Wizard.

The Answer Wizard window appears. In the first box, type the word, phrase, or question about which you want more information.

2   Type **Tables** and click the Search button.

A list of topics related to using Microsoft Access tables appears.

3   In the Tell Me About area, double-click "Tables: What they are and how they work."

Information about tables appears in the help window. Read the information, and then continue on to the next step.

4   Click the Close button on the Answer Wizard window to close it.

What Is a Database?

A *database* is a collection of information that's related to a particular topic or purpose. The key to efficient storage and retrieval of your data is the planning process. By first identifying what you want the database to do for you, you will be able to create a practical design that will result in a faster, more accurate data management tool.

Planning for a New Database

When you design your own database, you first go through a planning process that identifies what the database is for and what information you need to track. Before building your own database in Microsoft Access, consider the following questions:

- What information do I want to get from my database?
- What separate subject areas do I need to store facts about?
- How are these subjects related to each other?
- What facts do I need to store about each subject?

Microsoft Access helps you to manage your database by providing an efficient structure to store and retrieve information. The place you assemble the information about each subject you decide to track is called a *table*, and each category of facts collected in your table is called a *field*. Microsoft Access can automatically produce a *form* for you to fill in all your data. After you have entered some data, you can ask Microsoft Access to display a selected part of the information by using procedures called *find*, *sort*, or *query*. Finally, Microsoft Access helps you print just the part of the information you want to see in a *report*. At any time, you can customize the look or edit the contents of any part of your database.

Because Microsoft Access is a *relational database management system (RDBMS)*, you can organize data about different subject areas into tables, and then you can create relationships between the tables. This approach makes it easy to bring related data together when needed. By establishing relationships between individual tables instead of storing all of your information in one large table, you avoid a lot of duplication of data, you save storage space in your computer, and you maximize the speed and accuracy of working with your data.

Microsoft Access has many automated processes and on-line Help features to assist you in creating and enhancing each element of your database. These processes, which include wizards and toolbar buttons, are covered throughout the lessons in this book. More information about the Help features is contained in "Using Help with Windows 95" and "Use the Answer Wizard" earlier in this section.

Using an Existing Database

The primary elements of a database—tables, fields, forms, queries, and reports—are all included in the sample database used with this *Step by Step* book. To facilitate your learning about how to work with information in a database, you use the Sweet Lil's database throughout these lessons and then create new elements as needed.

The following illustration lists each table of the Sweet Lil's database with all of its fields and shows how the tables are related to each other.

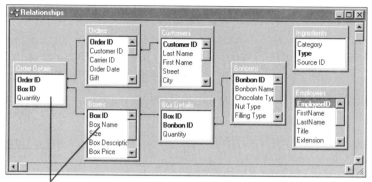

Tables in the Sweet Lil's Database

In the Sweet Lil's database, data about customers is stored in the Customers table and information about orders is stored in the Orders table. The two tables are related to each other, so Microsoft Access can easily show customer information with related order information (such as a customer's name and phone number with the customer's orders). Later in this book, you'll learn more about the advantages of organizing your data in this way.

When you look at the data contained in a table, each field is displayed as a column in the table. For example, if you want to see only Sweet Lil's 12-ounce boxes, you tell Microsoft Access to show you the boxes with 12 in the Size field. Microsoft Access shows you only those boxes. You'll have many opportunities to use this concept throughout this book.

You often use the values in fields to pinpoint the data that you want to see.

Each field in the Boxes table contains data that describes a box of chocolates that Sweet Lil's sells.

Box ID	Box Name	Size	Box Description	Box Price	Quantity on Hand
ALLS	All Seasons	8	Blueberries, raspberries, and strawberries to enjoy all season, both bitter and sweet.	$14.00	700
ALPI	Alpine Collection	12	Straight from the high Cascades, alpine blueberries and strawberries in our best chocolate.	$20.75	400
AUTU	Autumn Collection	16	Family-size box of Autumn favorites-- Marzipan Maple, Oakleaf, Finch, and	$43.00	200

Record: 1 of 18

Creating a New Database

Using Microsoft Access, you might want to create an entirely new database or to work with a database that has already been developed. In this *Step by Step* book, you will be using an existing database so that you can learn how to work with all the objects that are necessary for any database. You will also create new objects just as you would if you were starting a database from scratch.

When you need to do so, you can easily create a new Microsoft Access database using the Database Wizard. The first step in creating a successful database is to plan it out before you begin to use your software, as discussed earlier in this chapter.

In the following steps, you will learn how to create a new database from a template by using the Database Wizard. Then you will close the new database, and begin to use the Step by Step sample database.

Create a new database

Suppose you want to create a database for your personal address list, including related information like nicknames and hobbies. Microsoft Access includes a template for a personal address book, which you'll use to create your new database.

New Database

1   On the File menu, click New Database. Or, click the New Database button on the toolbar.

The New dialog box appears.

2   Make sure the Databases tab is active, and then double-click the Address Book icon.

The File New Database dialog box opens.

3   In the File Name box, type **My Address Book**, then click Create.

The Database Wizard starts. You will see a series of dialog boxes that ask you questions, then the Database Wizard will create your new database using the Address Book template and your answers.

4   The first dialog box tells you what kind of information your database will store. Click the Next button.

5   The next dialog box asks what optional fields you would like to include in your database. In the Fields In The Table list, scroll down and check the Nickname and Hobbies checkboxes. Click the Yes, Include Sample Data checkbox, then click Next.

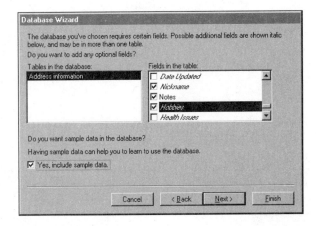

6 The next dialog box asks what style you would like for screen displays. Be sure Standard is selected, then click Next.

7 The next dialog box asks what style you would like for printed reports. Be sure Corporate is selected, then click Next.

8 In the next dialog box, click Next to accept the default title Address Book.

9 This is the last dialog box (the Next button is unavailable). Click Finish.

The Database Wizard creates your new database, including sample data and several forms and reports. The first window that is displayed, the Switchboard, is a form that the wizard created. To see the database window, click the Close button in the upper right corner of the Switchboard form. To close the Address Book database, click the Close button in the upper right corner of the database window.

After you complete the lessons in this book using the practice files, you will know how to work with the tables, forms, and reports in your new Address Book database.

NOTE Microsoft Access databases are different from Paradox or dBASE database files. In Paradox and dBASE, each table, form, and report is a separate file. In Microsoft Access, your data and all the tools you need to work with your data are stored in a single file.

Quitting Microsoft Access and Windows 95

Now that you are introduced to Windows 95 and Microsoft Access, you can proceed to Lesson 1. If you would like to quit Microsoft Access or Windows 95 for now, follow these steps.

Quit Microsoft Access

1 Hold down the ALT key, and press F4, or click Exit on the File menu.

2 If you see a message box asking whether you want to save changes, click the No button.

Quit Windows 95

Close

1 Close all open windows by clicking the Close button in the upper-right corner of each window.

2 Click Start, and then click Shut Down.

3 When you see the message dialog box, click the Yes button.

WARNING To avoid loss of data or damage to Windows 95, always quit Windows 95 using the Shut Down command on the Start menu before you turn your computer off.

New Features in Microsoft Access for Windows 95

The following table lists the major new features in Microsoft Access for Windows 95 that are covered in this book. The table shows the lesson in which you can learn about each feature. For more information about new features, on the Help menu, click Microsoft Access Help Topics; then click the Contents tab, and double-click What's New.

To learn how to	See
Get help from the Answer Wizard	Getting Ready
Get help while you work from ScreenTips	Getting Ready
Create a new database using the Database Wizard	Getting Ready
Filter records by selection	Lesson 4
Filter records by form	Lesson 4
Create a new table by entering data in a blank datasheet	Lesson 6
Import a text file using the Text Import Wizard	Lesson 7
Create a lookup field to relate two tables using the Lookup Wizard	Lesson 8
Change a table's properties from within the Relationships window	Lesson 8
Sort query data in datasheet view	Lesson 9
Create a new query using the new Query Wizard	Lesson 9
Change the format of an entire report with AutoFormat	Lesson 10
Create a form based on a filtered table using Inherited Filters	Lesson 11
Format controls to look raised, sunken, or etched using Special Effects	Lesson 11

To learn how to	See
Create a new form using the new Form Wizard	Lesson 11
Create a default control for a field with the DisplayControl property	Lesson 11
Format elements of forms with new formatting tools	Lesson 11
Copy control formatting with Format Painter	Lesson 11
Create custom ControlTips for controls	Lesson 11
Insert unbound pictures in a form using the new Image control	Lesson 12
Create a new form with a subform using the new Form Wizard	Lesson 13
Change a control's type quickly using Control Morphing	Lesson 14
Create a report with the new Report Wizard	Lesson 15
Add page numbering and date/time controls to a report or form	Lesson 16

Part
1

Data Basics

Adding Data to a Database

In this lesson you will learn how to:

Estimated time
20 min.

- Open a database.
- Open a form.
- Enter data.
- Select an option or a check box.
- Move from record to record.
- Open a table.
- Quit Microsoft Access.

The most convenient place to keep the information you need is right at your desk. You might keep stacking paper forms in a file folder next to the phone, as long as the stack doesn't get too big. But you have a problem if you try to keep all the information you need at your desk—pretty soon you can't find the desk!

You can use Microsoft Access to organize and store all kinds and quantities of information and have them available with only a few clicks of your mouse. In this lesson, you'll find out how to open a Microsoft Access database, use a form to add new data, and move from record to record.

What Is Data?

Data is anything you want to store and refer to again. In Microsoft Access, data can be text, numbers, dates, and pictures. For example, if you sell boxes of bonbons, you can store the names, pictures, and recipes of your bonbons, the prices and quantities of boxes, and the dates of sales.

In most cases, the easiest way to enter data is by using a *form*. Database forms resemble the paper forms we see in offices or find in junk mail. You type the data in the form, and then Microsoft Access stores it in a table.

A *record* is a set of information that belongs together, such as all the information on a magazine subscription card. A database can hold many records.

Setting the Scene

Sweet Lil's Chocolates, Inc., a fast-growing gourmet chocolate company, has switched to Microsoft Access to store data on its product lines and sales. To attract new customers, Sweet Lil's started a monthly newsletter called *The Chocolate Gourmet*. After seeing how much time the database saved and how many errors it prevented, the Newsletter Department wants to keep subscription information in the database as well.

You have been recruited to be the first person to enter data using a new form called "Subscriptions." The Sweet Lil's database contains the form you need. You'll open the database, open the Subscription form, and enter subscription data. The records you enter will be stored in the Customers table.

 NOTE If you have just completed the steps in "Getting Ready" earlier in this book for starting Microsoft Access and opening a database, skip "Opening a Database," and go to the following section, "Opening a Form."

Opening a Database

If you quit Microsoft Access at the end of "Getting Ready," or if you are just starting to use *Microsoft Access for Windows 95 Step by Step* with this lesson, perform these steps for starting Microsoft Access and opening a database.

Start Microsoft Access from Microsoft Windows

1 On the taskbar, click the Start button.

2 Point to Programs, and then click Microsoft Access.

The Microsoft Access startup window appears. From here, you can create a new database, open an existing database, or start the Database Wizard to help you create a new database.

After you have opened a database, the next time you start Microsoft Access you'll see the database name listed in the startup dialog box.

Open a database

To create a new database from scratch, see "Getting Ready," or refer to Microsoft Access online Help.

1 In the Microsoft Access startup window, be sure that the Open An Existing Database option button is selected, and then click OK.

The Open dialog box appears.

Look In Favorites

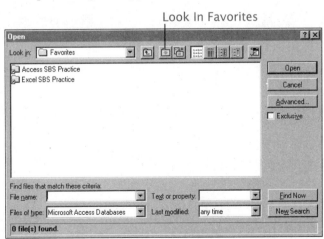

2   In the Open dialog box, click the Look In Favorites button.

The names of all folders and files that are contained within the selected folder are listed in the file list box.

3   Double-click the Access SBS Practice folder icon.

4   Double-click the Sweet Lil's filename.

The Database window for the Sweet Lil's database appears.

The Database window is a tabbed window—the Tables tab shows the tables that store data about Sweet Lil's business, the Forms tab shows the forms that were created for the Sweet Lil's database, and so forth. From the Database window, you can open and work with any object in the database.

Forms tab

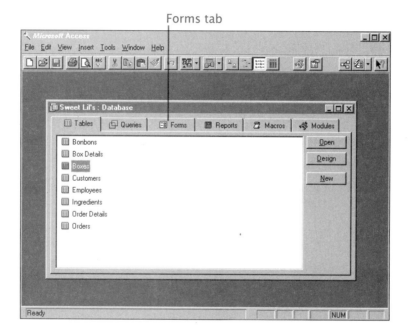

Opening a Form

Now that you're in the Sweet Lil's database, you can open the Subscription form to enter the subscription information for a new customer.

Open a form

1   In the Sweet Lil's Database window, click the Forms tab.

A list of the forms in the Sweet Lil's database appears.

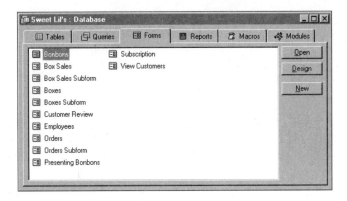

2   Double-click the Subscription form.

The Subscription form appears.

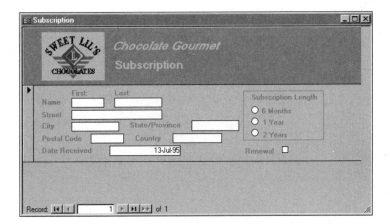

The Subscription form contains blank boxes—*fields*—where you type the information from the paper form. A field is an area on a form where you enter data, such as a last name or an address.

The *insertion point* indicates where the information appears when you type. You can move the insertion point by clicking a different field or by pressing the TAB key. In general, forms are set up so that when you press TAB, the insertion point moves among the fields from left to right or from top to bottom.

Microsoft Access fills in the current date in the Date Received field automatically so that you don't have to type it.

Entering Data

You'll use the blank Subscription form on your screen to enter the subscription for a fan of *The Chocolate Gourmet* from Ohio. Here's what his paper subscription form looks like.

Add a name

If you make a mistake, just press the BACKSPACE key, and then retype.

1   Type **Earl** in the First Name field.

As soon as you start typing, a new blank form appears below the one you're working in.

2   Press TAB to move the insertion point to the Last Name field (or click anywhere in the Last Name field).

When your hands are already on the keyboard, you press TAB to move to the next field or press SHIFT+TAB to move to the previous field.

3   Type **Lee** in the Last Name field.

Add an address

➤   Type the following address information, pressing TAB to move from field to field.

Street: **28 Dorothy**
City: **Fairborn**
State/Province: **OH**
Postal Code: **45324**
Country: **USA**

Selecting an Option Button or a Check Box

When you press TAB after typing "USA" in the Country field, Microsoft Access draws a dotted line around "6 Months" in the Subscription Length field instead of displaying the insertion point.

Subscription Length is an *option group*. Because an option group presents a set of options to select from, you don't have to type the data yourself—you just select an option. In this case, Earl Lee wants a 2-year subscription.

Option group

Check box

Select an option button

If you press TAB in this step, be sure the insertion point is in the Country field.

➤ Click the circle next to 2 Years. Or press TAB, and press the DOWN ARROW key twice.

A dot appears in the button next to 2 Years, indicating that this option is selected. Next, you'll fill out the Renewal field.

Select a check box

Earl Lee's subscription is a renewal. Renewal is a *check box*. When this kind of field is selected, you see a check mark in the box.

➤ Click the Renewal check box.

A check mark appears in the box.

 TIP To clear a selected check box, click it again. If you prefer to use the keyboard, you can press the SPACEBAR to select or clear a check box.

Moving from Record to Record

All the information in Earl Lee's subscription makes up one complete record. Now that you've entered Earl Lee's subscription, you're ready to start the next subscription.

Depending on the way a form is designed, you can see one or more records at a time while you use the form. If you can see the next record, you can move to it by clicking in it. Whether you can see the next record or not, you can move to it by pressing TAB from the last field in the current record (the record you're in now).

Save the record and move to the next record

➤ Click in the First Name field of the next record. Or in the Renewal field of the current record, press TAB.

Microsoft Access saves Earl Lee's subscription information automatically when you go to a new record. You don't have to do anything else to save the first subscription.

Return to the previous record

Looking over your first entry, you notice that you didn't type "St." in Earl Lee's street address. You'll return to the previous record to make the change.

You can also use the PAGE UP key to go to the first field in the first record. Then press TAB to move to the Street field.

1 In the Street field of Earl Lee's record, click after the "y" in "Dorothy" to return to the record.

Click here.

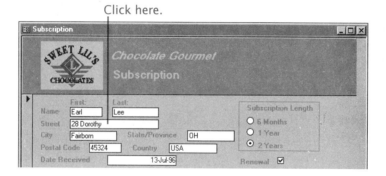

If you move to a field by pressing TAB, Microsoft Access selects the entire value in the field. To change from the selection mode and place the insertion point at the end of the field, press F2.

2 Press the SPACEBAR to insert a space after "Dorothy," and then type **St.**

3 Click in the First Name field of the next record.

Microsoft Access saves your change to Earl Lee's record.

While you were editing Earl Lee's record, you might have noticed that a pencil symbol appeared in the area on the left side of the form. The pencil indicates that you've changed data in the current record but your changes aren't saved yet. If you haven't changed data in the current record, a triangle appears instead of a pencil. You can see how this works while you add the next record from a customer named Becky Sawyer-Roundstone.

Add the first name

▶ Type **Becky** in the First Name field.

Notice that Becky's last name doesn't look as if it's going to fit in the Last Name field. If you were filling out a paper form, you'd have to squeeze the name in the space. But Microsoft Access forms can accommodate long names.

Add text to scrollable fields

1 Type **Sawyer-Roundstone** in the Last Name field.

As soon as you type one more letter than what fits in the Last Name field, Microsoft Access scrolls the name so that you can keep typing. The entire name is saved, even if you can't see it all at once.

2 Type **260 Kent Street Station 1551** in the Street field.

Finish entering the subscription

▶ Type the data below, pressing TAB to move from field to field.

City:	**Ottawa**
State/Province:	**Ontario**
Postal Code:	**K1A 0E6**
Country:	**Canada**
Subscription Length:	**6 Months**
Renewal:	**No**

It's almost break time. Before you stop, proofread your entries. When you're finished, close the Subscription form.

Close the form

▶ In the Subscription form window, click the Close button. Or, from the File menu, choose Close.

Be sure that you click the Close button for the form, not the Close button for the Microsoft Access window.

Click here.

Opening a Table

The records you just added using the Subscription form were saved in the Customers table in the Sweet Lil's database. Take a look at your new records in the Customers table.

Display table names in the Database window

➤ In the Database window, click the Tables tab.

The list of tables in the Sweet Lil's database appears.

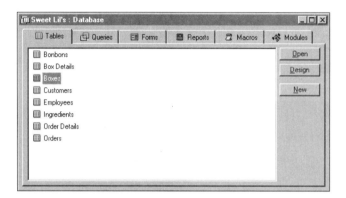

Open the Customers table

➤ Double-click the Customers table.

The Customers table opens, and its records appear.

The two records you added are at the end of the list of customers. You can use the navigation buttons at the bottom of the form window to move directly to the first, previous, next, or last record.

Move to the last record

> In the lower-left corner of the window, click the navigation button for the last record.

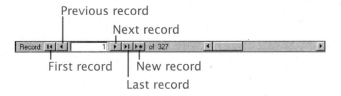

Previous record

Next record

First record   New record

Last record

The last records in the table appear. The last two records are the ones you just added for Earl Lee and Becky Sawyer-Roundstone. Microsoft Access automatically assigned Earl and Becky customer ID numbers. You'll learn how to set up a table that automatically assigns ID numbers in Part 2, "Expanding a Database."

TIP You can use the keyboard or the vertical scroll bar to move between records, but the fastest way to move in a large database is with the navigation buttons.

Quitting Microsoft Access

Since you're going on a break, it's best to quit Microsoft Access. That way, no one can damage your data while you're away. You can close the Customers table and quit Microsoft Access all in one step.

Quit Microsoft Access

> In the Microsoft Access window, click the Close button.

Click here.

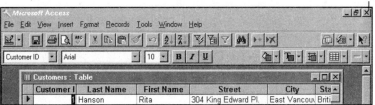

Before shutting down, Microsoft Access closes the Customers table (and any other database objects you might have open). If you made changes to the data in the Customers table before exiting, your changes are saved.

One Step Further: Moving Between Forms

You're ready to fill out more subscriptions. To make corrections faster, you can move between the forms quickly by using such keys as PAGE DOWN and HOME.

Enter two more subscriptions

Add information for two subscriptions to the Subscription form in the Sweet Lil's database.

1   Start Microsoft Access, and open the Sweet Lil's database.

After you open a database for the first time, it will appear in a list in the Microsoft Access startup window. You can save time by double-clicking the filename in the startup window instead of opening the Open dialog box.

2   In the Database window, click the Forms tab to see the list of forms. Then double-click the Subscription form to open it.

3   Add the subscription information for Hank Proctor as shown in the previous illustration.

4   Press PAGE DOWN to move to the next record.

You can immediately see a new blank form.

5   Add the subscription information for Rita Courqette.

In reviewing the paper form, you realize that Rita's last name is misspelled.

6 Double-click in the Last Name field.

7 To replace her name, be sure that the whole word is selected, and then type
Corquette

If you want to continue to the next lesson

➤ On the Subscription form, click the Close button. Or, on the File menu, click Close.

This closes the form, but it does not exit Microsoft Access.

If you want to quit Microsoft Access for now

➤ In the Microsoft Access window, click the Close button. Or, on the File menu,
click Exit.

This closes the form and exits Microsoft Access. The changes you made to the data
in the Subscription form are saved.

Lesson Summary

To	Do this
Open a database	From the Microsoft Access startup window, double-click the database you want to open. *or* From the Microsoft Access startup window, double-click More Files, then in the Open dialog, navigate to the folder where the database file is stored, and double-click the database filename.
Open a form	In the Database window, click the Forms tab, and then double-click the form you want to open.
Select an option in an option group	Click the Option button. *or* Press an ARROW key until the option is selected.
Select or clear a check box	Click the check box. *or* Press TAB to move to the check box, and then press the SPACEBAR.

To	Do this
Move to the next record on a form	Click the Next Record button at the bottom of the form. *or* From the last field, press TAB.
Move from field to field	Click the field you want to move to. *or* Press TAB to move to the next field; press SHIFT+TAB to move to the previous field.
Move to the previous record on a form	Press PAGE UP. *or* Click the Previous Record button at the bottom of the form.
Save data	Microsoft Access automatically saves your data. This usually happens when you move to another record or window, close the form, or exit Microsoft Access.
Open a table	In the Database window, click the Tables tab, and then double-click the table you want to open.

For online information about	Use the Answer Wizard to search for
Opening databases	**open**
Moving between records	**move between records**
Saving data	**save**
Opening tables	**open**

Preview of the Next Lesson

In the next lesson, you'll use a form to look at records in two ways: one at a time, arranged like a form; and several records at once, arranged like a table in row-and-column format. You'll copy data from one record to another and add a picture to a record.

Getting the Best View of Your Data

Estimated time
40 min.

In this lesson you will learn how to:

- Switch between Form view and Datasheet view of a form.
- Change the way a datasheet looks.
- Copy and move data.
- Select values from a list.
- Insert a picture in a record.

The best view of data isn't just one view—it depends on what you're doing at the time. When you add a new product, you might want to see all the details about that product at once. When you review a group of related products, you might prefer seeing all the products in a list. However the data is arranged, you need easy, convenient ways to add and edit data.

Microsoft Access forms have the flexibility to show you both kinds of views. In this lesson, you'll find out how to see different views of data using the same form, and you'll learn more techniques for adding and editing data on a form.

17

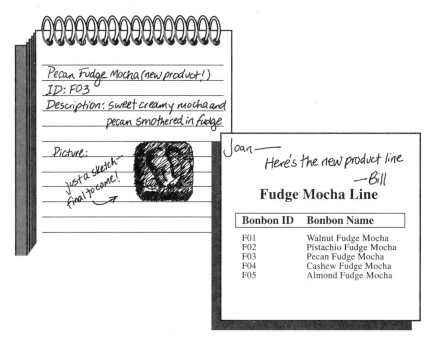

Understanding Views

A paper form shows one arrangement of your data. To see another arrangement, you have to use another form. A Microsoft Access form provides the flexibility of two views—Form view and Datasheet view. In Form view, the fields are arranged to show individual records to their best advantage. Datasheet view shows the same fields arranged in rows and columns, like a spreadsheet, so that you can see multiple records at the same time.

One form...

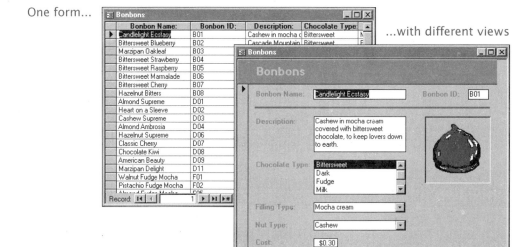

...with different views

In Datasheet view, you can rearrange columns and resize columns and rows. In either view, Microsoft Access provides powerful editing features you can use to keep your data current.

Start the lesson

➤ If Microsoft Access isn't already started, start it. Open the Sweet Lil's database as described in Lesson 1. If the Microsoft Access window doesn't fill your screen, maximize the window.

Switching Between Views of a Form

You've just been put in charge of Sweet Lil's new Fudge Mocha line. You'll use the Bonbons form to update existing records for Fudge Mocha bonbons and to add records for several new bonbons.

Open a form

1 In the Database window, click the Forms tab if it is not already active.

A list of the forms in the Sweet Lil's database appears.

2 Double-click the Bonbons form.

The Bonbons form opens, and the record for Candlelight Ecstasy appears.

In Form view, the fields on the Bonbons form are arranged so that you can see all the information about an individual bonbon at a glance. For your current task, a row-and-column format would make it easier to compare fields from different Fudge Mochas.

Switch to Datasheet view

Form View

The Form View button face will change depending on what was last selected from the drop-down list.

➤ On the toolbar, click the down arrow next to the Form View button, and then click Datasheet View.

The records in the Bonbons form appear in a row-and-column layout. The triangle next to the Candlelight Ecstasy record marks it as the current record.

You can see that two of the bonbons in the new Fudge Mocha line—Walnut Fudge Mocha and Pistachio Fudge Mocha—are already in the database (Bonbon IDs F01 and F02). These are the records you want to work with.

Move to a different record

➤ Click anywhere in the row for Walnut Fudge Mocha.

Now the record for Walnut Fudge Mocha is the current record. The triangle at the left edge of the datasheet is now pointing to the Walnut Fudge Mocha record. If you switch back to Form view, that's the record you'll see on the form.

19

Switch views

1   On the toolbar, click the down arrow next to the Form View button, and then click Form View to display the Form view.

The record for Walnut Fudge Mocha appears in the form.

2   Click the down arrow next to the Form View button, and then click Datasheet View to return to Datasheet view.

The form appears in Datasheet view. Walnut Fudge Mocha is still the current record.

Changing the Way a Datasheet Looks

The Bonbon Description field describes each bonbon in a sentence or two. You'll include these descriptions in Sweet Lil's catalog, so you want to make sure that the text is just right. With the datasheet laid out as it is now, you can see only part of each bonbon's description. To read an entire description, you'd have to use the arrow keys and the HOME and END keys to scroll through the text.

You'll change the datasheet layout so that you can read the entire description at once. To change the height of a row in a datasheet, you use the *record selector* on the left side of the record. You use the *field selector* at the top of a column to change the column width.

Field selector

Record
selector

You'll start by maximizing the Form window and then changing the row height so that you can see all of a bonbon's description at once.

Maximize the Form window

You can also double-click the Form window title bar to maximize the window.

➤   In the upper-right corner of the Form window, click the Maximize button.

The Form window is maximized.

Change the height of rows in a datasheet

1 Position the pointer on the lower border of any record selector (on the left side of the record).

Bonbon Name:	Bonbon ID:	Description:	Chocolate Type:	Filling Type:	Nut Type:
Candlelight Ecstasy	B01	Cashew in mocha c	Bittersweet	Mocha cream	Cashew
Bittersweet Blueberry	B02	Cascade Mountain	Bittersweet	Blueberry	None
Marzipan Oakleaf	B03	Marzipan shaped ir	Bittersweet	Marzipan	None
Bittersweet Strawberry	B04	Olympic Wilderness	Bittersweet	Strawberry	None
Bittersweet Raspberry	B05	Orcas Island raspbe	Bittersweet	Raspberry	None

The pointer changes shape to show that you can resize rows.

2 Drag the border downward to make the row higher.

Microsoft Access resizes all the rows. (You can't resize only one row.)

3 Adjust the height of the rows until you can read the entire description for Bittersweet Blueberry (Bonbon ID B02).

Now that you've resized the rows, you'll adjust the width of some of the columns.

Change the width of a column in a datasheet

The column for the Bonbon ID field is wider than necessary. If you make the column narrower, you'll be able to see more of the other fields in the datasheet.

1 Position the pointer on the right border of the field selector for the Bonbon ID field.

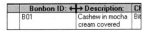

Bonbon ID:	Description:	C
B01	Cashew in mocha cream covered	Bit

You can also resize to a measurement you choose by dragging the border to the left to make the column narrower.

2 Double-click the right edge of the field selector.

Microsoft Access sizes the column to fit its widest value, but it also retains the complete field name at the top of the column.

Next, you'll make the Cost field narrower.

3 At the bottom of the form window, click in the scroll bar to see the rest of the fields.

Click here.

Microsoft Access scrolls the columns horizontally.

4 Click the arrows at either end of the scroll bar to scroll one field (one column) at a time.

5 Make the column for the Cost field narrower by double-clicking the right border of the field selector.

Hide a column

The Format menu also contains a Hide Columns command. When you choose the command, it hides the column that contains the insertion point.

The column for the Picture field doesn't show pictures for the bonbons in this view. (You can see pictures on forms in Form view but not in Datasheet view.) Because the pictures aren't visible anyway, you can hide the Picture column.

➤ Drag the right border of the Picture column all the way to its left border.

Microsoft Access hides the column.

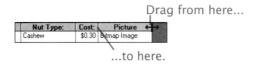

Drag from here...

...to here.

 TIP To display hidden columns, choose the Unhide Columns command from the Format menu. If the Unhide Columns dialog box indicates that the column is already showing, it might not be completely hidden. Make sure that you dragged the column's right border *all the way* to its left border.

Freeze a column

When you scroll to the fields on the right side of the datasheet, you can't see the Bonbon Name field, so you can't tell which bonbon records you're viewing. It would be more convenient to be able to scroll horizontally through the fields with the Bonbon Name field anchored, or frozen, on the left. You can do that by freezing the column.

If your screen resolution is greater than 640 by 480 pixels, you might not need to scroll and you will not see the scroll bars.

1 Scroll backward to the left side of the form.

Click here.

2 Click in any field in the Bonbon Name column.

3 From the Format menu, choose Freeze Columns.

Microsoft Access displays a bold line on the right border of the Bonbon Name column. Now the column is frozen.

4 Scroll horizontally to see the fields on the right side of the record, and then scroll backward to the left side of the form.

This column doesn't scroll.   All other columns scroll.

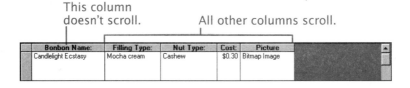

Save the layout of a form's datasheet

You can save this convenient layout so that the datasheet appears this way every time you use it.

 From the File menu, choose Save.

Scroll through a set of records

You're ready to work with the records in the Fudge Mocha line. But now that you've widened the rows in your datasheet, the records you want aren't visible. You can use either the vertical scroll bar or the PAGE DOWN key to scroll through the records.

1 In the vertical scroll bar, click below the scroll box. Or, press PAGE DOWN.

Bonbon Name:	Bonbon ID:	Description:	Chocolate Type:	Filling Type:	Nut Type:	C
Candlelight Ecstasy	B01	Cashew in mocha cream covered with bittersweet chocolate, to keep lovers down to earth.	Bittersweet	Mocha cream	Cashew	$
Bittersweet Blueberry	B02	Cascade Mountain	Bittersweet	Blueberry	None	$

Scroll box

Click here.

To scroll upward or downward one record at a time, click the arrows at the top or bottom of the scroll bar.

Microsoft Access scrolls downward one page (window).

2 Continue to click below the scroll box until you see the Fudge Mochas in the list.

Each time you click below the scroll box, the box moves down the scroll bar to show your relative position in the records.

 TIP If you know the relative position of the records you're looking for, you can move to them very quickly by dragging the scroll box. For example, if you're looking for a record in the middle of the list, drag the scroll box to the middle of the vertical scroll bar. You can see the records change as you drag the scroll box, and the ScrollTip tells you which record is at the top of the window.

Copying and Moving Data

You keep a database current and accurate by updating data in fields. Microsoft Access has convenient editing features that help you edit, move, copy, and delete data in fields. You'll find most editing features on the Edit menu and on the toolbar.

When you edit in Microsoft Access, keep in mind a principle called *select then do*. If you want to copy, delete, or change something, you first *select* it, and then you *do* it by choosing the action you want from the menu or by using buttons on the toolbar. There are also convenient keyboard shortcuts that you can use, which are listed to the right of many menu commands. For example, if you want to delete text, first you drag to select it, and then you choose Cut from the Edit menu (or press the shortcut keys CTRL+X).

When you cut or copy text or an object, Microsoft Access stores it in the Windows storage area called the *Clipboard*. When you paste, Microsoft Access pastes whatever is on the Clipboard at the current location of the insertion point. You can copy text from one field and then paste it into another field or into as many other fields as you need. That's because Windows keeps the Clipboard contents until you copy or cut something else.

Add text to a field

Market research tells you that chocolate fudge is a key ingredient for the success of your new line. You'll add the phrase "smothered in fudge" to the end of each bonbon description.

1 In the Description field for the Walnut Fudge Mocha bonbon, click between the "t" in "walnut" and the period.

The insertion point appears where you click.

2 Press the SPACEBAR to insert a space, and then type **smothered in fudge**

Copy text from one field to another

Rather than type the phrase again, you can copy it to the Description field for the Pistachio Fudge Mocha bonbon.

1 Select the phrase "smothered in fudge," including the space in front of "smothered" but not the period at the end.

Hint: Click in the space after the "t" in "walnut." Drag to select the text you want.

Copy

2 From the Edit menu, choose Copy. Or, click the Copy button on the toolbar.

Microsoft Access places a copy of the selected text on the Clipboard.

3 In the Description field for the Pistachio Fudge Mocha bonbon, position the insertion point between the "o" in "pistachio" and the period.

Paste

4 From the Edit menu, choose Paste. Or, click the Paste button on the toolbar.

Microsoft Access pastes the text from the Clipboard.

Cut

 NOTE You use the same steps to move text, except you choose Cut instead of Copy from the Edit menu (or click the Cut button to the left of the Copy button on the toolbar). Microsoft Access removes the text and places a copy of it on the Clipboard. Then you can paste the text where you want it.

Switch to Form view

Next, you'll enter records for Sweet Lil's three new Fudge Mochas—Pecan, Cashew, and Almond. You can add new records in either Datasheet view or Form view, but it's easier in Form view because you can see all the fields in a record at once.

Form View

On the toolbar, click the down arrow on the Form View button, and then click Form View.

The Bonbons form appears in Form view.

Begin a record

There's a new, blank record after the last record. You can use the navigation buttons to go to it quickly.

1 Click the New Record navigation button.

New Record button

The new record appears at the end of the last record.

2 Type this data in the first two fields:

Bonbon Name: **Pecan Fudge Mocha**
Bonbon ID: **F03**

3 In the Description field, type **Creamy sweet mocha and nutty pecan**

The next part of the description, "smothered in fudge," is still on the Clipboard. Instead of typing it, you can paste it again.

4 On the toolbar, click the Paste button.

5 Type a period at the end of the description.

Delete text

"Nutty" is redundant as an adjective for "pecan," so you'll delete it.

Select the word "nutty" and the space after it, and then press DELETE.

Replace text

To match the other Fudge Mocha descriptions, you want this description to start with "Sweet creamy" rather than "Creamy sweet." You can replace the old text at the same time that you type the new text, without deleting it first.

1 In the Description field, select "Creamy sweet."

2 Type **Sweet creamy**

Microsoft Access replaces the selected text with the text you type. Now your description is correct.

Selecting Values from Lists

A *value* is an individual piece of data, such as a last name, an address, or an ID number. Selecting a value from a list is often quicker than typing the value yourself. But lists have another advantage besides speed—they help keep your data accurate. When you select a value from a list, you know that it's spelled consistently and that it's a valid entry.

The Chocolate Type field on the Bonbons form is a special kind of field called a *list box*. List boxes display a list of values to select from. You can use either the mouse or the keyboard to select a value from the list.

The Nut Type and Filling Type fields are both *combo boxes*. With a combo box, you can either type the value yourself or select it from the list.

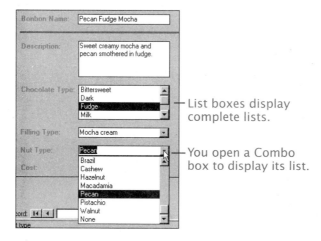

List boxes display complete lists.

You open a Combo box to display its list.

Select a value in a list box

➤ In the Chocolate Type field, click "Fudge" to select it, or press TAB to move to the Chocolate Type field, and then type **f**

"Fudge" is the only value in the Chocolate Type list box that starts with "f," so you can select "Fudge" by typing the first letter of the word. If the list box had more than one "f" value, you could type "f" to go to the first one and then use the DOWN ARROW key to move down the list.

Select a value in a combo box

You can either type the value you want in the Filling Type combo box, or you can select a value from the list. Often, it's easier and more accurate to select a value.

1 Click the arrow in the Filling Type field to display the list. Or, press TAB to move to the Filling Type field, and then press F4.

This list shows you the fillings that Sweet Lil's uses.

2   Select Mocha cream from the list.

To select the value without using the mouse, type **mo**, the first two letters in Mocha. Because Mocha cream is the only value that starts with those two letters, Microsoft Access selects it. If you wanted to select Marmalade instead of Marzipan, you'd type **marm**

3   Type **Pecan** in the Nut Type field, or select it from the list.

Enter the bonbon cost

➤   Type **.25** in the Bonbon Cost field, and then press TAB to move to the last field on the form.

When you leave the Bonbon Cost field, Microsoft Access automatically formats the value to show that it's a currency value.

You're ready to add the last value to this record—the bonbon's picture.

Adding a Picture to a Record

You can store most any kind of information in your database, including pictures, graphs, sounds, and other objects from other programs. An *OLE object* is any piece of information created with a program for Windows that supports *linking* and *embedding*. Microsoft Access stores OLE objects in a field in a table. You can store a different OLE object in each record, just as you can store a different name or address in a text field for each record. You can display the objects in any form or report.

Pictures stored in the Bonbons table...

...are displayed in the Bonbons form.

The Picture field on the Bonbons form is a special type of field called an *object frame*. You use this type of field to add, edit, or view OLE objects in your tables.

Insert a picture into a record

The picture for Pecan Fudge Mocha is in a file called Pecan.bmp. The Pecan.bmp file was copied to your Access SBS Practice folder when you copied the practice files to your hard disk. You'll insert the picture in the record for Pecan Fudge Mocha.

1   Be sure that the Picture field is selected, and then on the Insert menu, choose Object.

The Insert Object dialog box appears.

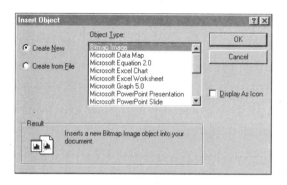

To draw a picture from scratch, you double-click Paintbrush Picture. Paint starts with an empty drawing area for you to draw in.

2   Scroll down the list of object types, and select Paintbrush Picture.

Because the picture already exists in a file, you need to tell Microsoft Access where to find it.

3   Select the Create From File option.

You can either type the name of the file you want to place or click the Browse button.

You'll learn more about using OLE in Microsoft Access in Lesson 12, "Using Pictures and Other Objects."

4   Click the Browse button.

5   If you're not in the Access SBS Practice folder, use the Directories list to switch to this folder, and then double-click Pecan.bmp.

The name and path of the picture file appears in the Insert Object dialog box. If you do not see all of the text, click in the text field and use the arrow keys to scroll through the text.

6   Click the OK button.

The picture appears in the Picture field.

28

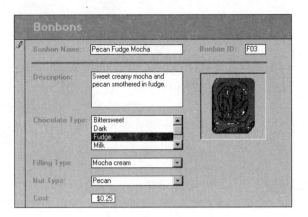

One Step Further: Adding Records to the Database and Editing a Picture

You're ready to add the other two Fudge Mocha bonbons to the database.

The fields for the Fudge Mocha line are all very similar. You could copy and paste the information and then edit it, but to speed up entry of data that is similar, you can use the Ditto key, CTRL+' (single quotation mark). You can also modify the pictures, if you want.

Add two more records

Use the datasheet view of the Bonbons form to add the records for Cashew Fudge Mocha and Almond Fudge Mocha to the database. The following tables show the data for the two records.

Remember that to display a new, empty record, you click the New Record button. The New Record button is in the lower-left corner of the form window.

If the Picture column is not visible, click Unhide Columns on the Format menu, click the check box for Picture, and then click Close.

1   Enter the data for Cashew Fudge Mocha.

Field	Data
Bonbon Name	**Cashew Fudge Mocha**
Bonbon ID	**F04**
Description	**Sweet creamy mocha and cashew smothered in fudge.**
Chocolate Type	**Fudge**
Filling Type	**Mocha cream**
Nut Type	**Cashew**
Cost	**.24**
Picture	**CASHEW.BMP**

2 Click the New Record button or the Next Record button to move to a new record. Then enter the data for Almond Fudge Mocha. Click each field, and use the Ditto key, CTRL+' (single quotation mark), to repeat any similar data from the Cashew Fudge Mocha record. Edit the information as necessary.

Field	Data
Bonbon Name	**Almond Fudge Mocha**
Bonbon ID	**F05**
Description	**Sweet creamy mocha and almond smothered in fudge.**
Chocolate Type	**Fudge**
Filling Type	**Mocha cream**
Nut Type	**Almond**
Cost	**.19**
Picture	**ALMOND.BMP**

Edit a picture

You can edit a bonbon's picture directly from the Bonbons form. The background of the picture for Almond Fudge Mocha doesn't match the other bonbon pictures, which all have light gray backgrounds. You'll fix the Almond Fudge Mocha picture to be like the others.

For help using Paint, press F1, or click Help Topics on the Help menu.

1 In the record for Almond Fudge Mocha, double-click the Picture field.

Paint starts, and the picture appears in the Paint window.

2 To change the background to light gray, click the light gray color in the palette at the bottom of the window, and then click the Fill With Color tool.

3 With the Fill With Color tool selected, click the white background of the picture. If you make a mistake, choose the Undo command from the Edit menu.

If you are editing the picture in Form view, click outside the picture when you are finished.

4 When you're finished editing the picture, click Exit & Return To Bonbons on the File menu.

If you want to continue to the next lesson

1 On the Bonbons form, click the Close button. Or, on the File menu, click Close.

2 If Microsoft Access asks whether you want to save your changes, click the Yes button.

This closes the form, but it does not exit Microsoft Access.

If you want to quit Microsoft Access for now

➤ In the Microsoft Access window, click the Close button. Or, on the File menu, click Exit.

This closes the form and exits Microsoft Access. The changes you made to the data in the Bonbons form are saved.

Lesson Summary

To	Do this	Button
Switch between Form view and Datasheet view	Click the down arrow on the Form View button, and then click Datasheet View or Form View.	
Change the height of rows or the width of a column in a datasheet	To resize rows, drag the lower border of any record selector. To resize a column, drag the right border of the column's field selector.	
Hide a column in a datasheet	Drag the right border of the column's field selector all the way to its left border. *or* Click in the column, and then click Hide Columns on the Format menu.	
Show hidden columns in a datasheet	On the Format menu, click Unhide Columns.	
Freeze the leftmost column or columns in a datasheet	Select the column or columns, and then click Freeze Columns on the Format menu.	
Copy text from one field to another	Select the text. On the toolbar, click the Copy button. Place the insertion point where you want the text to appear. On the toolbar, click the Paste button.	
Move text from one field to another	Follow the copy text procedure above, but use the Cut button instead of the Copy button.	
Insert a picture in a record	Select the field that will contain the picture, and then click Object on the Insert menu. In the Insert Object dialog box, select the object type, and then click OK. Or, in the Insert Object dialog box, select the Create From File option, and then double-click the picture you want. Click OK.	
Edit a Paint picture in a field	Double-click the picture.	

For online information about	Use the Answer Wizard to search for
Changing column widths	**resize column**
Hiding a column	**hide column**
Freezing columns	**freeze column**
Copying text from one field to another	**copy data**
Moving text from one field to another	**move data**
Inserting a picture in a record	**insert object**

Preview of the Next Lesson

In the next lesson, you'll use a form called "Boxes" to add a new box of bonbons to the database. This form contains a subform that shows which bonbons are in each box.

Saving Time with Forms

In this lesson you will learn how to:

**Estimated time
20 min.**

- Use a form with a subform to add and change data.
- Use a validation message to help you enter the right data.
- Undo your edits.
- Use a command button to perform a complicated task.
- Delete a record.

When you fill out a paper form, it's easy to make a small mistake that wastes a lot of time later, when you're ready to use the information. A simple subtraction error can result in a frustrating hour checking figures; a forgotten bit of information can eat up time while you look for the missing information and record it correctly. What you need is a form that does calculations for you, looks up missing information, and warns you if the data you enter isn't correct.

Microsoft Access forms can do all this for you. In this lesson, you'll find out how to use forms that help you start and stay with the right data.

Understanding Forms That Have Subforms

The form you'll use in this lesson—Boxes—is more complex than either the Subscription form or the Bonbons form that you used in the first two lessons. But with Microsoft Access forms, "more complex" doesn't necessarily mean "harder."

The Boxes form contains a *subform* that displays the contents of each box of bonbons. That means you can look at information about the whole box of bonbons on the main form at the same time you look at information about the bonbons on the subform. You can scroll through the records in the subform, adding and deleting bonbons, until the box of bonbons has the contents that you want.

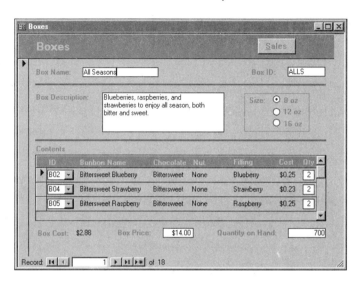

The advantage of using a form with a subform is that you can work with data from two different tables at the same time. In the Boxes form, data you enter on the main form is stored in the Boxes table. Data you enter on the subform is stored in the Box Details table. You'll learn how to create a form with a subform in Lesson 13, "Showing Related Records on a Form."

Start the lesson

> If Microsoft Access isn't started yet, start it. Open the Sweet Lil's database as described in Lesson 1. If the Microsoft Access window doesn't fill your screen, maximize the window.

Adding a Record to a Form That Has a Subform

You'll use the Boxes form to add a new box of bonbons called Winter Collection to Sweet Lil's line of products.

Open a form and go to the new record

1 Open the Boxes form. If the Tables tab is currently displayed in the Database window, be sure to click the Forms tab first. Otherwise, you'll open the Boxes table instead of the Boxes form.

Microsoft Access displays the record for All Seasons—the first box in the Boxes table.

2 Click the New Record navigation button at the bottom of the form.

The new blank record appears at the end of the existing records.

Enter data in the main form

1 Type the following data in the fields on the main form:

Box Name: **Winter Collection**

Box ID: **WINT**

Box Description: **Nuts and berries coated with chocolate and fudge for those long winter evenings by the fire.**

2 Select 12 oz in the Size option group.

3 Press TAB to move to the subform.

The insertion point moves to the first field in the subform. You'll add six different bonbons to the Winter Collection, each one containing either berries or nuts.

Enter a record in the subform

You'll learn how to create a combo box like this in Lesson 14, "Making Data Entry Easy and Accurate."

The first field in the subform will contain the Bonbon ID for the first bonbon in the Winter Collection box. The bonbon you want is Bittersweet Blueberry, but you're not sure of its ID number. The ID combo box can help you find the ID you want.

1 Open the list for the ID combo box.

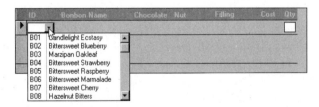

The list shows two columns: IDs in the first column and the corresponding bonbon names in the second column. When you select a row, only the ID is stored in the field. The names are there to help you make the right selection.

2 Select Bittersweet Blueberry.

The Bonbon ID, B02, appears in the ID field, and the Bonbon Name, Chocolate, Nut, Filling, and Cost fields are filled in automatically. The fields you fill in are displayed in white, and all others have a gray background.

3 Press TAB to move to the next field.

The insertion point skips fields that are already filled in and moves to the Qty field.

4 Type **3** in the Qty field, and then press TAB.

Microsoft Access saves the first record in the subform and moves the insertion point to the first field in the second record.

Enter more subform records

While you add the remaining bonbons to the subform in this exercise, the Box Cost field in the lower-left corner of the main form changes for each new record in the subform. How much a box costs Sweet Lil's depends on which bonbons are in the box. The Boxes form figures the box cost automatically while you're adding bonbons to the box.

1 Add the following two bonbons to the Winter Collection:

ID		Qty
B05	Bittersweet Raspberry	3
D03	Cashew Supreme	3

The record for the Cashew Supreme bonbon fills up the subform, but you have two more bonbons to add to the box. Look at the vertical scroll bar on the right side of the subform. The presence of the scroll bar means the subform can contain more records, and you can scroll upward and downward through the records to see them.

2 After filling in the quantity of the Cashew Supreme record, press TAB to move to the next record in the subform.

The subform scrolls to show another new, blank record.

3 Add the following three bonbons to the Winter Collection:

ID		Qty
D07	Classic Cherry	3
F01	Walnut Fudge Mocha	3
F02	Pistachio Fudge Mocha	3

4 When you're finished adding the records, scroll upward and downward in the subform to check your work. Make sure that each record is correct before going on.

Moving out of a subform

Now that you've added all the bonbons to the new box, you're ready to fill in the two fields in the lower portion of the main form—Box Price and Quantity On Hand.

➤ Press CTRL+TAB to move to the next field on the main form.

The insertion point moves out of the subform to the Box Price field on the main form. You can also move to the Box Price field by clicking it, but when you're entering new records, it's often easier to keep your hands on the keyboard rather than move back and forth between the mouse and the keyboard.

TIP   When you're using a form with a subform, you can think of the CTRL key as the "subform" key. Just as pressing TAB moves you to the next field within a subform or main form, pressing CTRL+TAB moves you from the subform to the next field in the main form. And just as pressing SHIFT+TAB moves you to the previous field within a subform or main form, pressing CTRL+SHIFT+TAB moves you from the subform to the previous field in the main form.

Entering the Right Data

You've already seen a number of ways that a Microsoft Access form can help you enter the right data. For example, the ID combo box in the subform helps you pick the right ID by showing you bonbon names as well as IDs. After you pick a bonbon, Microsoft Access automatically fills in fields, such as the Bonbon Name and Chocolate fields, saving you time and the possibility of data entry errors in those fields. While you're adding bonbons to the box, Microsoft Access automatically figures the cost of the box and displays it in the Box Cost field, saving you the effort of making the calculation yourself.

A form can also help you enter the right data by displaying a message when you enter incorrect information.

Get help correcting wrong data

The note you have from Sweet Lil's Marketing department says to start the new box at the special introductory price of $7.50.

1   Type **7.50** in the Box Price field, and then press TAB.

Microsoft Access displays a validation message that tells you the value you entered is incorrect and gives you information on how to correct the problem.

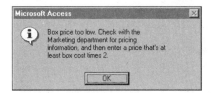

NOTE   If the message doesn't appear, the problem might be in the Box Cost field. The Box Price field checks the value in the Box Cost field and displays its message if the price is less than twice the cost. The Box Cost field is calculated automatically from the records entered in the subform. If you don't see the message, make sure that you entered the subform records correctly.

37

2   Click the OK button.

After calling the Marketing department, you find out that they made a mistake on their note and meant to start the box at $17.50.

3   Type a **1** before the 7 in the Box Price field, and then press TAB.

Microsoft Access accepts this price, adds a dollar sign, and moves the insertion point to the Quantity On Hand field.

4   Type **0** (zero) in the Quantity On Hand field.

This is a new box, so you don't have any in stock yet.

Microsoft Access rejected the price of $7.50 because the Box Price field has a *validation rule* attached to it. The value you enter in the field is checked against the rule; if the value breaks the rule, a message appears. You can't leave the field until you correct the invalid data.

Undoing Your Edits

With Microsoft Access, you can use the Undo button to undo changes you have made to the current field or record. You can also use the Undo commands on the Edit menu to undo recent actions.

Make changes and then undo your most recent action

1   Select "Nuts and berries" at the beginning of the description for the Winter Collection, and then type **Berries and nuts**

2   Place the insertion point in front of "fire," type **roaring**, and then press the SPACEBAR.

After looking over the changes, you decide that "roaring" doesn't sound quite right.

Undo

3   On the toolbar, click the Undo button.

Microsoft Access deletes "roaring," your most recent change.

Undo all edits in the current field

After making numerous changes to the text in a field, you might decide that you prefer the original text.

▶   On the Edit menu, click the Undo Current Field/Record command.

All the edits you made to the Box Description field since moving the insertion point into the field are undone, and the Undo button becomes unavailable because there are no more changes to undo in the Box Description field.

Using a Command Button

Sometimes one task turns into many related tasks. For example, you might be looking at information about the contents of a product on one form and realize that you want to see sales information for the product, too. So you open a sales form and find the appropriate sales information. This related task can require a number of steps to complete.

A *command button* on a form condenses related tasks into a single step. A command button can perform one action or a series of actions, depending on how the button is defined.

Now that you've added the Winter Collection box to the database, you'll use a command button to check on the sales of one of Sweet Lil's best sellers—the Autumn Collection.

Go to a specific record

The Autumn Collection is the third box in the Boxes form.

1   To the right of the word "Record," in the lower-left corner of the window, select the current record number, and then type **3**

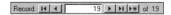

2   Press ENTER.

The record for the Autumn Collection—the third record in the table—appears.

Use a command button to perform a task

The Boxes form shows the contents of the Autumn Collection box. You can use the Sales command button to see the sales for this box.

1   Click the Sales button at the top of the Boxes form.

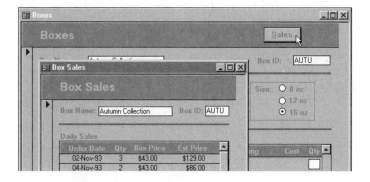

The Box Sales form appears. Like the Boxes form, the Box Sales form has a subform. The main form shows the name of the box at the top and the total sales for the box at the bottom of the form. The subform shows daily sales for the box.

2   Scroll through the records in the Daily Sales subform to see all the sales.

3   When you're finished looking at the sales of the Autumn Collection, click the Close button in the Box Sales form to close it (or choose Close from the File menu).

4   Close the Boxes form.

Deleting Records

In most databases, the only real constant is that data is constantly changing. You add records when you have to keep track of new people or things. You change records when the data changes. And you delete records when you no longer need to track the people or things that the records are about.

Sweet Lil's receives this note in the morning's mail:

Dear Sweet Lil's:

My son buys your chocolates frequently and loves them. In fact, he told me that he recently gave you my name to add to your customer list. I'm trying to lose some weight, so please don't add me to your list. No need to waste the catalog.

Thank you,

Francois Marcus

Go to the record you want to delete

Francois Marcus was just added to the Customers table last night. Using the View Customers form, you'll delete his record now.

1   Open the View Customers form.

2   Click the navigation button for the last record.

If you followed the steps in Lesson 1, the four new customers you added to the database are at the end of the records, and Francois Marcus's record is right before theirs. If you didn't do Lesson 1, Francois Marcus's record is the last record.

3   If necessary, click the Previous Record button until you see Francois Marcus's record (ID 436).

Delete a record

Delete Record

1   On the toolbar, click the Delete Record button. Or, click the Delete Record command on the Edit menu.

2   When Microsoft Access asks you to confirm the deletion, click the Yes button.

The record is deleted.

3   Close the View Customers form.

One Step Further: Adding a New Product and Deleting a Record in a Subform

You are ready to add one more season to the bonbon collections. If you change your mind about which items to include in the new collection, you can delete the information from the subform in the same way you did in the main form, or you can use a shortcut menu command.

Add a new box

Using the Boxes form, add a new box called Spring Collection.

1. Open the Boxes form.
2. Start a new record and enter the following data for the new box:

Box Name:	**Spring Collection**
Box ID:	**SPRI**
Box Description:	**Hearts and flowers make the perfect gift for springtime lovers.**
Size:	**12 oz**

3. In the Contents subform, enter the following data:

ID		Qty
D02	Heart on a Sleeve	3
D09	American Beauty	3
M06	Lover's Heart	3
M07	Apple Amore	3
M10	Forget-Me-Not	3
W02	Calla Lily	3
W03	Broken Heart	3

4. Finish the Spring Collection by entering this information on the bottom of the main form. Use CTRL+TAB to move to the main form.

Box Price:	**$23.50**
Quantity on Hand:	**0**

Delete a record in a subform

As you study the new collection, you decide to make some changes in what bonbons are included. Use the following steps to delete information in two different ways.

You decide to take the Lover's Heart and the Apple Amore bonbons out of this collection.

1   Delete the Lover's Heart bonbon from the Spring Collection. Use the same approach to delete a record in a subform as you did in the main form. First select the record by displaying it and clicking in any field (in this case, the ID or Qty fields). Then click the Delete Record button, and click Yes to confirm the deletion.

2   Use the same procedure to delete the Apple Amore record.

3   Add 1 to the quantity of the American Beauty, Forget-Me-Not, and Calla Lily bonbons so that the box contains four of each flower bonbon.

If you want to continue to the next lesson

1   On the Boxes form, click the Close button. Or, on the File menu, click Close.

2   If Microsoft Access asks whether you want to save your changes, click the Yes button.

    This closes the form, but it does not exit Microsoft Access.

If you want to quit Microsoft Access for now

➤   In the Microsoft Access window, click the Close button. Or, in the File menu, click Exit.

    This closes the form and exits Microsoft Access. The changes you made to the data in the Boxes and View Customers forms are saved.

Lesson Summary

To	Do this
Add a record with the New Record button	Click the New Record Navigation button at the bottom of the form.
Move from a main form to a field on a subform	Click the field in the subform. *or* From the last field on the main form before the subform, press TAB.
Move from a subform to a field on a main form	Click the field in the main form. *or* Press CTRL+TAB to move to the next field on the main form; press CTRL+SHIFT+TAB to move to the previous field on the main form.

To	Do this	Button
Respond to a validation message (a message that says you entered the wrong data in a field)	Click the OK button, and then correct the data in the field.	
Undo your most recent changes	On the toolbar, click the Undo button. *or* Use the Undo command on the Edit menu.	
Go directly to a specific record	Type the record number in the Record Number box between the navigation buttons at the bottom of the form, and then press ENTER.	
Delete a record	Select the record by displaying it and clicking in any field in the record. Then click the Delete Record button. *or* Select the record by displaying it and clicking in any field in the record. Then click Delete Record on the Edit menu.	

For online information about	Use the Answer Wizard to search for
Adding records to a form	**new record**
Undoing changes	**undo**
Deleting records	**delete record**

Preview of the Next Lesson

In the next lesson, you'll learn how to focus on finding the data that answers your questions. You'll find out how to filter records to get a set of related records, to sort records, and to find a record that contains a particular value in it.

Lesson

4

Finding Information

Estimated time
35 min.

In this lesson you will learn how to:

- Find a record with a particular value in it.
- Filter records to get a set of related records.
- Sort records.

You ask the questions; Microsoft Access provides the answers. When you're interested in milk chocolates, you don't want to look at data about bittersweets. When you're interested in your Toronto customers, you don't want to see all of your other customers.

While you're viewing data in forms, you can focus on the information you're interested in without wading through irrelevant data. In this lesson, you'll learn how to ask questions so that Microsoft Access displays only the data you want to see.

45

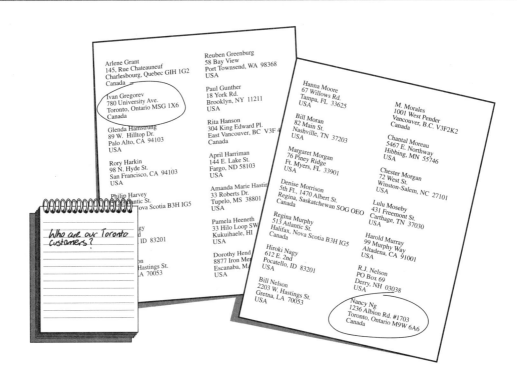

Finding One Record or a Group of Records

Microsoft Access is more helpful than a filing cabinet or a pile of paper, because you can find just the records you need, sorted the way you want them. Whether your database contains hundreds, thousands, or even millions of records, Microsoft Access finds just what you ask for and sorts the data just the way you want.

For quick searches, when you're looking for only one record, use the Find button on the toolbar. For example, you can find the record for the bonbon named Brazilian Supreme.

When you want to see a particular group of records, such as all the customers in Toronto, you create a *filter* to tell Microsoft Access which records you're interested in. When you create a filter, you give Microsoft Access a set of *criteria* that describe the records you want to see. Microsoft Access then displays the records in a form or in a form datasheet.

Records can be shown in a form...

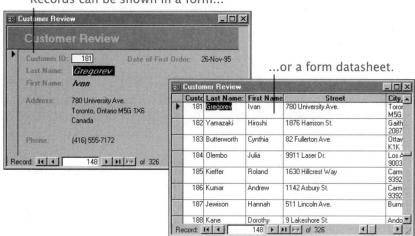

...or a form datasheet.

You can also *sort* records in alphabetical or numerical order. For example, you could sort your customers alphabetically by last name.

Start the lesson

➤ If Microsoft Access isn't started yet, start it. Open the Sweet Lil's database as described in Lesson 1. If the Microsoft Access window doesn't fill your screen, maximize the window.

Finding a Record

This morning you found on your desk a slip of paper that read "Call N. Valerio—she's going to cancel her order if you don't get back to her immediately!" But the note doesn't have a phone number on it. You need to look up her number in the Sweet Lil's database.

A fast way to get this customer's record is to use the Find button on the toolbar.

Open a form

> In the Database window, click the Forms tab if it is not already active, and then double-click the Customer Review form.

The form opens, and the first record appears.

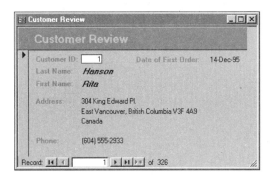

Find a record

1   Click in the Last Name field.

You don't need to select the entire last name—just click anywhere in the field. Even though the last name (Hanson) is on a gray background, you can still click in it to select it.

Find

2   On the toolbar, click the Find button.

The Find In Field dialog box appears. The title bar of the Find In Field dialog box shows the name of the field you're searching in—Last Name.

If the Find In Field dialog box blocks your view of the form, you can move it out of the way by dragging its title bar.

3   In the Find What box, type **Valerio**

You have the option of searching in all the fields for Valerio. Because you know the value is in the Last Name field (the current field), you can make the search go faster by searching only in the current field.

4   Click the Find First button.

The record for Nina Valerio appears.

This appears to be the customer you need to call, but you'd better check to make sure that there's not another customer with the same last name.

5   Click the Find Next button.

Microsoft Access doesn't find another Valerio.

6   Click OK to continue.

7   On the Find In Field dialog box, click the Close button to close the dialog box.

Now you know that you have only one customer named Valerio and that you can call her.

Find a record even if you don't know much about it

As soon as you hang up the phone with Nina Valerio, you get a call from a clerk in Sweet Lil's Shipping department. He's having trouble reading the address on a shipping label. All he can make out is part of the street name, which starts with "Stew." He asks whether you could find the name and address of the customer with this small amount of information.

1   In the Customer Review form, click in the field that contains the street address (the first line in the address).

You don't have to go back to the first record in the table—you can use the Find button from any customer's record.

2   On the toolbar, click the Find button.

The Find In Field dialog box appears. The Find What box still contains your last entry, Valerio.

3   Type **Stew** in the Find What box.

4   Click the down arrow next to the Match box, and select Any Part Of Field.

Because "Stew" is only part of the street name, you want to search for it no matter where it occurs in the field.

5   Click the Find First button.

Microsoft Access finds an address with "Stewart" in the street address.

You can make a search case-sensitive (find only text with the same uppercase and lowercase letters) by selecting the Match Case check box.

6   Click the Find Next button.

Microsoft Access finds a second record with "stew" in the address. This "stew" doesn't have a capital S, because it appears in the middle of a word.

7   Click the Find Next button again.

Microsoft Access doesn't find another "Stew," so you have two possible customers for the Shipping department.

8   Click the Close button to close the Find In Field dialog box, and then close the Customer Review form.

Filtering to Find a Group of Related Records

Suppose you're creating a promotional box of chocolates, and you want to include a bonbon that contains white chocolate. You'd like to review all the bonbons that contain white chocolate before making your choice. There are two new filtering methods in Microsoft Access for Windows 95: Filter by Selection and Filter by Form. You'll use both methods to filter the data you want.

 NOTE   If you followed the steps in Lesson 2, "Getting the Best View of Your Data," your datasheet will look a little different from the following illustration. The appearance of the datasheet doesn't matter, though—you can still follow the steps given in this lesson to create a filter.

1   Open the Bonbons form.

The form opens and displays the first record in the Bonbons table. The Bonbons form is designed to display a single record of data. In this case, you want to see all the bonbons that contain white chocolate, so you'll switch to the form's Datasheet view.

Form View

The Form View button face will change depending on what was last selected from the drop-down list.

2   On the toolbar, click the down arrow on the Form View button, and then click Datasheet View. Or, click Datasheet View on the View menu.

Bonbon Name:	Bonbon ID:	Description:	Chocolate Type:	Fill
Candlelight Ecstasy	B01	Cashew in mocha c	Bittersweet	Moch
Bittersweet Blueberry	B02	Cascade Mountain	Bittersweet	Bluet
Marzipan Oakleaf	B03	Marzipan shaped ir	Bittersweet	Marzi
Bittersweet Strawberry	B04	Olympic Wilderness	Bittersweet	Straw
Bittersweet Raspberry	B05	Orcas Island raspbe	Bittersweet	Rasp
Bittersweet Marmalade	B06	Marmalade covered	Dark	Marm
Bittersweet Cherry	B07	Royal Anne cherry	Bittersweet	Cherr
Hazelnut Bitters	B08	Classic hazelnut co	Bittersweet	None
Almond Supreme	D01	Whole almond han(	Dark	None
Heart on a Sleeve	D02	Dark chocolate witf	Dark	Cherr
Cashew Supreme	D03	Giant whole cashei	Dark	None
Almond Ambrosia	D04	Classic almond in a	Dark	Amar(
Hazelnut Supreme	D06	Whole hazelnut hai	Dark	None
Classic Cherry	D07	Whole cherry in cla	Dark	Cherr
Chocolate Kiwi	D08	Brazil nut surrounde	Dark	None
American Beauty	D09	Rich, dark chocola	Dark	None
Marzipan Delight	D11	Delicious marzipan	Dark	Marzi
Walnut Fudge Mocha	E01	Sweet creamy moc	Fudge	Moch

Record: 1 of 42

The Chocolate Type field shows the type of chocolate that each bonbon contains. For example, Candlelight Ecstasy has bittersweet chocolate.

To create a simple, quick filter, you'll use the new "filter by selection" method. You'll select the data you want to filter and then use the new Filter By Selection button on the toolbar.

3   Click anywhere in the Chocolate Type field.

First you'll use the Find button to find White in the Chocolate Type field.

Find

4   On the toolbar, click the Find button, and then search for "white."

The first record containing white chocolate is displayed. Close the Find In Field dialog box.

Filter By Selection

5   On the toolbar, click the Filter By Selection button.

All records containing "white" in the Chocolate Type field are displayed, and all other records are hidden. The navigation area at the bottom of the form window indicates that you are looking at filtered data.

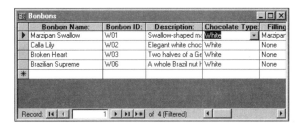

Add more criteria

Because you have to keep the cost of this promotional box down, you'd like to see only the white chocolate bonbons that cost less than $0.30 each. To use more criteria in your filter, you will use the new "Filter by form" method.

Filter By Form

1 On the toolbar, click the Filter By Form button.

The Filter By Form dialog box appears. The criteria "white" is already in the Chocolate Type field, because your previous filter is still applied. Next you'll add an additional criterion onto the Cost field.

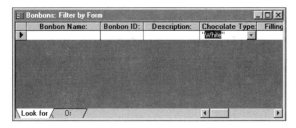

2 Using the scroll bar at the bottom of the dialog box, scroll to the right until you see the Cost field.

3 Click in the Cost field.

An arrow button appears in the Cost field. If you click the arrow, you can select a specific criterion from a list of the entries in the field.

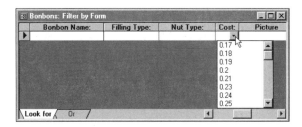

52

4 Click the arrow button in the Cost field. Then scroll down the list, and select 0.3.

This filter will show you records for all the bonbons that contain white chocolate and cost $0.30 each; but you want to see all the bonbons that contain white chocolate and cost *less than* $0.30, so you'll add a *comparison operator* to the filter.

5 Click on the left of the 0, and then type a less-than sign (<).

The comparison operator (in this case, the less-than sign) tells Microsoft Access to select all the white chocolate bonbons that cost less than $0.30. Next you'll apply the filter you've created.

Apply Filter

6 On the toolbar, click the Apply Filter button.

The filter is applied, and the two records that meet the filter criteria are displayed.

Bonbon Name:	Description:	Chocolate Type	Filling Type:	Nut Type:	Cost:
Calla Lily	Elegant white choc	White	None	None	$0.27
Brazilian Supreme	A whole Brazil nut	White	None	Brazil	$0.28

Record: 1 of 2 (Filtered)

Remove Filter

7 To see all the records again, click the Remove Filter button.

The Apply Filter button becomes the Remove Filter button after you apply a filter. All filters are removed, and all the records in the datasheet appear.

Sorting Records

Suppose you want to introduce your new assistant to the different kinds of bonbons that Sweet Lil's makes. She knows the names of the bonbons, but you'd like her to learn more about their ingredients, too. To make the bonbons easier for her to find, you'll sort them in alphabetical order.

Sort records alphabetically with a sort button

You can sort alphabetically directly in the form window, in either Form view or Datasheet view. In either case, you select the field that you want to sort and then click a Sort button.

1 In the Bonbons form window, click any record in the Bonbon Name field.

2 On the toolbar, click the Sort Ascending button. Or, point to Sort on the Records menu, and then click Ascending.

Sort Ascending

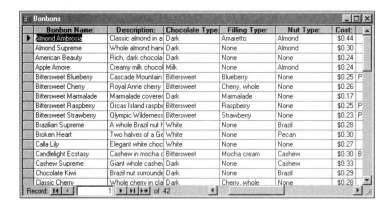

Ascending means that records are sorted from A to Z. Descending means that records are sorted from Z to A.

Sort records numerically with a sort button

Your assistant wants to know which bonbons are the most expensive. You'll sort the records so that the datasheet displays the most expensive bonbons first.

1   In the Cost field, click any record.

Sort Descending

2   On the toolbar, click the Sort Descending button. Or, point to Sort on the Records menu, and then click Descending.

Descending means that numerical records are sorted from highest to lowest, so the most expensive bonbon appears at the top.

3   Close the Bonbons form.

Microsoft Access for Windows 95 saves sorts with the form. The next time you open the Bonbons form, the records will still be sorted the way they were when you closed the form. Filters are not saved with forms, but in Part 3, "Asking Questions and Getting Answers," you'll learn how to create and use a *query*. A query is like a saved filter that you can use again and again, without having to reconstruct the filter each time.

One Step Further: Creating Additional Filters

Suppose it's spring of 1996. In late 1995, Sweet Lil's launched a marketing promotion in Canada. It's time to decide whether to recommend the promotion for the United States by studying how successful the Canadian campaign was. Working with filters allows you to quickly find and look at particular records. This exercise shows you more ways to specify information for your filter.

Find out who are the new customers from Canada

Create a filter that shows the Canadian customers who were added on or after December 15, 1995, the first day of the promotion.

1 Open the Customer Review form.

You'll build this filter in Form view instead of Datasheet view, so be sure that Form view is displayed.

Filter By Form

2 On the toolbar, click the Filter By Form button to begin building your filter.

The Filter By Form dialog box looks different this time, because you are building the filter in Form view.

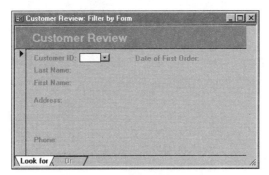

3 Press TAB four times so that the insertion point is in between Address and Phone.

A down arrow for a list box appears to the right of the insertion point.

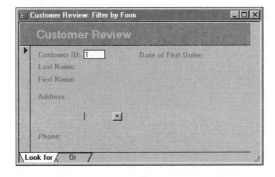

4   Click the down arrow, and select Canada.

"Canada" appears as a criteria in the Filter By Form dialog box. You could run a simple filter now by clicking the Apply Filter button, but for this exercise you'll add another, more complex criterion and a sort order.

5   On the Filter menu, click Advanced Filter/Sort.

The Advanced Filter/Sort dialog box appears, displaying the filter criteria you set in the previous steps. Next you'll add criteria for Date Of First Order and then sort the filtered records.

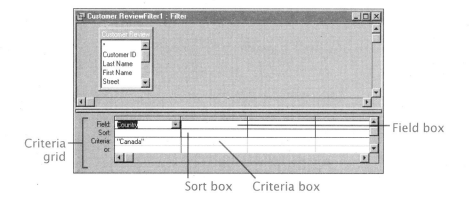

Criteria grid

Field box

Sort box   Criteria box

6   Press TAB to move to the next empty Field box in the criteria grid.

7   Click the down arrow for the empty Field box. Then scroll down, and select Date Of First Order.

8   Click in the Sort box below Date Of First Order. Then click the Sort box down arrow, and select Descending.

This sorts the records so that you see the newest customers (those with the most recent Date Of First Order) first.

9   To specify the dates you want to filter, click in the Criteria box under Date Of First Order. Then type the expression >=**15-Dec-95** and press ENTER.

The expression means "on or after December 15, 1995." After you enter the expression, Microsoft Access puts number signs (#) around the date, indicating that it is a date/time value.

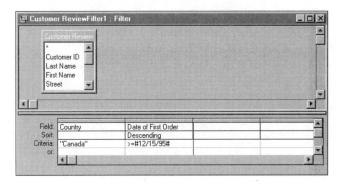

Apply Filter

10 On the toolbar, click the Apply Filter button to apply the filter.

The filter is applied, as indicated in the navigation area at the bottom of the form. You can use the navigation buttons to see each of the individual records resulting from the filter, or you can switch to Datasheet view to see all the filtered records at once. You can apply advanced filters in either Form view or Datasheet view.

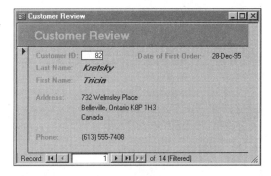

Form View

11 On the toolbar, click the down arrow on the Form View button, and select Datasheet View to see all of the filtered records at once. Or, click Datasheet View on the View menu.

If you want to continue to the next lesson

➤ On the Customer Review form, click the Close button. Or, on the File menu, click Close.

This closes the form, but it does not exit Microsoft Access.

If you want to quit Microsoft Access for now

➤ In the Microsoft Access window, click the Close button. Or, on the File menu, click Exit.

This closes the form and exits Microsoft Access.

Lesson Summary

To	Do this	Button
Find a specific record	On the toolbar, click the Find button, and fill in the dialog box.	
Apply a filter with Filter By Selection	Select a criteria in Form view or Datasheet view, and then click the Filter By Selection button on the toolbar.	
Apply a filter with Filter By Form	On the toolbar, click the Filter By Form button. Select criteria in the Filter By Form dialog box, and then click the Apply Filter button on the toolbar.	
Set criteria for an advanced filter	In the criteria grid of the Advanced Filter dialog box, select a field in the Field box, and then type a criteria expression in the Criteria box below the Field box.	
Sort records in a filter	With the form in Datasheet view, click in a field, and then click the Sort Ascending or Sort Descending button. *or* In the Criteria grid of the Advanced Filter dialog box, select Ascending or Descending in the Sort box below the field you want to sort on.	
Look at all records after you've applied a filter	Click the Remove Filter button.	

For online information about	Use the Answer Wizard to search for
Specifying criteria	**criteria**
Using expressions	**expression**

Preview of the Next Lesson

In the next lesson, you'll learn how to use reports to print information from your database. You'll print a sales report, and you'll create and print mailing labels.

Printing Reports and Mailing Labels

Lesson

5

Estimated time
25 min.

In this lesson you will learn how to:

- Open and preview a report.
- Print a report.
- Create and print mailing labels.

How many different ways do you use a customer's address or a product's name? The address might appear on an invoice and a mailing label. The product name might appear on the same invoice and on a sales report. Using Microsoft Access forms and reports, you can arrange and combine your data however you want. To present your data to its best advantage in print, use a report.

Reports can show all of the information in the database or just the information you want to highlight. Reports can also show other critical information, such as subtotals and totals. In this lesson, you'll open, preview, and print a sales report. Then you'll create a mailing label report and print your mailing labels.

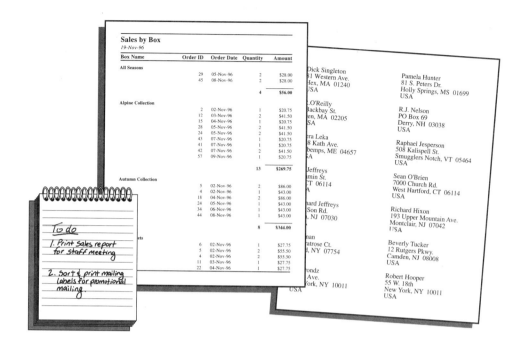

What Is a Report?

Up to now, you've used forms to put information in your database and to edit and find that information. Now you'll use reports to print the results of your work.

You can use either a form or a report to print detailed information, such as lists of records. For example, you could use either a form or a report to print a list of all your customers. A report is especially useful, however, when you want to print summary information, such as subtotals and totals. Microsoft Access calculates these for you and prints them on your report.

An additional advantage to using a report is that it gives you greater control than a form over exactly where the data prints on a page. For example, you can use a report to print records in snaking columns, like entries in a phone book. This type of layout is especially useful for printing mailing labels and phone lists.

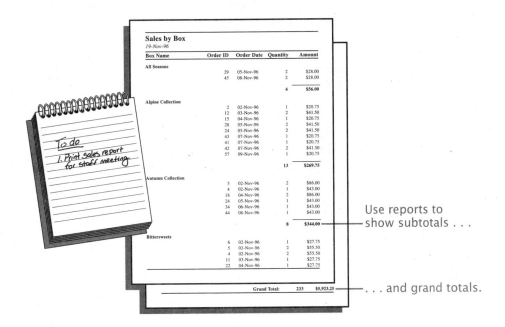

Use reports to show subtotals . . .

. . . and grand totals.

Start the lesson

▶ If Microsoft Access isn't started yet, start it. Open the Sweet Lil's database as described in Lesson 1. If the Microsoft Access window doesn't fill your screen, maximize the window.

Previewing a Report

Sweet Lil's marketing staff is planning a mail-order campaign to stimulate sales for assortments of chocolates that aren't selling well. You can print a report on recent box sales that will help you pick which boxes to promote. You'll use the Sales By Box report to see how the assortments have been selling during a one-week period in November.

Preview a report

1 In the Database window, click the Reports tab.

2 Double-click the Sales By Box report.

A dialog box appears that asks you to enter the dates for the period you want the report to cover.

3 Type **2-Nov-95** as a starting date, and then press ENTER.

To find out which country your computer is set for, open the Windows Control Panel, and double-click the Regional Settings icon.

Microsoft Access recognizes a number of ways to enter dates. For example, you could have used 11/2/95, another United States format. The Canadian (English) format is 2/11/95.

4 In the next dialog box, type **9-Nov-95** as an ending date, and then press ENTER.

Microsoft Access collects the appropriate data and opens the report in Print Preview (notice that your toolbar has changed).

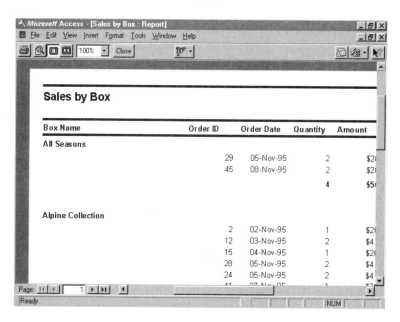

Look at a whole page at once

The report is magnified in Print Preview so that you can clearly read the data. The magnifying-glass pointer means you can switch views: Zoom out to see how the data is laid out on the whole page, and zoom in to see the magnified view.

Zoom

▶ Click anywhere on the report with the magnifying-glass pointer. Or, click the Zoom button on the toolbar to display the whole page.

Zoom in on the data

The layout looks fine. Now you'll make sure that you have the data you want.

➤ Click anywhere on the report. Or, click the Zoom button on the toolbar.

Now you're looking at the magnified view again.

Move around the page

If you want your report to have wider margins, click Page Setup on the File menu.

➤ Use the vertical scroll bar to move up and down the page, and use the horizontal scroll bar to move from left to right.

The data looks right—sales for the week of November 2, 1995.

Move from page to page

Before printing the report, take a quick look at each page. Your report is five pages long. The last page includes the grand total for all the boxes.

➤ Use the navigation buttons at the bottom of the window to page through the report.

Previous page   Last page

First page   Next page

The report looks great—it's ready to print.

Printing a Report

When you print a report, you have the option of specifying a range of pages if you don't want to print the entire report, and you can specify how many copies you want to print. If you print more than one copy, you can have Microsoft Access collate the copies for you. You can also print the report to a file on your disk instead of to the printer so that you can print the file at a later date.

If you're set up to print, you can print the Sales By Box report now.

Print a report from Print Preview

You can print a report quickly, using the default print settings, by clicking the Print button on the toolbar.

1 On the File menu, click Print.

The Print dialog box appears. In this case, you want to print one copy of the whole report, so you don't need to change any of the settings in the Print dialog box.

2 If you are set up with an active printer, click OK; otherwise, click Cancel.

3 Close the Sales By Box report.

TIP As you've seen, when you double-click a report in the Database window, Microsoft Access opens it in Print Preview so that you can see how the report will look on the page before you print it. To print a report without opening it first in Print Preview, select the report in the Database window; then click Print on the File menu, or click the Print button on the toolbar.

Creating Mailing Labels

Based on your report, you decide to promote the two slowest-selling boxes by discounting them in a special mailing to all customers. You'll create mailing labels and print the labels sorted by postal code.

To create mailing labels, you use an Access *wizard*. A wizard is like a database expert who asks you questions about the form or report you want, and then builds it for you according to your answers. You use Form Wizard to build forms and Report Wizard to build reports. Your mailing labels will be a new report in the database.

Create mailing labels

Because you just printed the Sales By Box report, the Database window is still showing the list of reports.

1   Click the New button.

The New Report dialog box appears.

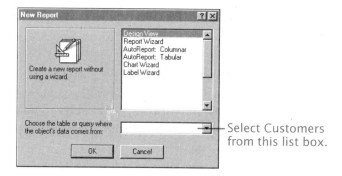

Select Customers from this list box.

2   In the list of wizards, select Label Wizard.

3   In the list box below the list of wizards, click the down arrow to display the list of tables and queries, and then select Customers.

The Customers table contains the names and addresses you want to print in the mailing labels.

4   Click OK.

The Label Wizard dialog box appears.

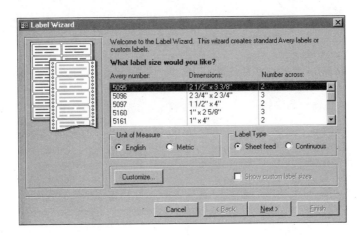

Select the mailing label size

You can choose from a wide range of label sizes, listed in either English measurements (inches) or metric measurements. If you have label stock on hand, use the Avery stock number to help you select the label size you want.

In the Label Type area, you can select the label paper type: sheet feed or continuous feed.

➤ Select Avery number 5260 (scroll down to find it), and then click Next.

The Label Wizard displays a dialog box for formatting the text in your labels.

Choose the font and color for the appearance of your text

You can make selections that will affect the appearance of your text. For now, accept the choices that Microsoft Access already has set.

➤ Click the Next button.

Define the label appearance

1 In the Available Fields box, double-click the First Name field.

Microsoft Access adds the field to the first line of your mailing label. You'll type spaces and punctuation marks in between the fields.

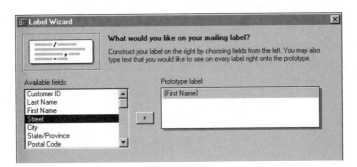

2   Press the SPACEBAR to put a space between first names and last names.

3   Double-click the Last Name field.

Microsoft Access adds the Last Name field to the first line of your mailing label, after the space you typed.

4   Press ENTER to go to the second line of the mailing label.

5   Define the second, third, and fourth lines of the mailing label as follows. If you make a mistake in a line of text, select the line, and use the BACKSPACE key to remove an item from the mailing label.

■ Street field in the second line.

■ City, State/Province, and Postal Code fields in the third line, with appropriate punctuation between them.

■ Country field in the fourth line.

When you're finished, the box for your mailing label prototype should look like the following illustration.

Type a comma and a space here...

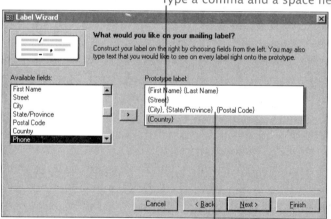

...and two spaces here.

The third line has three fields in it, with a comma and space after the first field and two spaces between the last two fields.

6   Click the Next button.

Now that you've defined the mailing label appearance, you'll tell Microsoft Access how to sort the printed labels.

Sort the labels

You want to sort the mailing labels by postal code so that all the labels with the same postal code are printed together.

1   In the Available Fields box, double-click the Postal Code field.

   Microsoft Access adds Postal Code to the list of fields that define the sort order.

2   Click the Next button.

Preview your mailing labels

   Click the Finish button.

   The labels appear as they will print on the page. If you want, you can scroll through the labels.

NOTE   If the labels don't appear lined up evenly, it might be due to a mismatch between your printer driver and the label size or format. Try different label sizes.

Because you know that you'll be making frequent mailings to your customers, you can save this mailing label report so that it's available any time you want customer labels.

Close the mailing label report

The report was automatically saved as Labels Customers when you created it, so you do not need to save it again.

   Close the Labels Customers report.

   Your new report appears in the list of reports in the Database window. Now whenever you need mailing labels for your customers, you can print this report.

When you created the Labels Customers report, you saved the definition of the mailing labels, but not the actual names and addresses that print on the labels. The data printed on the labels is stored in the Customers table. When Sweet Lil's gets a new customer, you add the customer's information to the Customers table. When a customer moves, you update the address in the Customers table. The next time you print the Labels Customers report, Microsoft Access automatically draws the most current data from the Customers table and prints a label for each customer.

One Step Further: Creating a Phone List

The Label Report Wizard makes it easy to create a variety of mailing labels. You can use the Label Report Wizard to create other types of reports as well.

Create a phone list

Use the Label Wizard to create a handy phone list that you can keep beside your phone or in your briefcase.

1 To create a new report, click the Reports tab in the Database window, and then click the New button.

2 In the list of wizards, select Label Wizard.

3 In the list box below the wizards, select Customers, and then click OK.

4 To answer the question "What label size would you like?" select Avery 5160 (or any 3-across mailing label), and then click Next.

5 To answer the question "What font and color would you like your text to be?" leave the default settings, and then click Next.

6 From the Available Fields box, specify the fields in the following illustration by double-clicking each one. Put punctuation between the appropriate fields by typing the commas and spaces. Press ENTER to move to a new line. When you have finished specifying the fields, click the Next button.

7 To answer the question "Which fields would you like to sort by?" double-click Last Name in the Available Fields box, and then click the Next button.

8 To answer the question "What name would you like for your report?" type **Customer Phone List**, and then click Finish.

9 To switch the magnification to preview your report, use the Zoom button on the toolbar, or click anywhere on the report with the magnifying-glass pointer.

10 When you're finished viewing the report, you can close it.

After you've created a report with a wizard, you can make changes and adjustments in the design to customize the report's appearance. You'll learn how to do this in the lessons in Part 5, "Customizing Your Reports."

If you want to continue to the next lesson

> If the Customer Phone List report is not closed, click the Close button. Or, on the File menu, click Close.

This closes the report, but it does not exit Microsoft Access.

If you want to quit Microsoft Access for now

> After closing the report, click the Close button in the Microsoft Access window. Or, on the File menu, click Exit.

This closes the form and exits Microsoft Access.

Lesson Summary

To	Do this	Button
Open and preview a report	In the Database window, click the Reports tab, and then double-click the report you want.	
Switch between a magnified view of a report in Print Preview and a view of the whole page	Click anywhere on the report. *or* On the toolbar, click the Zoom button.	
Move from page to page in a report in Print Preview	Use the navigation buttons at the bottom of the window.	
Print a report	In Print Preview, click Print on the File menu, or click the Print button on the toolbar. *or* To print a report directly from the Database window, select the report. Then either click Print on the File menu, or click the Print button on the toolbar.	
Create mailing labels	In the Database window, click the Reports tab, and then click the New button. Select Label Wizard, select the table or query that contains the data for the labels, and then follow the Label Wizard instructions.	

For online information about	Use the Answer Wizard to search for
Printing reports	**print reports**

Preview of the Next Lessons

Now that you know how to get data into and out of a database, you're ready to start creating tables and forms of your own. In Part 2, you'll learn techniques for expanding a database by adding and relating tables and by attaching and importing data. In the next lesson, you'll learn how to create a new table and use its datasheet to add records to the table.

Review & Practice

In the lessons in Part 1, you learned how to open a database, view and move within your data, use forms and filters, and sort records. If you want an opportunity to refine those skills before going on to Part 2, you can do so in the Review & Practice section that follows.

Review & Practice

Estimated time
35 min.

- Open a database and a database form.
- View your data and move between records.
- Use a form to enter and edit data.
- Use a filter to find specific records.
- Sort records alphabetically and numerically.
- Create a report.

Before you begin to expand your database by working with tables, you can use the steps in this Review & Practice section to practice the skills and techniques you learned in Part 1, "Data Basics."

Scenario

The Human Resources and Accounting departments have asked you to help them manage their information. You update the personnel records and answer questions posed by these departments.

Step 1: *Open a Database and View the Data*

To become familiar with the human resources information, you open a form called Employees. To look at the data in different ways, use the Form View button to select Datasheet view and Form view. Use the navigation keys at the bottom of the form window to move between records.

1 Start Microsoft Access, and open the Sweet Lil's database.

2 In the Database window, open the Employees form.

3 Browse through the data by using the navigation keys.

4 Look at a different view of this form by using the Form View button to select Datasheet view.

5 Change the width of the columns so that you can see more information in Datasheet view.

6 Switch back to Form view.

For more information on	See
Starting Microsoft Access	Getting Ready, Lesson 1
Opening a database	Lesson 1
Opening a form	Lesson 1
Moving between records	Lesson 1
Switching views of a form	Lesson 2

Step 2: *Enter and Edit Data in a Form*

The Human Resources department has given you some changes for the personnel files. Enter new data and change existing data.

1 A new employee has been hired. If necessary, switch to Form view, and then move to a new blank form.

2 Add the following information for the new employee.

First Name: **Joseph**
Last Name: **Wood**
Title: **Technician**

3 Add the following department information to the form.

Extension: **778**
Department: **Operations**
Birthdate: **4/5/58**
Date Hired: **3/1/96**

4 Ursula Halliday, employee ID number 6, has gotten married. Move to her record, and change the last name to Martin.

5 Adrienne Snyder, employee ID number 5, has left the company. Switch to Datasheet view. Select her record by clicking anywhere in the record, and then delete the record using the Delete Record button on the toolbar.

6 Switch back to Form view.

For more information on	See
Entering data in a form	Lesson 1
Moving around a form	Lesson 1
Choosing data from a combo box	Lesson 2
Editing text in a field	Lesson 2
Deleting a record from a form	Lesson 3

Step 3: *Find One or More Records*

An employee has put in a requisition for vacation, signed with a first initial and a last name, but the signature is hard to read. The Human Resources department can make out "Woo" at the beginning of the last name, and they ask you to determine from whom this memo might have come. Find and display records that match the information you have.

1 While in Form view, select the Last Name field, and then use the Find button to search for "Woo."

2 Note the first occurrence, and then search for any additional occurrences.

For more information on	See
Finding records	Lesson 4

Step 4: *Use a Filter to Find Specific Records*

The company adopted its current name, Sweet Lil's, in 1985. The Human Resources department would like to know which employees were with the company before the name change. Use a filter to specify dates to find the answer.

1 While in Form view, use a filter to learn which employees were hired prior to 1985 (Date Hired <1-Jan-85). Click in the Date Hired field, and then use the Advanced Filter/Sort feature.

2 Be sure that the Date Hired field name is in the Criteria grid. In the Criteria box below Date Hired, type an expression that indicates that the date hired was during or before 1984 (or prior to 1985).

3 Initiate an ascending sort. Use the navigation buttons to look at each record.

4 Switch to Datasheet view to see more records at one time.

For more information on	See
Using a filter to find records	Lesson 4
Using an expression	Lesson 4, Appendix A
Sorting records	Lesson 4

Step 5:   *Sort Records Alphabetically or Numerically with a Button*

The company accountant is checking a monthly phone bill and needs to know who has extension 787. Sort the records to make it easy to find out who it is.

1   While in Datasheet view, click in any row of the Extension column.
2   Sort the records by extension in ascending order.
3   Find extension 787 in the Extension column, and then close the Employees form.

For more information on	See
Sorting Records	Lesson 4

Step 6:   *Create a Report*

To facilitate the scheduling of department meetings, you are asked to produce a report that will contain the names, departments, and extensions of all the employees, sorted by the department name.

1   In the Database window, create a mailing label report.
2   Select the Employees table.
3   Use the Label Wizard to define a report that contains the following information:

Last Name, First Name
Department Name
Extension

4   Sort by Department Name and then by Last Name.
5   Name your report **Department List**
6   Choose Finish to end the Label Wizard, and then view your report.

For more information on	See
Using a Report Wizard	Lesson 5
Viewing a report	Lesson 5

If You Want to Continue to the Next Lesson

➤ On the Department List report, click the Close button. Or, on the File menu, click Close.

This closes the window, but it does not exit Microsoft Access.

If You Want to Quit Microsoft Access for Now

➤ In the Microsoft Access window, click the Close button. Or, on the File menu, click Exit to exit Microsoft Access.

Part 2

Expanding a Database

Adding a Table

Estimated time
35 min.

- Use a Table Wizard to create a table.
- Add records using a table's datasheet.
- Design a new table.
- Add fields to a table.
- Set field properties.

When information is well organized, it's easy to find and manage. Photographs arranged in family albums, for example, are easier to find than those jumbled together in a box in the attic. In a Microsoft Access database, information is organized in tables. You can display the information in a variety of formats, but it's all stored in tables. You have already examined and changed data displayed in a form, which is one way to look at data from one or more tables.

In this lesson, you'll learn how to create a table, define its fields, and add records in the table's datasheet.

What Is a Table?

A database *table* is a collection of data with the same subject or topic. One table might contain data about customers, such as each customer's name, address, and phone number. Another table might contain data about bonbons, such as each bonbon's name, picture, and cost.

A Microsoft Access database is a collection of tables—or at least one table—that you use to store related information. The tables in the Sweet Lil's database, for example, all contain data relating to different parts of Sweet Lil's business.

You worked with fields when you added records using the Boxes form in Lesson 3. In this lesson, you'll learn how to define the fields in a table, and you'll see how fields and records are displayed in tables.

Field

Bonbon ID	Bonbon Name	Chocolate Typ	Nut Type	Filling Type	Bonbon Des
B01	Candlelight Ecstas	Bittersweet	Cashew	Mocha cream	Cashew in m
B02	Bittersweet Blueber	Bittersweet	None	Blueberry	Cascade Mou
B03	Marzipan Oakleaf	Bittersweet	None	Marzipan	Marzipan sha
B04	Bittersweet Strawb	Bittersweet	None	Strawberry	Olympic Wild
B05	Bittersweet Raspbe	Bittersweet	None	Raspberry	Orcas Island
B06	Bittersweet Marma	Dark	None	Marmalade	Marmalade c
B07	Bittersweet Cherry	Bittersweet	None	Cherry, whole	Royal Anne c
B08	Hazelnut Bitters	Bittersweet	Hazelnut	None	Classic haze

Record

Each field appears as a column in the table and contains a category of information. For example, each field in the Bonbons table contains a different category of information that describes a bonbon, such as the name, chocolate type, or filling in the bonbon.

Each record appears as a row in the table and contains all the information about a particular person, item, or event (depending on the table's subject). Each record in the Bonbons table, for example, contains all the information about a particular bonbon. Each record in the Customers table contains all the information about a particular customer.

When you create a new table, you define how many fields the table has and what kind of data can be stored in each field. After naming and saving the table, you can add data to it.

Planning for New Tables

Sweet Lil's Chocolates is growing fast. More and more customers who order chocolates on Sweet Lil's toll-free telephone line want their gift orders to arrive very quickly, often overnight. To meet the increased demand, Sweet Lil's needs to increase the amount of candy they make and to speed up the process of getting candy to the customer. Therefore, Sweet Lil's has decided to make communication with its candy ingredient suppliers more efficient by having a main contact person at each supplier. To meet its customers' requirements for faster delivery, Sweet Lil's will begin using three shipping carriers instead of one so that customers can choose air delivery if they want.

First you'll use a Table Wizard to create a table in the Sweet Lil's database, called Suppliers. This table lists information about your primary contact person in each vendor company. Then you'll design a table, called Carriers, to hold data on the three carrier companies.

Creating a Table with a Table Wizard

Microsoft Access can guide you through the table creation process with a Table Wizard. It is a quick way to get started in a new database or to add a new table to an existing database. If you create a table with a Table Wizard, you can go back at a later time and edit or change anything in the table.

Start the lesson

You can also start Microsoft Access and open the Sweet Lil's database in a single step if you have opened the database recently. Click the Start button, point to Documents, and then click Sweet Lil's.

▶ If Microsoft Access isn't started yet, start it and open the Sweet Lil's database. If the Microsoft Access window doesn't fill your screen, maximize the window.

Create a table with a Table Wizard

1 In the Database window, be sure that the Tables tab is selected so that the list of tables appears, and then click the New button.

The New Table dialog box appears.

2 In the New Table dialog box, select Table Wizard, and then click OK.

The Table Wizard dialog box appears.

3 In the Sample Tables list, scroll downward, and select Suppliers.

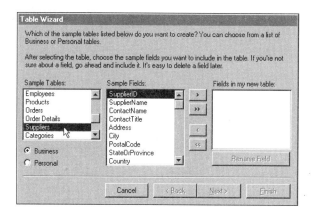

4 In the Sample Fields list, double-click each of the following fields to move it to the Fields In My New Table list:

SupplierName
ContactName
PhoneNumber
FaxNumber

5 Click the Next button.

Below "What do you want to name your table?" the name "Suppliers" appears. This is what you want to call your table, so you don't have to make any change.

A primary key is one or more fields that uniquely identify each record in a table. It is usually easiest to let Microsoft Access set the primary key.

6 With the option "Yes, set a primary key for me" selected, click the Next button.

7 The next question you see asks, "Is your new table related to any other tables in your database?" You don't have any tables to relate the Suppliers table to now, so click the Next button.

8 With the option "Enter data directly into the table" selected, click the Finish button.

Your new table opens in Datasheet view.

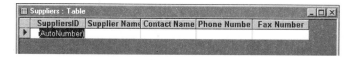

Adding Records in a Table's Datasheet

In the Datasheet view of a table, you add or look at your data. Later in this lesson when you design a new table, you'll enter data directly into a blank datasheet, and Microsoft

Access will analyze your data and automatically assign appropriate data types and formats for each field. You can also design tables from scratch and further customize any table by using Design view. You switch between Datasheet view and Design view by clicking the down arrow on the Table View button (on the left side of the toolbar) and selecting the view you want.

Switch to Datasheet view

Table View

The Table View button face will change depending on what was last selected from the drop-down list.

➤ If you are not in Datasheet view, on the toolbar, click the down arrow on the Table View button, and select Datasheet View.

Start a record

Microsoft Access has added a field called SuppliersID for you to use as the primary key. In the SuppliersID field is the word "AutoNumber," which lets you know that you don't have to fill in this field yourself. Microsoft Access will give each new record a number automatically. You will add the new information about suppliers to the other fields.

1 Press TAB to move to the SupplierName field.

As you begin typing, Microsoft Access gives the record an ID of 1.

2 Type **Chocolate World** and then press TAB to move to the Contact Name field.

3 Type **Becky Rheinhart** and then press TAB to move to the Phone Number field.

4 Type **(617) 555-5460** and then press TAB to move to the Fax Number field.

The Phone Number and Fax Number fields are formatted with an *input mask* that fills in the punctuation for you, so you type only the numbers.

5 Type **(617) 555-5459** to complete the record.

Save a record

The record is saved when you move to a new row. Before you move to another row, look at the record indicator in the field selector to the left of the SuppliersID field. The record indicator, which looks like a pencil, shows that you have added or changed data in the record but haven't saved the data yet.

Record indicator —

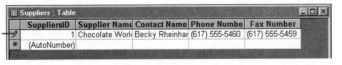

	SuppliersID	Supplier Name	Contact Name	Phone Number	Fax Number
	1	Chocolate Worl	Becky Rheinhar	(617) 555-5460	(617) 555-5459
*	(AutoNumber)				

➤ Press TAB to move to the next record.

When you move to the next record, Microsoft Access automatically saves the data in the previous record. You don't have to do anything else to save the record.

Add more records

➤ Press TAB to move to the SupplierName field, and then add these two records to the Suppliers table:

Supplier Name:	**Allfresh Nuts**	**Flavorly Extracts, Inc.**
Contact Name:	**Barney Cutter**	**Beverly Sims**
Phone Number:	**(313) 555-9987**	**(515) 555-9834**
Fax Number:	**(313) 555-9990**	**(515) 555-9888**

Close the table

➤ On the File menu, click Close. Or, click the Close button in the upper-right corner of the table.

The Suppliers table closes. The new Suppliers table now appears in the list of tables in the Database window.

Creating a New Table That You Design

Now that you have created a table by using a Table Wizard, you can create a table that is completely customized. Using the following steps, you can add a table to a new or existing database.

Create a New Table

1 In the Database window, be sure that the Tables tab is selected so that the list of tables appears, and then click the New button.

2 In the New Table dialog box, select Datasheet View, and click OK.

A blank datasheet with 20 columns and 30 rows appears.

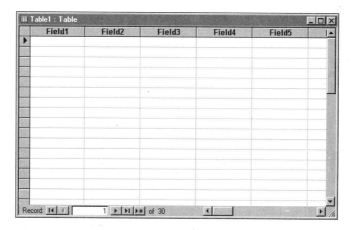

Naming Fields

You add a field to the new table by renaming the columns with the field names you want to use. To rename a column, you double-click the column name and type the new field name. You can insert more columns using the Column command on the Insert menu; Microsoft Access will delete any extra columns after you save the new table.

After you name your fields, you enter your data in the datasheet. Microsoft Access will create an appropriate *data type* and *display format* for the data you enter. The data type tells Microsoft Access what kind of data to accept in the field, and the display format specifies how data is displayed and printed. When you created a table with a Table Wizard, Microsoft Access automatically assigned a data type and display format for all of the fields based on the fields you selected from the list.

The following table shows examples of fields with different data types and the data each can hold.

Field	Data type	Data you might enter
Last Name	Text	Houlihan
Box Price	Currency	$18.75
Quantity on Hand	Number	500

Data types protect the accuracy of your data by restricting the type of information you can enter in a field. For example, you can't store a picture or a name in a field with the Currency data type.

Now, you're ready to add the first field to your new table. Later, when you save the new table, Microsoft Access will create a primary key and you will use that field to store an ID number for each carrier. To begin building the table, you'll just add data fields.

Name a field

 Double-click the default name Field1, and then type **Carrier Name**

A field name can contain up to 64 characters, including spaces. It can include any punctuation mark except a period (.), an exclamation point (!), or brackets ([ ]).

Add more fields

Next you'll add an additional field named Air Delivery.

1 Double-click the default name Field2, and then type **Air Delivery**

2 Move the pointer over the border between the names Air Delivery and Field3, and when the pointer changes to a two-headed arrow, double-click the border. The Air Delivery column will widen to fit the entire field name.

Your table should now look like the following.

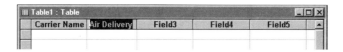

Your table is ready for you to start adding records to it.

Add records to the table

1 Click in the Carrier Name field for the first record, type **Wild Fargo Carriers**, and then press TAB to move to the Air Delivery field.

Air Delivery is a field that will have a Yes/No data type. Yes will mean Air, and No will mean Surface. No will be the default for the Air Delivery field. Wild Fargo Carriers uses surface as its delivery method, so you type No. After you have entered a few records with consistent data types, Microsoft Access will assign a data type to the field (which you can change later, in design view).

2 Type **No** in the Air Delivery field, and then click in the Carrier Name field for the next record.

3 Add two more records to the Carriers table:

Carrier Name: **Grey Goose Express**
Air Delivery: **Yes**
Carrier Name: **Pegasus Overnight**
Air Delivery: **Yes**

Your table should look like the following.

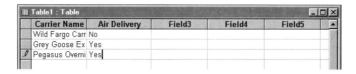

Save the table

Save

1 On the toolbar, click the Save button.

The Save As dialog box appears.

2 Name the table **Carriers**, and then click the OK button.

Microsoft Access asks whether you want to create a *primary key* for the new table. Every table in your database should have a primary key—one or more fields whose values uniquely identify each record in the table. The primary key helps Microsoft Access search, find, and combine data as efficiently as possible.

3 Click the Yes button.

Microsoft Access creates a primary key for the table and saves the table as Carriers. You will name the primary key field Carrier ID.

4 Double-click the field name "ID" at the top of the new primary key field. Type **Carrier ID** and then press ENTER.

Setting and Changing Field Properties

Each field in a table has *properties* that you can use to control how Microsoft Access stores, handles, and displays data in the field. For example, to display numbers in a field as percentages, you would set the field's Format property to Percent.

Each data type has a different set of properties associated with it. Fields with the Text and Number data types, for example, have a property called Field Size that sets the maximum size of data you can store in the field. Fields with the Yes/No data type, on the other hand, don't have a Field Size property, because the values stored in a Yes/No field have a fixed size.

Another property you can set or change for most fields is the default control type. For example, in the Air Delivery field your entry will always be either Yes or No, and you'd rather check a checkbox than type the word Yes. You can set the Display Control property for the Air Delivery field to be a checkbox by changing the Display Control field property.

Set field properties

Table View

1   On the toolbar, click the down arrow on the Table View button, and select Design View.

The Carriers table appears in Design view. The key symbol to the left of the Carrier ID field name indicates that Carrier ID is the primary key for the table. The Data Type column contains the data types that Microsoft Access set for you; you can change them easily by clicking in the Data Type column for a field and selecting a new data type from a drop-down list. You set or change field properties in the Field Properties dialog box at the bottom of the table.

2   Click anywhere in the row for the Air Delivery field.

The field properties appear in the Field Properties dialog box at the bottom of the table. You'll change the default control type for the Air Delivery field.

3   In the Field Properties dialog box, click the Lookup tab.

The Display Control property is on the Lookup tab and is set by default to Text Box.

For fast, detailed information on any property, click in the property box, and press F1.

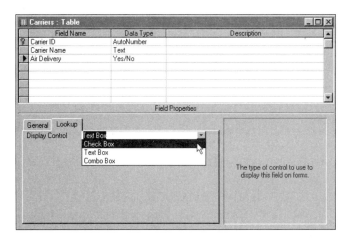

4   Click in the Display Control property box. Then click the down arrow that appears in the box, and select Check Box.

When you set a Check Box display control property, the default control in the table and in all forms based on the table will be a check box.

5   Switch to Datasheet view to see the new check box for the Air Delivery field. When Microsoft Access asks whether you want to save the table, click Yes.

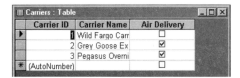

Close the table

▶ On the Carriers Table window, click the Close button.

The Carriers table closes. The table now appears in the list of tables in the Database window.

One Step Further: Setting New Field Properties and Filtering a Table

Before you begin another project with the Carriers table, you receive a note from Sylvia in the Shipping department. To accommodate the information she wants in the Carriers table, you will set some new types of field properties, and then add the data on her memo. Later you receive a call asking you to identify a carrier from just part of a contact person's name. You will use a filter to find the information.

SWEET LIL'S
CHOCOLATES

INTEROFFICE MEMO

Could you please add this information about our carriers to the database so we can look them up any time? Our contacts and their phones seem to change weekly, and we need a convenient place to keep them up-to-date.

Carrier	Contact Person	Contact Phone
Wild Fargo Carriers	Clyde Houlihan	(212) 555-7837
Grey Goose Express	Bella Lamont	(503) 555-9874
Pegasus Overnight	Morris Jantz	(206) 555-8988

Thanks,

Sylvia G.

Set field properties for new fields in a table

Add new field names and field properties to the Carriers table in Design view.

1 In the Database window, on the Tables tab, select the Carriers table.

2 Click the Design button to open the Carriers table in Design view.

3 In the Field Name column, add two new fields called Contact Person and Contact Phone by typing them into the Field Name column below Delivery Method.

After you add each new field and press ENTER or TAB, Microsoft Access will set the data type for each to the default data type, Text.

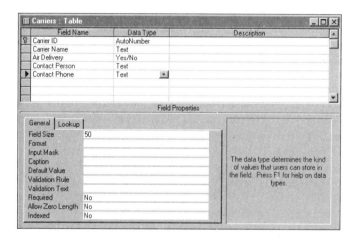

4 Click in the Contact Phone row. Then double-click in the Field Size box in the Field Properties dialog box, and type **24**

This sets the Field Size property of the Contact Phone field to a maximum of 24 characters. Next you'll create an input mask for the Contact Phone field so that you won't have to type punctuation when you enter a phone number in the table.

5 Click in the Input Mask field property box, and then click the ellipsis (...) button that appears on the right of the box. If Microsoft Access asks whether you want to save the table, click Yes.

The Input Mask Wizard appears.

6 Be sure that the Phone Number input mask is selected, and click the Finish button.

7 Use the Table View button to switch to Datasheet view, and then add the names and numbers from Sylvia's note to the Contact Person and Contact Phone fields. If Microsoft Access asks whether you want to save the table, click Yes.

8 Close the table.

When asked whether you want to save changes, click Yes.

Filter a table to find a record

You receive a call from the Shipping department telling you that someone took a message from a person named Clyde, who asked which orders are to be sent by air. The Shipping department needs you to identify which carrier called. Use a filter with a table as you did with a form in Lesson 4.

1   In the Database window, open the Carriers table in Datasheet view.

2   On the Records menu, point to Filter, and then click Advanced Filter/Sort.

3   In the Carriers table in the upper part of the Filter window, double-click the Contact Person field.

    Contact Person is entered in the Field box in the Criteria grid.

4   Because Clyde could be either a first or last name, type ***clyde*** in the Criteria box to indicate that the name Clyde is only part of the field.

5   Click the Apply Filter button to see the results of your filter.

Apply Filter

If you want to continue to the next lesson

➤ On the Carriers table, click the Close button. Or, on the File menu, click Close.

    If you're asked whether you want to save changes, click Yes. This closes the table, but it does not exit Microsoft Access.

If you want to quit Microsoft Access for now

➤ In the Microsoft Access window, click the Close button. Or, on the File menu, click Exit.

    If you're asked whether you want to save changes, click Yes. This closes the table and exits Microsoft Access.

Lesson Summary

To	Do this
Create a table	In the Database window, click the Tables tab, and then click the New button. Select Table Wizard, and follow the prompts.
	or
	In the Database window, click the Tables tab, and then click the New button. Select Datasheet View. Change the default field names to your names, enter data for a few records, and then save the table. You can customize the table in Design view.

To	Do this
Add records to a table	Display the table in Datasheet view. Then type the data in the fields.
Add a field to a table	In the first empty row in Design view, type a field name in the Field Name box. Select a data type from the drop-down list in the Data Type column.
Set properties for a field	Click the row that defines the field in the upper portion of the Design view window, and then set the property in the Field Properties dialog box in the lower portion of the window.
Get Help on any field property	Click in the property box, and then press F1.
Add or modify fields in a table	Select the table in the Database window, and then switch to Design view. Move to the Field Name column, and then make your changes.

For online information about	Use the Answer Wizard to search for
Creating a table	**create table**
Adding fields to a table	**add field**
Making changes to a field in a table	**change table**
Adding records to a table	**add records**
Setting or changing a table's primary key	**primary key**
Setting properties for a field	**field properties**

Preview of the Next Lesson

In the next lesson, you'll learn how to use data that's stored outside your Microsoft Access database in a different file format, and you'll learn how to import the data to make a new Microsoft Access table.

7

Linking and Importing Data

Estimated time
30 min.

In this lesson you will learn how to:

■ Link an external table.

■ Work with data in a linked table.

■ Use a Form Wizard to create a form for a linked table.

■ Import a file from a different database.

In previous versions of Microsoft Access, linking was referred to as "attaching."

Suppose you have sales data in a file that's not part of a Microsoft Access database. Can you use Microsoft Access to work with the data? The answer is probably *yes*. If the data is in Microsoft Excel, Lotus 1-2-3, dBase, Microsoft FoxPro, Paradox, Btrieve, Microsoft SQL Server, or a text file, you can either import it or link it. If you import the data, you create a new Microsoft Access table to hold the data; if you link the data, the data remains in its current file format for updating and sharing, but you can work with the data using Microsoft Access.

In this lesson, you'll learn how to link a table in a different database format to your Microsoft Access database and how to use Microsoft Access to work with data in the external table. You'll also learn how to import data into your Microsoft Access database and export data from Microsoft Access to a different file format.

Using Data from Different Sources

When you *import* data into your Microsoft Access database, Microsoft Access copies the data from its source into a table in your database. You can import data from these file formats:

- A spreadsheet file, such as a Microsoft Excel or a Lotus 1-2-3 file.

- A text file, such as a file you might create with a word processing program or a text editor.

- A file in another database format, such as a Microsoft FoxPro file; a Paradox version 3.*x* or later file; a dBASE III or later file; a Btrieve file (with an Xtrieve dictionary file); a Microsoft SQL Server file; or another Microsoft Access database file.

You also have the choice of *linking* to files in any of these formats. A linked table isn't copied into your Microsoft Access database; the table stays in its original file format. You create a link between your Microsoft Access database and the external table, including other Microsoft Access tables. That way, you can use Microsoft Access to work with the data, and someone else can still use the table in its original program.

You can also start Microsoft Access and open the Sweet Lil's database in a single step. Click the Start button, point to Documents, and then click Sweet Lil's.

In this lesson, you'll start by linking a Paradox table to the Sweet Lil's database. Later, you'll import the data so that it's a Microsoft Access table.

Start the lesson

> If Microsoft Access isn't started yet, start it and open the Sweet Lil's database. If the Microsoft Access window doesn't fill your screen, maximize the window.

Linking an External Table

If you link an external table to your Microsoft Access database, you can view and update the data even if others are using the data in the table's source program. You can create Microsoft Access forms and reports based on the external table. You can even use a query to combine external data with the data in your Microsoft Access tables. You'll learn more about using a query to combine data from different tables in Lesson 9, "Selecting the Records You Want."

As a small company, Sweet Lil's charged a flat shipping rate. Now that it has expanded nationwide and uses three carriers, you plan to base shipping charges to customers on the destination state or province and the selected carrier. A colleague in the Shipping department has a Paradox version 3.5 table that contains the data.

Your colleague wants to continue using Paradox for the time being to keep track of his shipping data, so instead of importing the table into the Sweet Lil's database, you'll link it. That way, your colleague can continue to work with the table using Paradox while you work with it using Microsoft Access.

Link an external table

1   On the File menu, point to Get External Data, and then click Link Tables.

The Link dialog box appears.

2   Click the Look In Favorites button, and then double-click the Access SBS Practice folder.

3   In the Files Of Type list box, select Paradox.

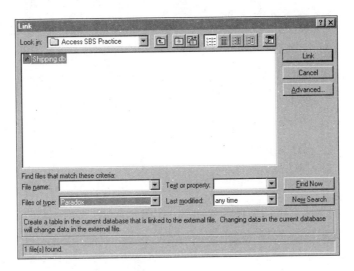

The Paradox version 3.5 file, Shipping.db, appears in the list of files. Shipping.db was copied to your Practice folder when you copied the practice files to your hard disk.

4   Click the Link button.

Microsoft Access links the table to your database, and then displays a message to let you know that the table was successfully linked.

5   Click OK to close the message box, and then in the Link dialog box, click the Close button.

Now the SHIPPING table appears in the Database window along with the other tables in the Sweet Lil's database. The Px symbol identifies the table as a linked Paradox table.

NOTE In addition to Shipping.db, a Paradox index file, named Shipping.px, was copied to your Practice folder when you copied the practice files to your hard disk. Paradox stores information about the table's primary key in this file. To open the linked table, Microsoft Access needs the .px file. If you delete or move the .px file, you won't be able to open the linked table. See Microsoft Access online help for more information about linking Paradox tables.

Working with Data in the Linked Table

After you link an external table to your Microsoft Access database, you can use it much as you would a regular Microsoft Access table. You can't change the structure of a linked table (add, delete, or rearrange fields), but you can set field properties in Design view to control the way Microsoft Access displays data from a field. You can also use field properties to give a field a default value or to check new data entered in a field to be sure it meets a rule you specify.

Open a linked table

> In the Database window, double-click the SHIPPING table.

The table opens in Datasheet view.

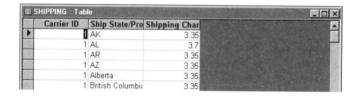

Change a field property

You'd like to see the data in the Shipping Charge field displayed as currency. One of the Microsoft Access data types is Currency; maybe you can use this data type to display the data the way you want.

Table View

1 On the toolbar, click the down arrow on the Table View button, and select Design View.

Microsoft Access displays a message to let you know that you can't modify some properties of a linked table. It asks whether you want to open the table anyway.

2 Click Yes.

The SHIPPING table appears in Design view.

3 Click the Data Type box for the Shipping Charge field.

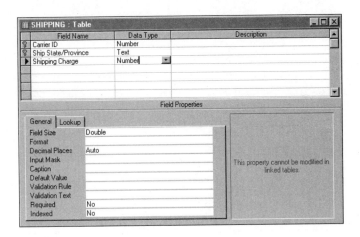

The properties of the Shipping Charge field appear in the lower portion of the window. The Hint box beside the properties says that this property (Data Type) can't be modified in linked tables. But you can still modify how Microsoft Access displays the data by setting the field's Format property.

4   In the lower portion of the window, click in the Format property box.

Now the Hint box displays a hint about setting the Format property.

5   In the Format property box, click the down arrow, and then select Currency.

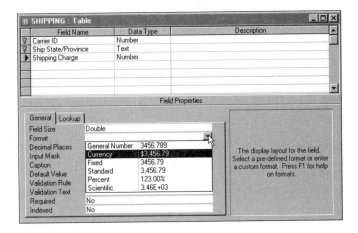

6   On the toolbar, click the Table View button to switch to Datasheet view. In the message box, click Yes to save your changes.

Now the data is formatted the way you want.

7   Close the SHIPPING table.

95

Importing a Table

Your colleague in the Shipping department has decided to use Microsoft Access instead of Paradox to manage his shipping data. This means you don't need to keep the Paradox file of shipping charges anymore; you can import the file so that it's part of the Sweet Lil's database. Remember that when you link a table, it retains its original file format. When you import a table, the data is converted to Microsoft Access format.

Import a table

1 On the File menu, point to Get External Data, and then click Import.

The Import dialog box appears.

2 In the Files Of Type list box, select Paradox.

The Shipping.db file appears in the list of files.

3 Double-click the Shipping.db file.

4 When you see the message that the file has been successfully imported, click the OK button.

5 Close the Import dialog box.

In the Database window, the imported table has been added to the list. Because your linked table is named SHIPPING, Microsoft Access gives the imported table the name SHIPPING1. (You can't have two tables with the same name in one database.)

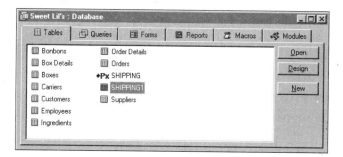

Delete a table or a link

Now that the data is stored in a Microsoft Access table, you don't need the linked SHIPPING table in Paradox format, so you can delete it from your list of tables.

1 In the Database window, select the linked SHIPPING table, and then press DELETE.

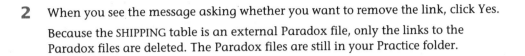

2   When you see the message asking whether you want to remove the link, click Yes.

Because the SHIPPING table is an external Paradox file, only the links to the Paradox files are deleted. The Paradox files are still in your Practice folder.

 NOTE You can import and link both delimited (each field is separated by a unique character, such as a tab or comma) and fixed-width (each field has exactly the same number of characters) text files using the new Text Import Wizard. On the File menu, click Import/Link. In the Files Of Type box, select Text Files. Double-click the text file you want to import or link, and then follow the steps in the Text Import Wizard.

Rename a table

Because you now have only one table with shipping data, you can rename the imported file from SHIPPING1 to Shipping.

You can also use the right mouse button to click the table icon and then click Rename.

1   In the Database window, select the SHIPPING1 table.

2   Click the filename (not the icon).

A box appears around the name, and the name is highlighted for changing.

3   Type **Shipping**, and then press ENTER.

Working with Data in the Imported Table

The data in the imported table is now part of your Microsoft Access database, but you want to change some aspects of the table. You can customize the table's design, as you would with a table you created yourself. In this case, you will change some of the properties so that the values are displayed in a format you choose.

Change properties

1   Open the Shipping table in Design view by clicking the Design button in the Database window.

2   Click in the Field Size property box for the Carrier ID field, click the down arrow, and then select Long Integer.

Long Integer limits values in the field to whole numbers. In addition, it allows you to create a relationship between the Carriers table and the Shipping table. You'll learn more about this in Lesson 8, "Relating Tables."

3   Click in the Data Type box for the Shipping Charge field, click the down arrow, and then select Currency.

Your table should look like the following.

Record selector

```
Shipping : Table                                    _ □ ×
    Field Name          Data Type              Description        ▲
  Carrier ID          Number
  Ship State/Province Text
▶ Shipping Charge      Currency      ▼

                         Field Properties

 General  Lookup
 Format
 Decimal Places   Auto
 Input Mask
 Caption                                    The data type determines the kind
 Default Value                              of values that users can store in
 Validation Rule                           the field. Press F1 for help on data
 Validation Text                                        types.
 Required         No
 Indexed          No
```

Delete and add a primary key

When Microsoft Access imported the data, it also imported the primary key information from the original Paradox table. The key symbols on the left of the field names indicate those fields are primary keys. You might wonder why the table uses two fields (Carrier ID and Ship State/Province) as primary keys. These two fields make a good primary key, because, taken together, their two values are unique for each record in the table. To see how this works, look at the table in Datasheet view. Each carrier ID appears in the table 59 times—once for every state and province. And each state or province appears in the table three times—once for every carrier. But the combination of a specific carrier ID and a specific state or province—1 and AK, for example—appears in the table only once.

Adding primary keys is quite simple. You open a table in Design view, click the record selector for the record you want to use as a primary key, and click the Primary Key button on the toolbar. To delete primary keys, you click the record selector for the field containing the primary key and then click the Primary Key button on the toolbar.

Primary Key

1 Click the record selector for the Carrier ID field.

2 On the toolbar, click the Primary Key button.

Both primary keys are deleted because they act together to uniquely identify each record in the table.

3 Click the record selector for the Carrier ID field again, and then click the Primary Key button on the toolbar.

Only the Carrier ID field is set as the Primary key.

Save

4 On the toolbar, click the Save button, and then click Yes to remove the warning message.

The first warning message refers to the changes you made in the previous exercise. You won't lose data in this case because the data in the fields is smaller than the new size limits you set.

5 Click OK to remove any further warning messages.

Microsoft Access will not allow you to save the table because the Carrier ID field alone does not uniquely identify each record in the table.

6 Click the record selector for the Carrier ID field. Then press and hold down the CTRL key while you click the record selector for the Ship State/Province field.

Both records are selected.

7 On the toolbar, click the Primary Key button.

Both records are set as primary keys, and each record is now uniquely identified.

8 On the toolbar, click the Save button. Then on the table, click the Close button.

Using AutoForm to Base a Form on a Table

A table datasheet is a convenient way to work with all the records in the table at the same time, but for ease and reliability of data entry, you might prefer to use a form. To create a simple form based on a table, Microsoft Access provides a fast way called AutoForm.

Create a form with AutoForm

All three of Sweet Lil's carriers are now shipping to both Puerto Rico and Guam. You want to create a form to enter the new shipping information. The AutoForm Wizard will create a simple new form based on the Shipping table for you.

1 In the Database window, be sure that the Tables tab is selected, and select the Shipping table.

New Object

The New Object button face will change depending on what was last selected from the drop-down list.

2 On the toolbar, click the down arrow on the New Object button, and then select AutoForm.

The new Shipping form, based on the Shipping table, is created for you.

New Record button

Add information with the new form

Add the new shipping information using the new form.

1 At the bottom of the form, click the New Record button to move to the next new record.

2   Enter the new information, using PR for Puerto Rico and GU for Guam. (You do not need to type the dollar signs in the Shipping Charge field, because the display format was automatically set to Currency when Microsoft Access created the form.)

Carrier ID	Ship State/Province	Shipping Charge
1	PR	$3.85
1	GU	$10.50
2	PR	$5.36
2	GU	$4.30
3	PR	$8.52
3	GU	$7.51

3   Close the Shipping form when you have finished entering the information.

4   When you see the message "Save changes to the design of 'Form1'?" click Yes. Name the form **Shipping** in the Save As dialog box.

One Step Further: Exporting Data to Microsoft Excel

You will need to have Microsoft Excel installed on your computer to do the next exercise.

You might want to use a spreadsheet program to analyze the data in one of your database tables. For example, you can export the whole table, or just part of the table, to a Microsoft Excel file.

Export data from a table to a Microsoft Excel file

You want to examine some price breakdowns for the sizes of the boxes that Sweet Lil's sells compared with the prices of the boxes. You are interested in all boxes that sell for less than $30.00. You could export the whole Boxes table to Microsoft Excel, but since you don't need the information from all of the fields, you can export only the information you select. All you need is the information from the Box Name, Size, Box Description, and Box Price fields.

1   In the Database window, click the Tables tab, and then double-click the Boxes table to open it.

Sort Descending

2   To see all the prices of the boxes you need, click in the Box Price column, and then click the Sort Descending button on the toolbar.

The records are sorted by box price, from highest to lowest.

3   To select only the data you need, drag through the entries for all of the records that have a box price less than $30.00. Include only the information from the Box Name, Size, Box Description, and Box Price fields.

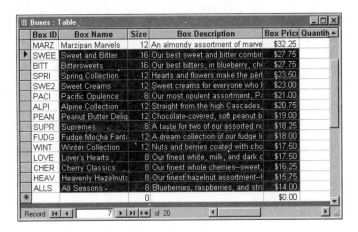

4   On the Tools menu, point to OfficeLinks, and click Analyze It With MS Excel.

Microsoft Excel opens with a worksheet named Boxes that contains the selected data. Microsoft Excel has already saved the new worksheet in your Access SBS Practice folder.

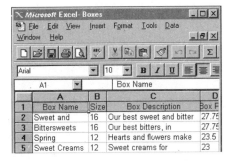

5   In the Microsoft Excel window, click the Close button to close Microsoft Excel.

If you want to continue to the next lesson

➤   On the Boxes table, click the Close button. Or, on the File menu, click Close.

Click No if a dialog box appears asking whether you want to save changes to the design of the Boxes table. This closes the table, but it does not exit Microsoft Access.

If you want to quit Microsoft Access for now

➤   In the Microsoft Access window, click the Close button. Or, on the File menu, click Exit.

Click No if a dialog box appears asking whether you want to save changes to the design of the Boxes table. This closes the table and exits Microsoft Access.

Lesson Summary

To	Do this	Button
Link an external table to a Microsoft Access database	Open the Database. On the File menu, point to Get External Data, and then click Link Tables. Navigate to the file you want to link, and then click the Link button.	
Change field properties of a linked table	In Design view, click the property you want to change. (The Hint text will let you know if it's a property you can't change.)	
Import a table	Open the Database. On the File menu, point to Get External Data, and then click Import. Select the file type, double-click the filename, and then click OK.	
Rename a table	Select the table in the Database window. Then click the name (not the icon), type the new name, and press ENTER.	
Delete a link to an external table	In the Database window, select the linked table, and then press DELETE. Microsoft Access deletes only the link, not the external table.	
Use AutoForm to create a form based on a table	In the Database window, click the Tables tab, and then select the table. Click the down arrow on the New Object button on the toolbar, and then select AutoForm.	

For online information about	Use the Answer Wizard to search for
Linking an external table	**link table**
Creating a form based on a table	**create form**
Importing a table	**import table**

Preview of the Next Lesson

In the next lesson, you'll learn how to create relationships between tables so that they're automatically joined in queries. You'll also learn more about designing tables for a relational database.

Relating Tables

Estimated time
40 min.

In this lesson you will learn how to:

- Create a relationship between two tables.
- Relate tables that contain multiple-field primary keys.
- Detect a many-to-many relationship and use a linking table.

Some encounters are temporary; others last a lifetime. You might have many things in common with the person sitting next to you on an airplane, for example, but that doesn't mean you'll ever see the person again. In contrast, you probably have daily contact with a co-worker, a friend, a parent, or a child. It's similar with relationships between tables. If you want to see related information from two tables again and again, you can create a permanent relationship between them. That helps Microsoft Access automatically associate the information in the two tables whenever you use them together in a query, form, or report.

There are two ways to create a relationship between tables: by using a lookup field and by creating a table join. There are advantages to both methods, depending on what you want to do. When you use the Lookup Wizard to create a lookup field in a table, the wizard creates a permanent relationship between two tables, and it also creates an automatic *combo box* for fast, accurate data entry in the table and in all forms based on the table. Creating a relationship between two tables by joining them in the Relationships window is a more advanced method, but it offers a few different options, such as the opportunity to study the overall relationship picture and the option to enforce *referential integrity* between tables (referential integrity ensures that relationships between records in related tables are valid, and that you don't accidentally delete or change related data).

In this lesson, you'll learn how to create a relationship between two tables using both methods. You'll also learn how to evaluate relationships and to structure your tables so that they're related correctly.

Understanding Relationships

Microsoft Access is a relational database, so you can use data from more than one table at a time. After you create tables in your database and set each table's primary key, you can create relationships between the tables. A relationship can help Microsoft Access associate the data in any new query, form, or report that includes the two related tables.

You can create two types of relationships in Microsoft Access: a *one-to-many relationship* or a *one-to-one relationship*. The most common type by far is the one-to-many relationship. In this type of relationship, one record in one table can have many related records in another table. For example, one customer can place many orders. Similarly, one record in a Customers table (called the *primary table* in the relationship) can have many matching records in an Orders table (called the *related table*).

Customers is the primary table (the "one" side)...

Customer ID	Last Name	First Name	Street	City	State/Pro
263	Lincoln	Elizabeth	98 Bluehills Hwy.	Frankfort	KY
268	Harriman	April	144 E. Lake St.	Fargo	ND
269	Smith	Hillary	89 N. 18th St.	Freemont	CA
270	Jones	Norman	17331 Fairhaven St.	Tallahassee	FL
271	Eddington	George	8804 14th Ave.	Tallahassee	FL
272	Beauregard	Donna	71 36th Ave.	Lachine	Québec

Record: 214 of 326

Order ID	Customer ID	Carrier ID	Order Date	Gift	Order Method	Ship Last Na
67	399	2	11-Nov-95	Yes	1	Nixon
68	63	3	11-Nov-95	No	1	Valerio
69	269	1	11-Nov-95	No	2	Smith
70	49	3	11-Nov-95	No	1	Carruthers
71	209	2	11-Nov-95	No	1	Santorini
72	319	1	12-Nov-95	Yes	1	Leach

Record: 67 of 407

...and Orders is the related table (the "many" side).

In a one-to-one relationship, on the other hand, one record in the primary table can have only one matching record in the related table. This type of relationship is less common than the one-to-many relationship. One reason you might use a one-to-one relationship would be when you want to separate information about employees into public and restricted data. For example, you might put public information, such as names and job titles, in one table and restricted information, such as salary information, in another table. These two tables would have a one-to-one relationship, because each record in the public table would have only one matching record in the restricted table.

NOTE You can also have relationships between your tables that help ensure that the data in the relationship makes sense—for example, that you don't have orders in the Orders table with no matching customer in the Customers table. For details, look up "Referential Integrity" in Microsoft Access online Help.

You can also start Microsoft Access and open the Sweet Lil's database in a single step. Click the Start button, point to Documents, and then click Sweet Lil's.

Start the lesson

In this lesson, you'll use the Lookup Wizard to create a relationship between the Orders table and the Employees table, and then you'll use the Relationships window to create a relationship between the Carriers table created in Lesson 6 and the Shipping table imported in Lesson 7. If you don't have the Carriers table and Shipping table, see Lessons 6 and 7 for instructions on adding them to the Sweet Lil's database. Then you can complete the exercises in this lesson.

➤ If Microsoft Access isn't started yet, start it and open the Sweet Lil's database. If the Microsoft Access window doesn't fill your screen, maximize the window.

Creating a Lookup Field to Relate Employees to Orders

Customers call Sweet Lil's to place orders for boxes of bonbons. The Sweet Lil's database includes an Orders table that contains a record for each order, with information such as when the order was placed, where it should be shipped, and how the customer paid for it. The database also has an Employees table that includes a record for each employee, with information such as the employee's name, phone number, and date of hire.

So that you can easily find out the name of the employee who took an order, you will create a relationship between the Employees table and the Orders table.

To create a relationship between these two tables, you'll use the Lookup Wizard. You will create a lookup field in the Orders table that looks up names of employees in the Employees table. In addition to creating a relationship between the two tables, the Lookup Wizard will create a *combo box* control in the Orders table so that employees can select a name from a list instead of typing it. This will make data entry easier and more accurate for Sweet Lil's employees.

Create the lookup field

1   In the Database window, click the Tables tab, and then double-click the Orders table.

    The Orders table will contain the lookup field, and the lookup field will look up names in the Employees table.

2   On the Insert menu, click Lookup Column.

    The Lookup Wizard starts, and the first dialog box appears. You want the new field (the lookup column) to look up values in another table, so leave the default option selected.

3   Click the Next button.

The wizard asks which table or query should provide the values for your lookup column.

4   Be sure the Tables option is selected under View, select Employees, and then click Next.

The wizard asks which fields should be included in your lookup column. You can include more than one field to make the selection process easier (for example, Last Name and First Name), but only one field value (Employee ID) will be stored in the Orders table.

5   Double-click Last Name, double-click First Name, double-click Employee ID, and then click Next.

The Lookup Wizard displays your lookup column layout. You can resize the columns to a best fit by double-clicking the right border of each column header. The wizard has hidden the Employee ID number (the "key column") because you don't need to see the number when you look up a name, but the Orders table retains the Employee ID information.

Double-click here to resize the columns.

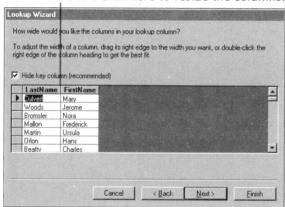

6   Click Next.

7   To answer the question "What label would you like for your column?" type **Employee**, and then click Finish.

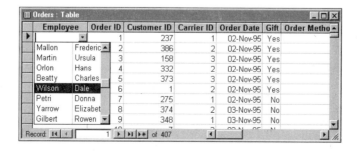

You'll learn how to create a combo box control without creating a lookup column in Lesson 14.

The Orders table appears in Datasheet view, with the new lookup column at the beginning of the table. Now Sweet Lil's employees can enter employee names in the table quickly and accurately by clicking the down arrow and selecting a name from the list. In addition, when a form is created that uses the Orders table, the Employee ID field will automatically be a combo box on the form.

Move the new field and look at field properties

You want to place the Employee ID field at the end of the table instead of at the beginning, so that when you enter data, Employee ID is entered last.

1 Switch to Design view.

2 Click the record selector for the Employee ID field, which is at the top of the list, to select the field.

3 Drag the Employee ID field to the bottom of the list of fields.

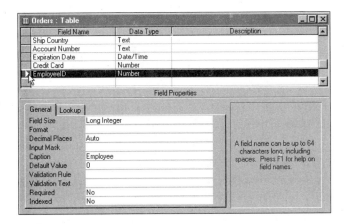

Save

4 On the toolbar, click the Save button to save changes to the Orders table.

5 In the Properties dialog box at the bottom of the Design view window, click the Lookup tab.

The Lookup Wizard has set the field's Display Control property to Combo Box.

6 Close the Orders table.

Creating a Relationship in the Relationships Window

Creating relationships in the Relationships window is a little more complex than using the Lookup Wizard, but it also offers a few more options. For example, you have the option of enforcing referential integrity between the two joined tables, and you can select different types of joins. (For more information, click Answer Wizard on the Help menu and search for **referential integrity** or **join type**.) Relationships created in the Relationships window will not set an automatic Display Control property, such as the combo box the Lookup Wizard created earlier in this lesson, but you can create joins between fields that have different names, and you can see the "big picture" of relationships in your database.

Before you can create a relationship in the Relationships window, the tables must contain matching fields. You relate the primary key field in the primary table (on the "one" side of the relationship) to a matching field in the related table (on the "many" side). The matching field is sometimes called a *foreign key*.

Before creating a relationship, determine which table is the primary table and which is the related table. If the related table doesn't contain a field with data that matches the data in the primary key field in the primary table, add the field to the related table so that you can create the relationship.

After you create a relationship between two tables, you can't modify or delete the fields on which the relationship is based without deleting the relationship first.

Display the Relationships window

In the relationship between the Carriers and Shipping tables in the Sweet Lil's database, the Carrier ID field is the matching field.

Carrier ID is the primary key of the Carriers table...

Carrier ID	Carrier Name	Air Delivery	Contact Person	Contact Phone
1	Wild Fargo Carr	No	Clyde Houlihan	(212) 555-7837
2	Grey Goose Ex	Yes	Bella Lamont	(503) 555-9874
3	Pegasus Overni	Yes	Morris Jantz	(206) 555-8988
(AutoNumber)		No		

Record: 1 of 3

Carrier ID	Ship State/Province	Shipping Charge
1	AK	$3.35
1	AL	$3.70
1	Alberta	$3.35
1	AR	$3.35
1	AZ	$3.35

Record: 1 of 192

...and the matching field in the Shipping table.

This is a one-to-many relationship. One carrier can have many different shipping charges, depending on the destination of the package, so the Carriers table is the primary table in the relationship. When you create the relationship between these two tables, you'll relate Carrier ID in the Carriers table to Carrier ID in the Shipping table.

Relationships

➤ On the toolbar, click the Relationships button. Or, on the Tools menu, click Relationships.

The Relationships window appears.

Clear Layout

NOTE For this exercise, the Relationships window should be empty. If yours is not, click the Clear Layout button on the toolbar. Or, on the Edit menu, click Clear Layout. Then click Yes to clear the Relationships window.

Add tables to the Relationships window

Show Table

1   On the Relationships menu, click Show Table; or, on the toolbar, click the Show Table button.

2   On the Tables list, select the Carriers table, and then click the Add button.

3   Select the Shipping table, and then click the Add button.

A window of each table with its list of fields appears in the Relationships window.

4   Click the Close button to close the Show Table dialog box.

Create a relationship between tables

1   In the Relationships window, drag the Carrier ID field from the field list in the Carriers table to the Carrier ID field in the Shipping field list.

You drag the field from the field list of the primary table (Carriers) to the field list of the related table (Shipping).

When you release the mouse button, the Relationships dialog box appears. Be sure that the matching field is listed for both tables. If it is not, you can click the list box down arrow and select the proper field.

2   Click the Create button.

The Carriers table is now related to the Shipping table. You see a line between the matching fields in the two tables. This relationship remains intact until you delete it.

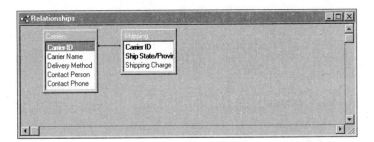

3   On the Relationships window, click the Close button.

When you close the Relationships window, a message asks whether you want to save changes to the Relationships layout. This decision affects only what is graphically displayed in the Relationships window. Any relationships between tables you have created or deleted remain in your database.

4   Click the Yes button to save the layout of the Relationships window.

The next time that you open the Relationships window, you will see the display you just saved.

Related fields don't necessarily have to have the same name as the primary key fields they're related to. However, they do have to contain matching data. In addition, they must have the same data type (with two exceptions), and if they have the Number data type, they must have the same field size. The exceptions are that you can match an Increment AutoNumber field with a Long Integer Number field, and you can match a Replication ID number field with a Replication ID AutoNumber field. For example, the Carrier ID field in the Carriers table has the AutoNumber data type, with New Values set to Increment. The Carrier ID field in the Shipping table has the Number data type, with its Field Size property set to Long Integer.

Delete and restore a relationship between tables

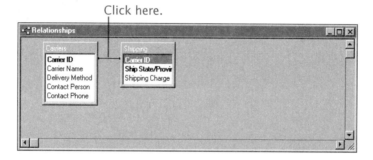

Relationships

1   On the toolbar, click the Relationships button to see the layout of the Relationships window that you saved.

2   Click the line between the Carriers table and the Shipping table.

Click here.

The line appears heavier.

3   Press DELETE to delete the relationship.

4   In the message box, click the Yes button to delete the relationship.

Microsoft Access erases the line between the two tables. They are no longer related.

5   Re-create the relationship by dragging the Carrier ID field from the Carriers table to the Carrier ID field in the Shipping table and then choosing the Create button in the Relationships dialog box.

6   Close the Relationships window.

If you see a message box asking whether you want to save changes to the layout, you can click either Yes or No.

Relating Tables with Multiple-Field Primary Keys

A table's primary key can consist of one or more fields. If a table with a multiple-field primary key is the primary table in a relationship, you must relate *all* the fields in its primary key to matching fields in the related table. To see why, look at the Shipping and Orders tables in the Sweet Lil's database. These two tables have a one-to-many relationship, with Shipping as the primary table.

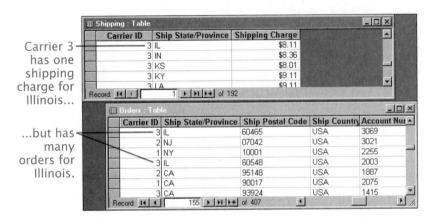

Carrier 3 has one shipping charge for Illinois...

...but has many orders for Illinois.

The primary key for the Shipping table consists of two fields: Carrier ID and Ship State/Province. Before Microsoft Access can correctly relate a shipping charge to an order, it must be able to find matching data for *both* fields. That's because a shipping charge is based on both the carrier that the customer chooses and the destination of the order.

Relate a multiple-field primary key to matching fields

Create a relationship between the Shipping and Orders tables so that Microsoft Access can automatically look up an order's shipping charge.

Relationships

Clear Layout

Show Table

1 On the toolbar, click the Relationships button.

The Relationships window appears, showing the layout you last saved.

2 On the toolbar, click the Clear Layout button, and then click Yes to proceed.

3 On the toolbar, click the Show Table button.

4 In the Show Table dialog box, select and add both the Shipping table and the Orders table to the Relationships window. Then close the Show Table dialog box.

5 In the Relationships window, drag the Carrier ID field from the Shipping table to the Carrier ID field in the Orders table.

When you release the mouse button, a Relationships dialog box appears. Be sure that the Carrier ID field is listed for both tables. If it is not, you can click the list box down arrow and select the proper field.

111

6   Click the cell under Carrier ID for each table, and then click the list box down arrow to select Ship State/Province.

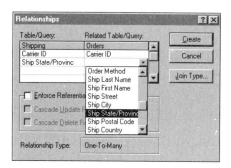

7   Click the Create button.

The Relationships window displays the relationship between the two tables. To see the relationship more easily, you can drag the Orders table farther away from the Shipping table and drag the border of the Orders table downward to show both fields without having to scroll.

NOTE   If Microsoft Access says that you can't relate the tables, close the Relationships dialog box, and then check the design of your Shipping table. Its primary key should consist of *both* the Carrier ID field and the Ship State/Province field. The Carrier ID field should have the Number data type, and its Field Size property should be set to Long Integer. The Ship State/ Province field should have the Text data type. For help defining the table, see Lesson 7, "Attaching and Importing Data."

---

8   On the Relationships window, click the Close button. When Microsoft Access asks whether you want to save the layout, click Yes.

Because the tables are now related, Microsoft Access can use the values in both tables to find information you ask for.

See how your relationships work

You've created one relationship between the Carriers and Shipping tables and another relationship between the Shipping and Orders tables. You can see how the relationships work when you need information that requires data from more than one table.

You have already learned to use a filter to request information from the Sweet Lil's database that meets specific criteria. With a filter, you were able to set criteria and display the selected data, but from only one table.

By using a query, you can take advantage of relationships between tables by drawing on information from two or more tables. In the following steps, you can see how related tables are used in a query. In Lesson 9, you create new queries and use the query grid to refine the selection of the information you want.

Use the Carrier ID and Ship State/Province fields in the Orders table to find the appropriate shipping charge for an order.

1 In the Database window, click the Queries tab to display the list of queries, and then click the New button.

2 In the New Query dialog box, double-click Simple Query Wizard.

The Simple Query Wizard dialog box appears.

3 From the Tables/Queries listbox, select Table: Orders. Then in the Available Fields list, double-click Order ID to add it to the Selected Fields list.

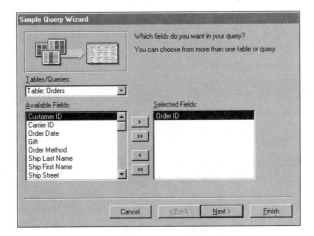

4 Add these fields to your Selected Fields list:

From the Carriers table, the Carrier Name field

From the Shipping table, the Shipping Charge field

Microsoft Access uses the relationships you created to automatically join the tables in the query.

5 Click the Next button.

6 Be sure the Detail option is selected, and then click Next.

7 Change the title to Carriers Query, making sure that the option "Open the query to view information" is selected, and then click Finish.

The related data from all three tables appears in the Query window.

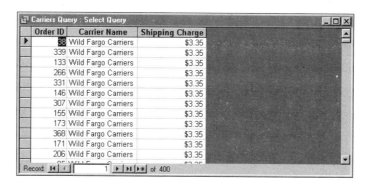

8   Close the query.

Microsoft Access has saved the query automatically, and the name Carriers Query appears in the list of queries in the Database window.

Identifying Many-to-Many Relationships

When you evaluate a relationship between two tables, it's important to look at the relationship from both sides. You might think at first that you have a one-to-many relationship when you actually have a *many-to-many relationship*. A many-to-many relationship occurs when one record in either table can have more than one matching record in the other table. In those cases, you need a third table that links the two tables before you can create the relationships.

The Boxes and Bonbons tables in the Sweet Lil's database are a good example. At first glance, you might think that boxes and bonbons have a one-to-many relationship, because one box can contain many different bonbons. But take a look at the relationship from the bonbons side. One bonbon can appear in more than one box.

You'd have a problem if you tried to create a one-to-many relationship between the Boxes table and the Bonbons table. Which is the primary table in the relationship?

Suppose you made Boxes the primary table in the relationship. You'd add a Box ID field to the Bonbons table to hold the matching values. But in the record for the Bittersweet Blueberry bonbon, you'd have to enter box IDs for both the All Seasons and Alpine Collection boxes, because the Bittersweet Blueberry bonbon appears in both boxes. If you do that, Microsoft Access can't relate the Bittersweet Blueberry record with the right boxes—you can have only one value in each matching field. The same thing happens if you try putting a Bonbon ID field in the Boxes table.

The solution is to create a *junction table* that contains the primary keys of the two tables you want to relate. In a junction table, you can add another field that is in neither of the original tables but gives you an additional piece of information relevant to both of the other tables. In the Sweet Lil's database, the junction table is called Box Details. The primary key of the Box Details table consists of Box ID and Bonbon ID—the primary keys of the two tables you're trying to relate. The Box Details table also contains a Quantity field, which tells you how many of each bonbon are in a box.

The Box ID relates
the Boxes table...

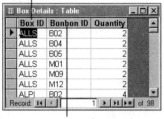

...to the Bonbon ID
in the Bonbons table.

One Step Further: Using Junction Tables

When you create a junction table, you don't add fields to it that really belong in one of the two related tables. For example, you might be tempted to add the Box Name field to the Box Details table. But that field is already in the Boxes table; it shouldn't be repeated. The only fields that belong in the Box Details table are those needed to define the link (Box ID and Bonbon ID) and any field whose data describes the relationship between the records in the other two tables. The Quantity field qualifies because its data relates to both of the other tables—it tells how many of each bonbon are in each box.

See how a junction table relates two other tables

The Boxes table has a one-to-many relationship with the Box Details table, and so does the Bonbons table. The Box Details table serves as a junction table between the two tables involved in the many-to-many relationship.

Relationships

1 In the Database window, click the Tables tab. Then on the toolbar, click the Relationships button.

2 On the toolbar, click the Clear Layout button, and then click Yes to proceed.

Clear Layout

3 On the toolbar, click the Show Table button.

The Show Table dialog box appears.

Show Table

4 Add the Bonbons table, the Box Details table, and the Boxes table to the Relationships window, and then close the Show Table dialog box.

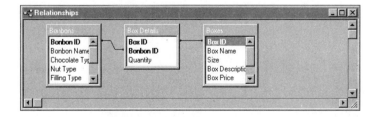

You can see the links between the tables.

If you want to continue to the next lesson

➤ On the Relationships window, click the Close button, and then click No. Or, on the File menu, click Close, and then click No.

This closes the window, but it does not exit Microsoft Access.

If you want to quit Microsoft Access for now

➤ In the Microsoft Access window, click the Close button, and then click No. Or, on the File menu, click Exit, and then click No.

This closes the window and exits Microsoft Access.

Lesson Summary

To	Do this	Button
Create a lookup column to relate two tables	Open the table that will contain the lookup column. On the Insert menu, click Lookup Column. Follow the steps in the Lookup Wizard.	
Create a relationship between two tables	On the toolbar, click the Relationships button to open the Relationships window, and then click the Show Table button on the toolbar. In the Show Table dialog box, select the primary table on the Tables tab, and click Add. Select the related table, and click Add. Close the dialog box. In the Relationships window, drag the common field from the primary table to the related table. Click Create.	
Delete a relationship between tables	Open the Relationships window. Click the line linking the tables, press DELETE, and then click Yes to confirm.	
Use a junction table to create a many-to-many relationship	Open the Relationships window. Click the Show Table button. In the Show Table dialog box, select the tables, click Add, and then close the dialog box. In the Relationships window, drag the field you want to relate from the primary table, to the junction table. Click Create.	

For online information about	Use the Answer Wizard to search for
Creating or deleting relationships between tables	**relationships**
Using a junction table	**relationships**

Preview of the Next Lessons

In Part 3, you'll learn about creating and using queries. You'll join tables, and add fields to a query, set criteria for a query, and sort query data. You'll create a parameter query and use parameters to find a range of records and create a report. In the next lesson, you'll limit the records you see to those that meet your criteria, and you'll show totals and other calculations in a query.

Review & Practice

In the lessons in Part 2, you learned how to create tables, establish relationships, and work with related tables. If you want an opportunity to refine those skills before going on to Part 3, you can do so in the Review & Practice section that follows.

Review & Practice

Estimated time
35 min.

You will review and practice how to:

- Create a table.
- Create a relationship between two tables.
- Set a primary key in a table.
- Identify a many-to-many relationship.
- Create a linking table.
- Delete a table from a database.

Before you begin to learn about asking questions of your database, you can use the steps in this Review & Practice section to practice the skills and techniques you learned in Part 2, "Expanding a Database."

Scenario

The Marketing department is planning for the next quarter. They will run advertising promotions for selected boxes of bonbons. You create and relate tables to keep track of their information. When you're finished, you delete an unneeded table from the database.

Step 1: *Create a Table*

The Marketing department wants to use Microsoft Access to keep track of advertising promotions for different boxes of bonbons and the Marketing employee who is responsible for each promotion. The promotion name will be unique to each project.

If you are using the Table Wizard, a good sample table to use is Projects.

1 Create a new table that has fields for Employee ID, Promotion Name, Start Date, and Box ID.

Do *not* allow Microsoft Access to create a primary key for you.

2 Save the table with the name **Promotions**

3 Select AutoNumber as the data type for the Employee ID field.

4 Set the Promotion Name field as the primary key.

5 Close the table, and verify that the Promotions table is listed in the Database window.

For more information on	See
Creating a table	Lesson 6
Selecting a data type	Lesson 6
Setting a primary key	Lesson 6, Lesson 8

Step 2: *Relate Tables with a One-to-Many Relationship*

Each promotion will be handled by one employee, but one employee might handle more than one promotion. Create a one-to-many relationship between the Employees table and the Promotions table, where the Employee ID field is the matching field.

1 Determine which table is the primary table and which is the related table.

2 Use the Relationships window to create a relationship between the Employees table and the Promotions table.

3 Do not save the layout of the Relationships window when you close it.

For more information on	See
Understanding relationships between tables	Lesson 7
Displaying relationships in the Relationships window	Lesson 7

Step 3: *Relate Tables with a Many-to-Many Relationship*

The Marketing department is interested in the dates and locations of orders for certain boxes. The Orders table contains a record for each order, with information such as when the order was placed, where it should be shipped, and how the customer paid for it. The Boxes table contains a record for each box in the product line, with information such as the box name, size, description, and price. An order could include more than one kind of box, and a box could appear on more than one order.

How would you relate the Orders and Boxes tables so that you could easily find the names of all the boxes in an order?

1 Analyze the relationship between the Orders and Boxes tables from both sides.

2 Open the Order Details table, which is a junction table between the Orders and Boxes tables based on their primary keys. It also contains a Quantity field.

3 Close the Order Details table, and view the relationship between the Orders, Boxes, and Order Details tables in the Relationships window.

For more information on	See
Identifying a many-to-many relationship	Lesson 8
How a junction table works	Lesson 8

Step 4: *Delete a Table from a Database*

The Marketing Department has notified you that, for the next quarter, they will use an outside consultant for their promotions. Therefore, they do not need to track the promotions information in the Sweet Lil's database.

1 In the Relationships window, delete the relationship between the Employees table and the Promotions table.

2 In the Database window, delete the Promotions table from the database.

For more information on	See
Deleting relationships	Lesson 8
Deleting a table from a database	Lesson 7

If you want to continue to the next lesson

Switch to the Relationships window, and then click the Close button. Or, on the File menu, click Close.

This closes the window, but it does not exit Microsoft Access.

If you want to quit Microsoft Access for now

In the Microsoft Access window, click the Close button. Or, on the File menu, click Exit.

This closes the table and exits Microsoft Access.

Asking Questions and Getting Answers

Part

3

Selecting the Records You Want

Estimated time
45 min.

In this lesson you will learn how to:

- Create a query based on a table or another query.
- Set criteria to get a set of related records.
- Sort data and hide a field in a query.
- Create a query that shows related data together.
- Join tables in a query and summarize data.
- Change a field name in the datasheet.
- Show calculations in a field.

If your business changes from day to day, you'll frequently want to look at your data from different angles. Before calling your customers for a marketing campaign, you'll want to create a list of selected names and phone numbers. To review sales trends, you'll want to find out how many orders you received for a specific month. To facilitate express orders of supplies, you'll want to identify a contact person's name and phone number quickly.

In this lesson, you'll create a variety of queries that select the data you want. You'll also calculate total values using a query, and you'll use a query to answer a "what if" question.

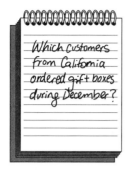

Customer	State/Province	Gift	Order Date
Adams, Cathy	CA	Yes	23-Dec-95
Fogerty, Sam	CA	Yes	09-Dec-95
Harkin, Rory	CA	Yes	03-Dec-95
Kennedy, Brian	CA	Yes	10-Dec-95
Kimball, Mary	CA	Yes	23-Dec-95
Kimball, Mary	CA	Yes	02-Dec-95
Kumar, Andrew	CA	Yes	19-Dec-95
Lopez, Maria	CA	Yes	10-Dec-95
Olembo, Julia	CA	Yes	15-Dec-95
Pence, Stephen	CA	Yes	23-Dec-95

What Is a Query?

A query defines a group of records you want to work with. You can think of a query as a request for a particular collection of data, such as "Show me the names and phone numbers for our carriers with their shipping charges." The answer to the request is called a *dynaset*. The records in a dynaset can include fields from one or more tables.

Dynaset of the Shipping Charges query

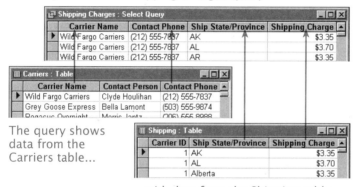

The query shows data from the Carriers table...

...with data from the Shipping table.

You might wonder why you don't just include all the data you need in one large table. The answer holds the secret to the power of a relational database. When you create a separate table for each subject of data—for example, customers or products—the result is a system that provides extraordinary flexibility in how you can bring related data together.

You use queries in much the same way as you use tables. You can open a query and view its dynaset in a datasheet. You can base a form or a report on a query. You can also update the data in a query's dynaset and have the changes saved back to the table where the data is stored.

Because of the flexibility of queries, you might find that you use queries more often than tables. That's because you can use a query to sort data or to view a meaningful subset of all the data in your database. You can look at only the customers in your region, for example, instead of wading through all the customers in the Customers table, and you can see information about their purchases at the same time.

When you worked with a filter in Lesson 4, you found information from a single table. By using a query, you can ask questions of your data that require information from more than one place in your database. You can also save the query to use again, and you can use an existing query to build a new query.

You can create one query that shows which customers bought which products, another query that shows which products sold best in Europe, and another that shows postal codes sorted according to product sales. You don't have to store the product information three times for the three different queries—each piece of information is stored in its table only once. Using queries, you can access the same information in many different ways.

How Do You Create or Modify a Query?

In Microsoft Access, you can create a query by using the new Simple Query Wizard and then modify the query by using a feature called graphical *query by example* (*QBE*). You can also create a query by using graphical QBE; but for simple queries, the Simple Query Wizard is faster.

With graphical QBE, you modify queries by dragging fields from the upper portion of the Query window to the QBE grid. You place the fields in the QBE grid in the order you want them to appear in the datasheet. In this way, you use the QBE grid to show Microsoft Access an example of what you want the results of your query to look like.

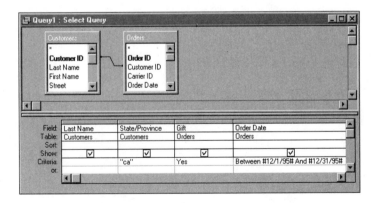

Graphical QBE makes it easy to build on an existing query. Often, one question leads to another, and you find that you want to keep changing a query. For example, you might start by finding all your customers from California. Then, by making small changes to the QBE grid, you can find all the California customers who ordered gifts and, finally, all the California customers who ordered gifts in December. And you can keep going, refining the query until you get it just right.

You can also start Microsoft Access and open the Sweet Lil's database in a single step. Click the Start button, point to Documents, and then click Sweet Lil's.

In Lesson 8, you got a preview of working with a query when you created relationships for three tables, and then displayed data from all three tables simultaneously. In this lesson, you learn to create queries, and then refine your requests for more specific data.

Start the lesson

▶ If Microsoft Access isn't started yet, start it and open the Sweet Lil's database. If the Microsoft Access window doesn't fill your screen, maximize the window.

Creating and Saving a Query

You're in charge of a telephone survey of Sweet Lil's customers in your sales region. Your region is New York State, so you'll use a query to get a list of the names and phone numbers of the New York customers. The information you need is stored in the Customers table.

Create a query

1   In the Database window, click the Queries tab.

2   Click the New button.

3   In the New Query dialog box, double-click Simple Query Wizard.

The Simple Query Wizard opens to help you create your query.

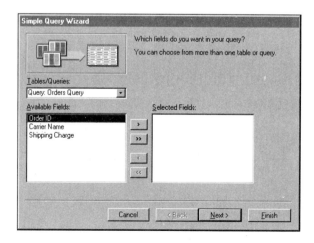

4   In the Tables/Queries list box, scroll upwards and select Table: Customers.

The Customers table fields are listed in the Available Fields box. You use this list to select the fields you want to display in your query.

Add fields to a query

1 Double-click the Customer ID field.

   The Customer ID field is added to the Selected Fields list.

2 Add the Last Name, First Name, State/Province, and Phone fields to the Selected Fields list. When you finish, the Selected Fields list has five fields.

Name and save a query

1 On the Simple Query Wizard, click the Next button.

2 In response to the question, "What title do you want for your query?" type the name **NY Customers** and click the Finish button.

   The finished query is displayed in Datasheet view, and the name of the query appears in the title bar. Microsoft Access also saves this query and adds it to the list of queries in the Database window for you to use again.

Setting Criteria for the Records You Want

The current query displays records for all customers in the Customers table. But you're interested only in the customers from New York, so you'll set criteria to limit the result of the query to only those records for New York customers.

For more information, see the Appendix, "Using Expressions."

You set criteria for a query using an *expression*, a type of formula that specifies which records Microsoft Access should retrieve. For example, to find fields with a value greater than 5, you'd use the expression >5. You use an expression in a query, which was covered in Lesson 4, in exactly the same way as you do in a filter.

Specify criteria

Query View

The Query View button face will change depending on what view is currently selected. You can find the Query View button on the left side of the toolbar—use the ToolTips to help you find it.

1 On the toolbar, click the down arrow on the Query View button, and then select Design View.

2 Click in the Criteria box in the State/Province column.

3 Type **NY** and press ENTER.

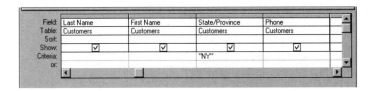

After you press ENTER, Microsoft Access automatically places quotation marks around what you typed, indicating that it is text.

Run your query

Query View

> On the toolbar, click the down arrow on the Query View button, and select Datasheet View to check the results of this query.

Microsoft Access displays the customers from New York State with their phone numbers.

Add more criteria

Now you have a list of customers in your sales region. But you want to call only your most recent customers—customers with customer IDs greater than 200. To find these customers, you'll add another criterion to the query.

1   On the toolbar, click the down arrow on the Query View button, and select Design view.

2   In the Criteria box in the Customer ID column, type the expression >**200**

By adding this criterion, you're telling Microsoft Access, "Find customers who have customer IDs greater than 200 and who live in New York."

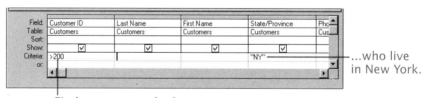

...who live in New York.

Find customers who have
Customer IDs greater than 200...

For more information on operators, see the Appendix, "Using Expressions."

3   Use the Query View button to switch to Datasheet view and see the customers you're going to call.

Sorting in a Query

For more sorting examples, see Lesson 4, "Finding Information."

To make it easier to find a phone number for a specific customer, you can list the customers in alphabetical order. A new feature of Microsoft Access for Windows 95 is the ability to sort a query in datasheet view.

Sort records alphabetically

Sort Ascending

1 Click anywhere in the Last Name column.

2 On the toolbar, click the Sort Ascending button.

The Last Name field is sorted from A to Z.

Customer ID	Last Name	First Name	State/Province	Phone
310	Brownlee	Jason	NY	(914) 555-0931
249	Gunther	Paul	NY	(212) 555-4934
298	Hendricks	Louise	NY	(516) 555-2067
280	Kahn	Juliet	NY	(212) 555-9424

Record: 1 of 8

Hiding a Field

In the NY Customers query, you don't really need to see the State/Province field in the datasheet because the query shows only the customers from New York. This field has to be included in the Design view of the query, because you use it to set criteria. However, you don't need to see this field repeated for every record in the dynaset. You'll use the Show check box in the QBE grid to hide this field so that it doesn't appear in the datasheet.

Hide a field

1 On the toolbar, click the down arrow on the Query View button, and select Design View.

2 In the Show box in the State/Province column, click the check box to clear it.

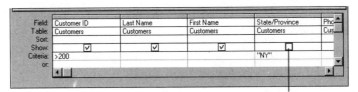

Click the Show check box in the State/Province column.

The query will use any criteria or sort information in this field, but it will not show the field in the datasheet.

Query View

3   On the toolbar, click the down arrow on the Query View button, and select Datasheet View.

The State/Province field no longer appears.

4   On the query window, click the Close button to close the query. Click Yes to save the changes.

5   Scroll through the list of queries in the Database window, if necessary, and see that the query you created, NY Customers, is now included in the list.

Creating a Query Based on Related Tables

To associate data in different tables correctly, Microsoft Access uses matching values in equivalent fields in the two tables. To create a relationship between two tables, you draw a *join line* between two matching fields in the Relationships window. In most cases, the primary key from one table is joined to a field in another table that contains the matching values.

Lesson 8, "Relating Tables," showed you how to create relationships between tables. Now you can create a query based on tables that are related.

Lillian Farber, the president of the company, is analyzing the company's orders for the month before the holidays. She has asked you to give her a list of all orders that were placed in November. She wants to know the order IDs, the customers' names, and the dates of the orders.

Create a query using related tables

The information that Lillian Farber needs is contained in two different tables, the Orders table and the Customers table. You create a new query by using these tables in the graphical QBE grid (without the Simple Query Wizard).

1   In the Database window, click the Queries tab if it is not already active, and then click the New button.

2   In the New Query dialog box, double-click Design View.

The Select Query window opens, and the Show Table dialog box appears.

3   On the Tables tab, double-click the Orders table, and then double-click the Customers table.

4 On the Show Table dialog box, click Close.

The Orders and Customers tables are placed in the Select Query window. A join line automatically appears between the Customer ID fields in the two tables. This is because a relationship already exists between these two tables.

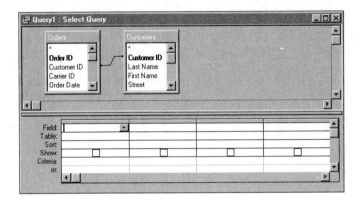

5 On the File menu, click Save.

6 Name the query **Order Information**, and then click OK.

Add fields from two tables to the query

You add fields from the related tables to the query.

1 In the Orders table, double-click the Order ID, Customer ID, and Order Date fields.

The three fields appear in the QBE grid.

2 On the Customers table, double-click the Last Name field.

The Last Name field appears in the QBE grid.

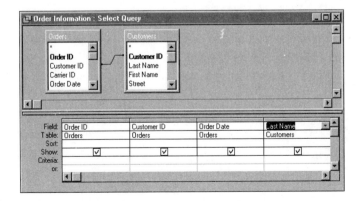

133

Specify criteria and check the results

You use an expression to select records for the month of November. This expression includes the *Between...And operator.*

1 In the Criteria box in the Order Date column, type **Between 1-Nov-95 And 30-Nov-95** and then press ENTER.

The format of the date changes and number symbols (#) appear around the dates automatically. Because this is a long expression, you might want to widen the Order Date field in the QBE grid so that you can see the entire expression after you've typed it.

2 To size the column to its "best fit," double-click the right border at the top of the Order Date column in the query grid.

Double-click here to widen
the Order Date column.

Query View

3 Use the Query View button to switch to Datasheet view and see the orders for November.

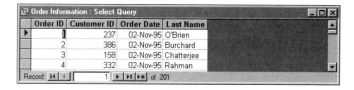

4 Save the query again, and then close it.

Joining Tables in a Query

As you have just seen, when you add related tables from the Sweet Lil's database to a query, join lines automatically appear between them in the Query window.

Join lines also appear automatically in a query for tables that do not have an existing relationship but that do have a field with the same name and data type, and where one of the join fields is a primary key. In this case, the join lines indicate that the matching fields will relate the data for the purposes of the query, but a permanent relationship between them is not established.

If no relationship exists between the tables you want to use, and one is not automatically created when you add the tables to a query, you can still use related data by joining the tables in the Query window when you create the query. For the join to work, the tables must contain fields with matching data.

> **NOTE** When you draw a join line between two tables in the Query window, the join applies to that query only. If you want to use the same two tables in another query, you'll need to join them again in the new query.

Join two tables in a query

You need a quick way to look up the contact names of the suppliers of the ingredients for Sweet Lil's products.

The Ingredients table lists categories and types of ingredients that bonbons are made of, and it contains a field called "Source ID" that identifies where the ingredient is purchased. The Suppliers table has detailed information about the suppliers of ingredients for Sweet Lil's products, and it contains a field called "Suppliers ID." You can join these two fields in a query because they contain matching data.

The Suppliers table was added in Lesson 6, "Adding a Table."

1 In the Database window, click the Queries tab, and then click the New button.

2 Double-click Design View, add the Ingredients table and the Suppliers table to the query, and then close the Show Table dialog box.

3 From the Ingredients table, drag the Source ID field to the Suppliers ID field in the Suppliers table.

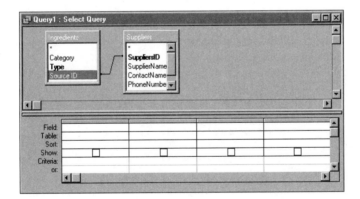

A join line connects the two fields to associate the data correctly between the two tables.

4 On the Ingredients table, double-click the Category and Type fields to add them to the QBE grid.

5 On the Suppliers table, double-click Contact Name to add it to the grid.

6 On the Ingredients table, double-click the Source ID field to add it to the grid.

7 In the Source ID column, click in the Sort box, and then click the down arrow and select Ascending.

135

View the datasheet

Query View

1 Use the Query View button to view the results of your query in Datasheet view.

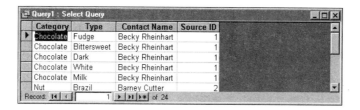

2 Scroll down the records to see the information in the Contact Name field change according to which supplier (Source ID) is used.

Save and name your query

1 On the File menu, click Save.

The Save As dialog box appears.

2 Name the query **Ingredient Source**, and then click OK.

3 Close the query.

4 Check that your query appears in the Database window.

Your query is saved in the Sweet Lil's database. You can open it anytime by double-clicking the query name in the Database window. When you open the Ingredient Source query, Microsoft Access gets the most current data stored in the Ingredients and Suppliers tables and brings it together in the query's dynaset.

Summarizing Data

When you design a query, you can specify which fields to use for grouping records and which fields to use for totals (calculations). For example, you can calculate the total number of bonbons (the type of calculation) within each box (the group).

For each box...

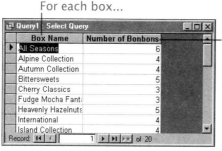

...find the total number of bonbons.

You could begin a new query, but in this case you can use an existing query as the foundation of your new query.

You'll create a new query by modifying the existing Order Information query. The new query will find the total number of orders by country. Then you find the totals of each state or province in each country.

Use an existing query to create a new query

The Order Information query shows you a list of orders by customer. Often, you'll want more than just a list of orders; you'll also want to know the total number of orders placed by country or the total value of all boxes within one order. You can use Microsoft Access queries to perform these calculations for you.

1 In the Database window, click the Queries tab if it is not already active, and select the Order Information query.

2 In the Database window, click the Design button.

3 On the File menu, click Save As/Export.

4 Name the query **Total Orders by Country** and click OK.

The name of the query appears on the title bar of the query and also in the list of queries in the Database window.

Add and delete fields in a query

To specify the information you want, you need to change the fields included in the query.

1 Delete the Last Name field from the query by selecting the field selector at the top of the column and then pressing DELETE.

2 Delete the Customer ID field and the Order Date field from the query.

3 Add the Country field from the Customers table to the query by dragging it and releasing it on top of the Order ID field in the grid.

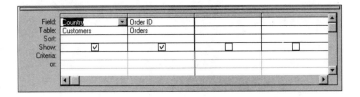

When you release the mouse button, the Country field becomes the first field listed in the query grid, and the Order ID field moves to the right.

Calculate totals in your query and group the results

Totals

1 On the toolbar, click the Totals button.

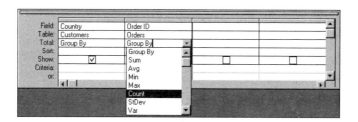

A row called Total appears in the QBE grid. Each box contains the designation "Group By."

2 Click the Total box in the Order ID column, and then click the down arrow. From the list, select Count.

Because there is one order ID for each order, you are counting the number of orders. You're grouping by country, so the count will be the count of orders for each country.

Query View

3 Use the Query View button to view the results of your query in Datasheet view.

The datasheet shows the total number of orders for each country. The second column automatically displays the name CountOfOrder ID.

Group totals by two fields

You'd like to investigate further. So far, you have grouped the results of your query by country. But you also want to know how many orders you've received from each state or province within each country. You can group by a second field.

1 Use the Query View button to switch to Design view.

2 From the Customers table, add the State/Province field to the QBE grid. Place the field between the Country and Order ID fields.

"Group By" appears in the Total row.

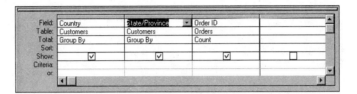

3 Use the Query View button to switch to Datasheet view.

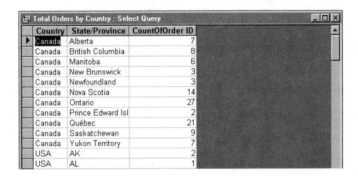

Microsoft Access groups first by country (because this is the first Group By field in the QBE grid) and then by state or province. The totals are calculated for each state or province within each country.

Changing a Name in the Datasheet

By changing the name of a field in a query, the datasheet shows a relevant column heading, and you can use the new field name for referring to the field in forms, reports, and other queries.

Change a field name

In the Total Orders By Country query, CountOfOrder ID is a generic field name assigned by Microsoft Access. You can easily change it to a more meaningful name, such as Total Orders.

1 Use the Query View button to switch to Design view.

2   In the QBE grid, place the insertion point immediately to the left of the Order ID field name, and then press the mouse button. Type **Total Orders:** to the left of the field name. (Be sure to include the colon. A space after the colon is optional.)

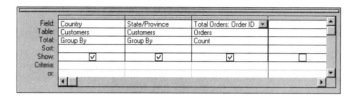

3   Use the Query View button to switch to Datasheet view.

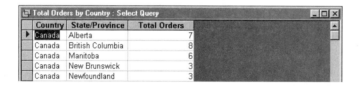

4   Save the query, and then close it.

Showing Calculations in a Field

When you're running a business, your most common questions begin with "What if." Sweet Lil's is no exception. The chocolates are selling so well that the sales manager wants to know, "What if I raise prices on our boxes by 5 percent?"

Because the tables in the Sweet Lil's database don't contain a field that shows prices raised by 5 percent, you'll use a query with a calculated field to answer this question.

Create the query

The new query is based on the Boxes table. Use the New Query graphical QBE grid to create the query.

1   Create a new query, and add the Boxes table.

2   Add the Box Name and Box Price fields to the QBE grid.

The query you've just created will display the current price for each box.

3   On the toolbar, use the Query View button to look at the query in Datasheet view.

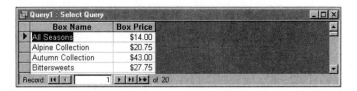

4   Save the query, and name it **Raise Prices**

Add a calculated field

Now you'll add a calculated field that will show what prices would be if you raised them by 5 percent.

1   Switch to Design view, and place the insertion point in the empty box to the right of the Box Price column in the Field row.

In an expression, the square brackets indicate that this is a field name. Brackets automatically appear around a single-word field, but here, you must type the brackets because the field name contains a space. For more details on using expressions in calculated fields, see the Appendix, "Using Expressions."

2   Type **[Box Price]*1.05** and press ENTER.

Multiplying by 1.05 is the same as raising the price by 5 percent. After you press ENTER, Microsoft Access adds a name for the field: Expr1. This is the name that will appear as the heading for this row in the datasheet.

3   To see the whole expression, double-click the right border of the field selector.

Microsoft Access adds Expr1 as the field name.

This expression will show the box price raised by 5%.

4   Switch to Datasheet view to see your results.

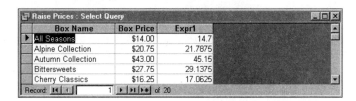

Change the name and format of the calculated field

Because Expr1 is a generic field name that doesn't describe your data very well, you will change the name of this field to "New Price." You also want to show the new price information formatted as currency, and you want a description that readily explains what the new prices mean. You use the Properties sheet to customize the characteristics of your query.

Properties

1 Switch to Design view, and then double-click the term Expr1 to select it.

2 Replace Expr1 with **New Price**

3 Click the Properties button to open the Field Properties dialog box.

4 To change the display of the new price information, click in the Format box, and then click the down arrow to display the list of formats.

5 Select Currency to format the prices with dollar signs and decimals.

6 Click in the Description box, and type **Shows prices raised by 5%**

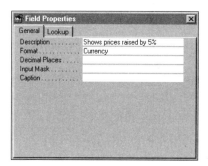

7 Close the Field Properties box.

8 Switch to Datasheet view to see the new prices with the properties you specified.

Box Name	Box Price	New Price
All Seasons	$14.00	$14.70
Alpine Collection	$20.75	$21.79
Autumn Collection	$43.00	$45.15
Bittersweets	$27.75	$29.14
Cherry Classics	$16.25	$17.06

The new prices appear as currency, and you can see the New Price caption at the top of the column. When you click in the New Price field, the description appears on the status bar at the bottom of the Datasheet window.

9 Save and close the query.

One Step Further: Creating a Form Based on a Query

Because new bonbons are being added to Sweet Lil's collection, you want to create a new form to add information about the suppliers of additional ingredients. Because of the popularity of some advertised specials, you'd like to have the phone number of a supplier readily available to confirm the express shipment of an ingredient order. You can use the Ingredient Source query as the basis for your new form.

First you'll add the Phone Number field from the Suppliers table to the Ingredient Source query for quick reference when you are working with ingredient orders. Then you'll delete the Source ID field from the query, and you'll create a new form to help you track ingredient information.

Add a field to a query

You want to be able to quickly find the phone number of a supplier's contact person in case you need to check the shipment of an ingredient.

1 Open the Ingredient Source query in Design view.

2 Drag the Phone Number field from the Suppliers table to the QBE grid and drop it on the Source ID field (so that it is positioned between the Contact Name field and the Source ID field).

Delete a field from a query

Now that you can see the contact name and phone number in your query's dynaset, you don't need to see the Source ID number.

1 Click the field selector for the Source ID column, and then press the DELETE key.

2 Save your changes to the query.

3 Switch to Datasheet view to see the results of the query.

Create a form based on a query

You'll use the New Form dialog box to create a simple form based on the Ingredient Source query.

New Object

1 With the Ingredient Source query open, click the down arrow on the New Object button, and then select New Form.

The New Form dialog box appears with the Ingredient Source query already selected in the list box at the bottom of the dialog box.

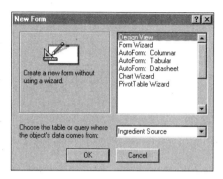

*The Form
Wizard creates
a simple
columnar form
based on the
Ingredient
Source query.*

2 Double-click AutoForm: Columnar.

3 Save the new form as Ingredient Source, and then close the form.

If you want to continue to the next lesson

➤ On the Select Query window, click the Close button. Or, on the File menu, click Close.

Be sure that the Database window appears on your screen.

If you want to quit Microsoft Access for now

➤ On the Microsoft Access window, click the Close button. Or, on the File menu, click Exit.

This closes the table and exits Microsoft Access.

Lesson Summary

To	Do this	Button
Create a new query	In the Database window, click the Queries tab. Click the New button, and then double-click Design View or Simple Query Wizard.	
Add a table to a query	Create a new query by selecting Design View in the New Query dialog box. In the Show Table dialog box, double-click the table you want to add. Click Close. To add a table after you have closed the Show Table dialog box, click the Show Table button on the toolbar.	

To	Do this	Button
Add a field to a query	Double-click the field in the table in the upper portion of the Query window.	
Save and name a query	On the File menu, click Save. In the Save As dialog box, type a name and click OK.	
Set criteria	In the QBE grid, enter criteria in the Criteria box for any field in the query.	
Sort the records in a query	In the QBE grid, click in the Sort box for the field you want to sort, and select Ascending or Descending. *or* In Datasheet view, click in the column by which you want to sort, and then click the Sort Ascending or Sort Descending button on the toolbar.	
Hide a field in a query	In the QBE grid, click the Show check box under any field so that the check mark disappears.	
Find a range of data	In the QBE grid, enter criteria using the Between...And operator.	
Join tables in a query	Use the Show Table dialog box to add the tables to the QBE grid. The two tables must contain fields with matching values. Drag the matching field from one table, and drop it on the matching field in the other table.	
Delete a field from a query	Click the field selector in the QBE grid to select the field, and then press DELETE.	
Calculate totals	On the toolbar, click the Totals button. Click in the Total cell for the field you want to calculate. Click the down arrow, and select a total function (such as Count).	Σ
Give a field a custom name	In the QBE grid, place an insertion point to the left of the field name. Then type a custom field name followed by a colon.	
Show calculations in a field	In the Field cell, add an expression that calculates a value.	

145

To	Do this	Button
Change the properties of a field	Click in the cell with the properties you want to change, and then click the Properties button. Select a property, and either type your data or choose an option if there is a list.	

For online information about	Use the Answer Wizard to search for
Creating queries	**queries**
Adding or deleting fields and tables in a query	**queries**
Joining tables in a query	**join tables**
Setting criteria in a query	**criteria**
Changing field properties	**field properties**
Calculating in a query	**calculations**

Preview of the Next Lesson

In the next lesson, you'll learn how to make queries easier to use. You'll create a query that displays a dialog box that prompts you for criteria. When you run the query, the criteria you enter will appear in the datasheet.

Creating User-Friendly Queries

Lesson

10

Estimated time
20 min.

In this lesson you will learn how to:

■ Create a parameter query.

■ Use parameters to find a range of records.

■ Base a report on a parameter query.

■ Use the Query Wizard to create a crosstab query.

How often do you ask the same types of questions about your data? At Sweet Lil's, a customer might ask for information about the contents of the 12-ounce boxes of candy; later another customer might ask for information about the 8-ounce boxes. Similarly, a customer might ask how many boxes of each kind of candy are in stock and then want to know how many of each size there are. These requests might occur over and over again, and only the details differ. In this lesson, you will learn two ways to work with repetitive queries to make answering questions easier.

Instead of creating numerous queries to answer different but related questions, you can create a *parameter query*. A parameter query prompts you for criteria each time you run the query, so you can use the same query over and over again with a change in criteria. You'll create parameter queries, and you'll create a report based on a parameter query.

To look at a large volume of data in a more readable format, you can create a *crosstab query*. A crosstab query selects the information you want and rearranges it in a spreadsheet format, so you can immediately pick out the answer to a question. A crosstab query can also calculate totals. You'll use a Query Wizard to create a crosstab query so you can see at a glance how many boxes are in stock.

147

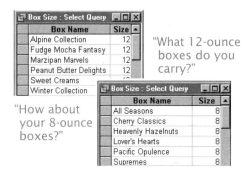

"What 12-ounce boxes do you carry?"

"How about your 8-ounce boxes?"

What Is a Parameter Query?

A parameter query asks you to enter one or more parameters—or criteria—when you run the query. For example, a parameter query might ask you to enter a beginning date and an ending date. Microsoft Access runs the query using your parameters as criteria and then displays the datasheet. Typically, you create a parameter query when you expect to run a query frequently, but you'll be using different criteria each time you run it.

When you run the query, Microsoft Access prompts you for the criteria...

...and then displays the datasheet.

Parameter queries save time, and they're easy to use. Because the query displays dialog boxes that prompt you for criteria, you don't have to change the design of your query every time you want to use different criteria.

You can also start Microsoft Access and open the Sweet Lil's database in a single step. Click the Start button, point to Documents, and then click Sweet Lil's.

Parameter queries are especially helpful as the basis for reports. For example, suppose you run a sales report at the end of every week. You can create a parameter query that prompts you for the dates you're interested in. You fill in the dates you want, and then they are automatically included in the report.

Start the lesson

➤ If Microsoft Access isn't started yet, start it and open the Sweet Lil's database. If the Microsoft Access window doesn't fill your screen, maximize the window.

Creating a Parameter Query

You're designing new boxes of bonbons, and you want to feature a different type of chocolate in each box. Today you might want to run the query to see a list of dark chocolate bonbons; tomorrow you might want to take a look at milk chocolates. You'll design a parameter query that asks you which type of chocolate you're interested in.

Create the query

The new query is based on the Bonbons table.

1 In the Database window, click the Queries tab if it is not already active, and then click the New button.

2 Double-click Design View to display the Select Query window and the Show Table dialog box.

3 Add the Bonbons table to the query, and close the Show Table dialog box.

4 Add the Bonbon Name, Chocolate Type, Bonbon Cost, and Bonbon Description fields to the QBE grid.

5 In the Sort box below the Bonbon Name field, select Ascending to display the bonbon names in alphabetical order.

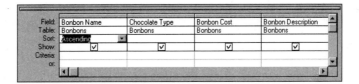

6 Save the query, and name it **Bonbon Information**

Set criteria with a parameter

Now that you've created a query and added fields, you're ready to specify criteria. To do this, you type the prompt that you want to appear in the dialog box when you run the query. Then you define the data type of the value that should be entered in the dialog box.

> In the Criteria box in the Chocolate Type column, type [**Enter Chocolate Type**]

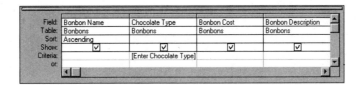

This is the prompt that appears in the dialog box when you run the query.

Define the data type of the parameter

Define the data type of the parameter so that the data entered at the prompt will be of the right kind. If someone tries to enter the wrong type of data in the query's dialog box, Microsoft Access displays a message and won't allow the query to proceed.

1 On the Query menu, click Parameters.

   The Query Parameters dialog box appears.

2 In the first box in the Parameter column, type the same prompt as you entered in the Criteria box, but without the brackets: **Enter Chocolate Type**

3 Press TAB to go to the first box in the Data Type column.

   A down arrow appears, which when clicked will display a list of data types.

   The default data type is Text, which is the correct data type for the Chocolate Type field.

4 Click OK to save the information and close the Query Parameters dialog box.

Run the parameter query

A parameter query prompts you for information anytime you open it from the Database window or display its datasheet.

Query View

The Query View button face will change depending on what view is currently selected. You can find the Query View button on the left side of the toolbar—use the ToolTips to help you find it.

1 On the toolbar, click the Query View button to switch to Datasheet view.

   The Enter Parameter Value dialog box appears.

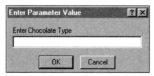

2 Type **Bittersweet** and then click OK or press ENTER.

   The datasheet for the query displays the records for bittersweet bonbons.

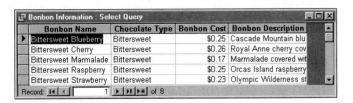

Using Parameters to Find a Range of Records

When you're running the Bonbon Information query, you might want to limit the bonbons to a specific cost range. To do this, you'll add two new parameters to the Bonbon Information query. These parameters will specify the lowest and the highest cost of bonbons that will appear in the datasheet.

Add a range of parameters

Before displaying the datasheet, Microsoft Access will need two parameters: the lowest cost and the highest cost. To add a range of parameters, you'll use the Between...And operator.

1 Use the Query View button to switch to Design view.

2 Click in the Criteria box in the Bonbon Cost column.

3 To be able to see the whole expression as you type it, press SHIFT+F2 to open the Zoom window.

4 Type **Between [Enter low cost] And [Enter high cost]** and click OK.

You have added two prompts: one for the lowest cost and one for the highest cost.

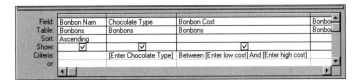

Define the data type of the parameters

Define the data type of these parameters so that the data entered at the prompts will be of the right kind.

1 On the Query menu, click Parameters.

The Query Parameters dialog box appears.

2 In the second box in the Parameter column, type the prompt **Enter low cost** and then press TAB to move to the Data Type column.

The default data type, Text, appears. Because the Box Cost field has a Currency data type, you need to change the data type to Currency.

151

3 Click the down arrow in the Data Type box, and then select Currency from the drop-down list.

You might need to scroll up the list to find Currency.

4 In the third box in the Parameter column, type **Enter high cost** and then press TAB and change the data type to Currency.

5 Click OK.

Save

6 On the toolbar, click the Save button to save the Bonbon Information query with the two new parameters.

Run the query

Now when you run the query, you'll be prompted for all three parameters, with a different dialog box for each.

Query View

1 Use the Query View button to switch to Datasheet view and run the query.

The Enter Parameter Value dialog box appears.

2 Type **Dark** and click OK or press ENTER.

The second dialog box prompts you for the low cost.

3 Type **.25** to find bonbons that cost a minimum of $0.25, and then click OK or press ENTER. You don't need to type a dollar sign ($).

The third prompt appears.

4 Type **.35** to find bonbons with a maximum cost of $0.35, and then click OK or press ENTER.

The datasheet displays the records for dark chocolate bonbons that cost between $0.25 and $0.35.

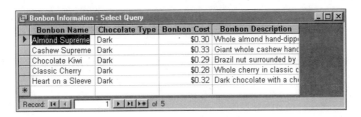

5 Close the query.

Basing a Report on a Parameter Query

Your research has shown that there's a huge market for moderately priced boxes that feature milk chocolate bonbons. Suppose you're proposing a new line of boxes to Lillian Farber, the company president. As part of your presentation, you'll hand out an attractive report that lists milk chocolate bonbons that cost between $0.15 and $0.22.

You base the report on the Bonbon Information query. Because you want it to contain all the fields of the query, you can use the AutoReport Wizard to automatically create the report.

Create the report

For your report, you want the information about each bonbon displayed in a single-column list. You'll select the query that contains the data you want to print in your report, and then you have the AutoReport Wizard build the report for you.

New Object

The New Object button will change depending on what object was previously selected. The button is located on the right side of the toolbar—use the Tool-Tips to find it.

1 In the Database window, click the Queries tab if it is not already active, and then select Bonbon Information.

You don't have to open the query; just select it.

2 On the toolbar, click the down arrow on the New Object button, and then click AutoReport.

The AutoReport Wizard automatically builds the report with the default choices and then prompts you for the three parameters.

3 Enter the following parameters:

Chocolate type: **Milk**
Low cost: **.15**
High cost: **.22**

A single-column report appears that includes all the values from all the fields and records of the Bonbon Information query.

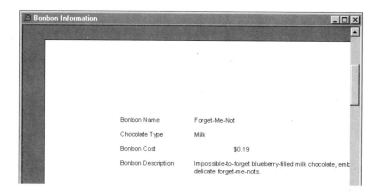

4 To see what a page will look like when it is printed, click anywhere on the page (the pointer looks like a magnifying glass). Click anywhere on the page again to see a close-up view of the report.

5 Save the report with the name **Bonbon Information** and then close the report.

AutoFormat the report

If you don't like the look of the report that the AutoReport Wizard has created, you can select a new AutoFormat.

1 Click the Reports tab, and then open the Bonbon Information report in Design view.

2 On the Format menu, click AutoFormat.

The AutoFormat dialog box opens.

3 Select an AutoFormat from the AutoFormats list, and then click OK.

The report is displayed in Design view again.

4 Switch to Print Preview to see the new report format (you'll have to enter parameters again if the report is based on a parameter query).

5 Close the report, and save the changes.

Creating a Crosstab Query

Every time that a holiday approaches, orders start to pour in for specific boxes of candy. Customers want to know how many boxes you have on hand and also how many of each size. The questions are similar, but the names and sizes of boxes change. To respond to volume orders, you need a convenient way to see the total number of boxes for each bonbon collection you have in stock, in addition to how many boxes you have in each size.

You could study the Boxes table, and then create a number of queries to answer the questions, but a crosstab query can summarize your data in a compact, spreadsheet-like format. A crosstab query can show a large amount of information arranged in a way that is easy to review.

Use a Query Wizard to create a crosstab query

A Query Wizard creates a crosstab query for you, calculates the totals you need automatically, and then displays the data in a readable format.

1 In the Database window, click the Queries tab, and then click the New button.

2 Double-click Crosstab Query Wizard.

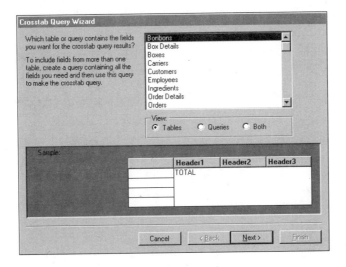

The Crosstab Query Wizard appears.

3 In the View area, be sure that the Tables option button is selected. Then select the Boxes table on the list, and click the Next button.

4 Double-click the Box Name field to make it the leftmost column of the query, and then click the Next button.

5 Select the Size field so that the values in the Size field will be used for column headings, and then click the Next button.

6 In the Fields list, select the Quantity On Hand field for the data you want in the middle.

7 In the Functions list, select Sum, and then click the Next button.

8 Name the query **Boxes in Stock** and then click the Finish button.

The datasheet for the crosstab query appears, showing the layout of the names and quantities of boxes, as well as how many of each size you have in stock.

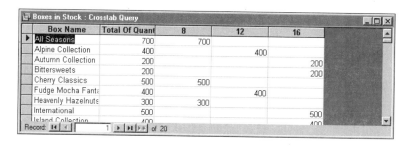

If you want to change anything about the crosstab query, you can switch to Design view and modify it as you would any other query.

9 Close the query.

One Step Further: Creating a New Query from an Existing Query

To track rising costs, you are asked to query the Sweet Lil's database for costs of bonbons according to the type of nut used.

You can base the new query on the Bonbon Information query. You delete a parameter, and then you add a new parameter for Nut Type. You also change the order in which you want the parameters to appear when you run the query.

Create a new query based on an existing one

To use the Bonbon Information query as the basis for a new query, open it and then save it with a new name.

1 In the Database window, select the Bonbon Information query, but do not open it.

2 Click the Design button.

3 On the File menu, click Save As/Export, and name the query **Nut Information**

Delete a parameter from the query

To delete a parameter from a query, delete the prompt from both the QBE grid and the Query Parameters dialog box.

1 In the Criteria box in the Chocolate Type column, select the parameter including the brackets, and then press DELETE.

2 On the Query menu, click Parameters to display the Query Parameters dialog box.

3 If it is not already selected, select "Enter Chocolate Type," and then press DELETE.

The Data Type value will automatically be deleted when you click OK.

4 Click OK to return to Design view.

Add a new field and a new parameter to the query

Add the Nut Type field to the query, and create a parameter that displays a prompt when the query is run.

1 Drag the Nut Type field to the QBE grid, and drop it so that it is to the left of Bonbon Cost.

2 In the Criteria box in the Nut Type column, type **[What type of nut?]**

3 Widen the cell so that you can read the whole parameter if necessary.

You can save time by copying the parameter to the Query Parameters dialog box. By copying instead of typing, you can also be sure that the text matches exactly.

4 Select **What type of nut?** not including the brackets. Press CTRL+C to copy the text.

5 On the Query menu, click Parameters to display the Query Parameters dialog box.

6 Click in the first box in the Parameter column, and then press CTRL+V to paste the text.

7 Press TAB to go to the Data Type cell, and then verify that the data type is set to Text.

8 Click OK to save the information and close the Query Parameters dialog box.

Run the query

Now you are ready to see the results of your new query.

1 Switch to Datasheet view, and run the query.

2 Answer the prompts by entering the following information:

Nut type: **Hazelnut**
Low cost: **.20**
High cost: **.33**

Change the order of the parameters

The order in which the prompts appear depends on the order in which they are listed in the Query Parameters dialog box. You can change the query so that the prompts for the range of bonbon prices come before the prompt for the type of nut.

1   Switch to Design view.

2   On the Query menu, click Parameters.

3   Select the parameter **What type of nut?** and press CTRL+X to cut the text.

4   Click in the box below "Enter high cost" and press CTRL+V to paste the text.

5   Press TAB and verify that the data type is set to Text, and then click OK.

6   Switch to Datasheet view to run the query with the parameters in the new order.

If you want to continue to the next lesson

➤   On the Nut Information query, click the Close box, and then click Yes to save your changes. Or, on the File menu, click Close.

This closes the query, but it does not exit Microsoft Access.

If you want to quit Microsoft Access for now

➤   In the Microsoft Access window, click the Close box. Or, on the File menu, click Exit, and then click Yes to save your changes.

This closes the table and exits Microsoft Access.

Lesson Summary

To	Do this
Set criteria with parameters	Display the query in Design view. In the Criteria box in the appropriate column, type the prompt that will appear when you run the query. Enclose the prompt in square brackets.
Define the parameter	On the Query menu, click Parameters. Enter the same prompt from the Criteria box, but without the square brackets. Then select the data type, and click OK.
Run a parameter query	In the Database window, click the Queries tab, select a query, and then click the Open button. Type a value in the Enter Parameter Value dialog box.
Base a report on a parameter query	Create a parameter query, and save it. In the Database window, click the Queries tab, and select the Query you want to base the report on. On the toolbar, click the down arrow on the New Object button, and then click AutoReport. The report is created.
AutoFormat a report	Open the report to be formatted in Design view. On the Format menu, click AutoFormat. Then select an AutoFormat style, and click OK.
Create a crosstab query	In the Database window, click the Queries tab, and then click the New button. Double-click Crosstab Query Wizard. Select a table or query from the list, and click Next. Select fields for the row and column headings, and then select the field for the data in the middle. If you want, select a function. Click Finish.

For online information about	Use the Answer Wizard to search for
Creating crosstab queries	**crosstab queries**
Creating parameter queries	**parameter queries**

Preview of the Next Lessons

In Part 4, you'll learn to use controls to customize your forms. You'll create controls to show text and data, and you'll show a picture on a form. By using a Form Wizard, you'll be able to create a form based on two tables, and you'll create a combo box with a list of choices that will make your forms easier to use. In the next lesson, you'll add graphical controls to a form to make data entry quick and convenient.

Review & Practice

In the lessons in Part 3, you learned how to select records by using a query and how to adjust queries so that they answer complicated questions easily. The following Review & Practice section gives you an opportunity to gain more experience with building and fine-tuning your queries.

Part

3

Review & Practice

Estimated time
25 min.

You will review and practice how to:

- Create a query and set criteria.
- Sort information and find a range of data in a query.
- Create a query with related tables.
- Summarize data in a query.
- Set parameters in a query.
- Create a report based on a parameter query.

Creating queries is one of the fundamental ways you can unlock the power of a database. Before you go on to the next lesson to learn how to customize the forms you use, this Review and Practice section gives you an opportunity to apply some of the techniques you have learned about querying for information.

Scenario

Sweet Lil's has asked its departments to gather data for a plan to increase their production while lowering their costs. The Marketing department wants to find out what products could be promoted to a wide group of customers who want to give high-quality boxes of candy as gifts but are watching their budgets. The Shipping department has questions about the carriers and the shipping methods it has been using. Both departments ask you to help them design queries for the information they need.

161

Step 1: *Create a query and set criteria*

The Marketing department staff wants to focus on increasing the orders from customers who request boxes of candy that fall within a certain price range. They ask you to identify those boxes larger than the 8-ounce size, but with a price under $30.00.

1 Create a new query using the Boxes table.

2 Add fields to the query so that you can see the names, sizes, and prices of the possible boxes.

3 Create an expression that will find boxes with sizes larger than 8 ounces.

4 Create an expression that will find boxes costing less than $30.00. You don't need to enter the dollar sign in the expression.

5 Run the query.

6 Close the query without saving it.

For more information on	See
Creating a query and setting criteria	Lesson 9
Using an expression in a query	Lesson 9 Appendix, "Using Expressions"

Step 2: *Sort and find a range of data in a query*

To move existing merchandise quickly, the company is planning a large-scale campaign to promote medium-priced assortments of bonbons ("Quality Everyone Can Afford"). You want to advertise only boxes that have prices between $17.00 and $25.00 inclusive and for which you have more than 200 boxes on hand. You'd like to list the boxes in alphabetical order.

1 Create a new query based on the Boxes table.

2 Add fields to the query to show the names, prices, and quantities of the boxes on hand.

3 Sort the query alphabetically by the names of the boxes.

4 Use an expression with comparison operators to find prices between $17.00 and $25.00, but do not include dollar signs. (Hint: Type **>=17 and <=25**)

5 Create an expression that shows only those boxes with quantities of more than 200 in stock.

6 Run the query.

7 Save the query with the name **Mid-Priced Boxes** and then close the query.

For more information on	See
Sorting data in a query	Lesson 9
Finding a range of data	Lesson 9
Using an expression in a query	Lesson 9 Appendix, "Using Expressions"
Naming and saving a query	Lesson 9

Step 3: *Create a query with related tables*

The Shipping department staff has asked you to help compile some statistics for their quarterly budget report. They have a question about the services they have used from a particular carrier. Create a query that shows all orders shipped by air within the United States.

1   Create a new query, and add the tables for Orders and Carriers.

You created the Carriers table in Lesson 6.

2   Add a field to the query that shows the order identification numbers.

3   Add a field and criteria to the query that shows "USA" as the ship country.

4   Add a field to the query that shows the carrier name.

5   Add a field for the delivery method, and then type **Yes** in the Criteria box to show that air is the selected method.

6   Run the query.

7   Because all the results of your query are from the United States, you don't need to see USA in the dynaset. Return to Design view, and hide the Ship Country column.

8   Save the query with the name **Shipping USA**, and then close it.

For more information on	See
Creating a query with related tables	Lesson 9
Hiding a field in a query	Lesson 9

Step 4: *Summarize data in a query*

The Shipping department staff are now interested in how much money they have spent on shipping by air in the United States by carrier. Modify the Shipping USA query, which summarizes shipping charges by carrier, for destinations in the United States.

1   Add the Shipping table to the Shipping USA query.

You imported the Shipping table in Lesson 7. This table is already related to the other two, with a join line drawn from the Carrier ID field.

2 Add the Shipping Charge field to the query.

3 From the View menu, choose Totals to add the Total row to the query grid, and then select Sum from the list for the Shipping Charge total.

4 Because you don't need the Order ID field for this query, delete this field, and then run the query.

5 Hide the columns for Ship Country and Air Delivery for a better view of the relevant data.

6 Close the query, and save your changes.

For more information on	See
Summarizing data in a query	Lesson 9

Step 5: *Add parameters to a query*

Bob in the Shipping department has been using the Order Review query in the Sweet Lil's database so that he can routinely check on orders for each customer. The query always shows *all* the orders, but he would like to see orders only for a specific range of dates. Modify the Order Review query so that Bob will be prompted for a beginning and ending date each time he runs the Order Review query.

1 In Design view, open the Order Review query.

2 Add a parameter to the Criteria box in the Order Date column that will prompt Bob to enter information between one date and another date.

3 Open the Query Parameters dialog box, and type the prompts.

4 Set the data type for the prompts to Date/Time to match the data type of the Order Date field.

5 Run the query and find orders between the dates of December 26, 1995, and December 31, 1995.

6 Save and close the query.

For more information on	See
Setting parameters in a query	Lesson 10

Step 6: *Create a report based on a parameter query*

To target customers for a "buy before the rush" promotion, the Marketing department has asked you to identify who ordered boxes of bonbons during the last two days before Christmas. The parameters you just added to the Order Review query are exactly what you need to get this information. You can use the Report Wizard to quickly create a report based on the Order Review query.

1   Use the AutoReport Wizard to automatically build a report for you, based on the Order Review query.

2   When prompted for dates, query for records between December 23, 1995, and December 24, 1995.

3   Look at both magnified and reduced views of your report.

4   Save your report, and name it **Order Review**

For more information on	See
Creating a report based on a parameter query	Lesson 10

If you want to continue to the next lesson

➤   On the Order Review report, click the Close button. Or, on the File menu, click Close.

This closes the report, but it does not exit Microsoft Access.

If you want to quit Microsoft Access for now

➤   In the Microsoft Access window, click the Close button. Or, on the File menu, click Exit.

This closes the table and exits Microsoft Access.

Part

4

Customizing Your Forms

Using Controls to Show Text and Data

Estimated time
50 min.

In this lesson you will learn how to:

- Add a text label to a form.
- Change the size of text and the colors on a form.
- Add a field (bound control) to a form.
- Create a check box.
- Set the properties of a control.
- Align controls.

When you want a quick form with standard features, an automatic form that you create using *Form Wizards* is perfect. It is already formatted and prompts you for all the basic elements of a form. But what if you're looking for a form that provides a more custom fit? For example, you might want to add your own text, use colors to match your corporate look, or replace a standard field with a check box to make the form easier to use. All the tools you need are available in Design view.

In this lesson, you'll learn how to add text and fields to a form, and you'll use the graphical tools available in Design view to enhance your form.

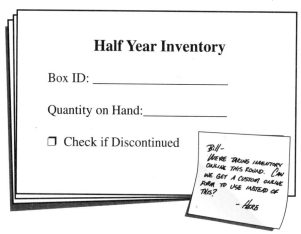

What Is a Control?

A *control* is a graphical object on a form or report that displays data, performs an action, or improves readability. The most common type of control used to display data from a field is called a *text box*. A text box can display text or numbers, and you can use it to type in new data or change existing data. Another type of control, called a *check box*, provides a graphical way to display Yes/No data. A third type of control, called a *label*, can display text or numbers that you use to identify fields or as a title for a form.

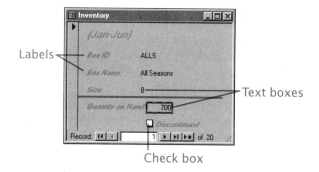

Microsoft Access provides many types of controls that you can use to customize your forms, including lines, rectangles, and command buttons. It also provides controls that display lists of values, as well as pictures, graphs, or other objects.

Each control on a form is a separate object. This means that when you're working on the design of a form, you can select any control, drag it to another location on the form, resize it—even copy it onto the Clipboard and paste it onto a different form.

In addition, each control has a set of properties, such as its color and position on the form, that you can set to determine how the control looks and operates. In the previous illustration, for example, each label and text box has a gray background that matches the background of the form. The background color of a text box or label is a property that you can set.

Start the lesson

➤ If Microsoft Access isn't started yet, start it and open the Sweet Lil's database. If the Microsoft Access window doesn't fill your screen, maximize the window.

Changing the Design of a Form

A new feature in Microsoft Access is Inherited Filters. If you base a form on a filtered table, the form will "inherit" the table's filter.

Before you create a form, it's a good idea to figure out the purpose of the form and plan how it should look and function. If other people will use the form, talk to them and find out how they'll use it. Will they change the data on the form or only view the data? Do they intend to print the form? What fields should the form include? How will you arrange the fields so that the data is displayed most effectively? By planning the creation of your form carefully, you'll save time.

Sweet Lil's is about to conduct its semi-annual inventory count. Herb, from the warehouse, stops by your office and asks you to design an online inventory form for him. He explains that his workers will use the form to update the quantity on hand of each box in inventory. "All we need on the form is the box ID code and the quantity on hand so that we can find the right box and update its quantity," says Herb. "Real simple. But can you make it look like all the other online forms? You know, with the blue and gray colors and everything?" You assure him that his inventory form will be exactly what he needs.

Create a form

You'll use a Form Wizard to create the basic form, and then you'll switch to Design view to customize its appearance.

1   In the Database window, click the Forms tab, and then click the New button.

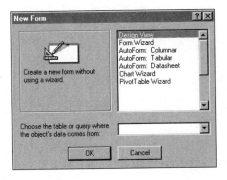

The New Form dialog box appears. Because Herb's workers will use the form you're creating to change the data in the Quantity On Hand field in the Boxes table, you'll make Boxes the underlying table for the form.

2　In the list box at the bottom of the New Form dialog box, click the down arrow, and select Boxes.

3　In the list of wizards, double-click Form Wizard.

The Form Wizard dialog box appears.

4　In the Available Fields list, double-click Box ID, and double-click Quantity On Hand to add these fields to the form. Then click the Next button.

5　Select the Columnar layout option for the form, and then click the Next button.

6　For a style, select Colorful1, and then click the Next button.

7　For the title of the form, type **Inventory**, and then click the Finish button.

The form opens in Form view. In a columnar form, you see the field name and the data from one record of the Boxes table aligned vertically.

8　On the toolbar, click the Save button.

Save

Switch to Design view

You use *Form view* and *Datasheet view* to look at and change data. Like tables and queries, a form has one more view—*Design view*—that you use to look at and change the design of the form.

On the toolbar, click the arrow on the Form View button, and then click Design View.

You might need to adjust the size of the Form to display the information in the following illustration by dragging the edge of the Form footer downward.

Form View

The Form View button face will change depending on what view is currently selected. You can find the Form View button on the left side of the toolbar—use the ToolTips to help you find it.

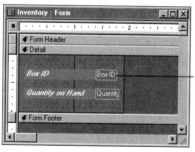

In Design view, you see the Field name instead of data in the control.

172

In Design view, the form is divided into three sections. When you're viewing data, the form header appears at the top of the window, and the form footer appears at the bottom. The *detail section* makes up the main body of the form and contains the fields from the Boxes table. The form footer and header are empty, but you could add information to them that you want to appear at the bottom and top of the form when you're viewing data on screen and when you see it in print.

Adding a Label

A label is a control that contains text you want to display on the form. The text in the label doesn't come from a field; instead, you just type the text right in the label control.

To add a label to a form, you use the Label tool in the *toolbox*. The toolbox contains a tool for every type of control you can use on a Microsoft Access form.

If the toolbox isn't visible, click Toolbox on the View menu.

When you switch to Design view for the first time, Microsoft Access displays the toolbox near the left side of the window. You can move the toolbox by dragging or double-clicking its title bar.

Add a label

Herb wants a label on the Inventory form that tells what period of time the inventory covers.

Label

1   On the toolbox, click the Label tool.

2   In the form detail section, click above the Box ID label.

Click here. ⎯

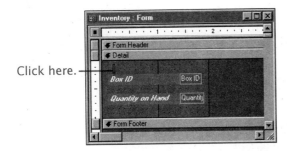

3   Type **(Jan-Jun)** and then press ENTER.

After you press ENTER, Microsoft Access selects the control. You can tell the control is selected because it has sizing handles around it. You can resize a control by dragging one of its sizing handles.

Sizing handle

You don't need to resize this control, but you might want to move it to a different position in the form detail section.

Move a control

If your new label seems crowded, you can move the new label. You move a control by dragging it with the mouse.

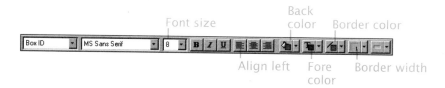

Hand

1   Click on the selected label control, but don't release the mouse button.

2   While the pointer is a hand icon, drag the control into a better position. When the control is where you want it, release the mouse button.

Aligning the labels exactly at this point is not important—you'll learn about aligning controls later in this lesson. You can also drag the bottom of the detail section downward to make more room for all of the labels and then rearrange them.

Changing the Size of Text and Setting Colors

If the toolbar isn't visible, click Toolbars on the View menu. Click the Form Design check box, and then click Close.

The toolbar that appears in Design view contains options you can use to set the size of text in a control and the colors used in a control.

Font size   Back color   Border color

| Box ID | MS Sans Serif | 8 | **B** *I* U |

Align left   Fore color   Border width

For quick help on options on the toolbar, you can press SHIFT+F1 and then click the toolbar.

Change the text size and resize the label

You'd like the text in your new label to be bigger than it is. To change the point size, you use the Font Size box on the toolbar.

1   Select the label, and verify that the sizing handles are visible.

2   With your new label selected, set the Font Size box to 12 points. You can either type **12** in the box or select 12 from the drop-down list.

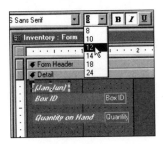

 NOTE If you click the label after it's already selected, Microsoft Access puts an insertion point inside the label so that you can edit its text. As long as the insertion point is inside the label, you can't change the point size. If that happens, click outside the label, and then click the label once to select it again.

After you change the point size, the label is no longer big enough to show all the text. There's a fast way that you can resize the control to make it fit the text perfectly.

3 Be sure that the label is still selected. Then on the Format menu, point to Size, and then click To Fit.

Microsoft Access resizes the control so that it fits the new text size.

4 If necessary, move the labels to create some space between them.

Change a section's background color

Sweet Lil's corporate style calls for form details to have a light gray background with dark blue text in the labels. To change your Inventory form so that it matches the corporate style, you'll select colors using the color buttons on the toolbar. The color buttons display floating palettes of colors, which can be dragged away from the toolbar to float on your work area; you use the floating palettes to change the appearance and colors of a control. To see an example of the corporate style, you can open the Bonbons form; be sure to close the form before working on this exercise.

1 Click the detail bar of the Inventory form.

The detail bar is highlighted; the form header and form footer bars are not.

175

Click here to
select the
Detail bar.

2   On the toolbar, click the arrow on the Back Color button.

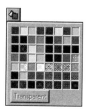

Back Color

3   Select light gray as the Back Color.

The background color of the detail section changes to light gray.

Change the color of text

You want to change the text in the labels to dark blue. You can do all three labels at once by selecting all three labels.

1   Click the (Jan-Jun) label to select it. Then hold down SHIFT, and click the Box ID and Quantity On Hand labels.

You can see handles on all three labels, indicating that they are selected.

To drag the palette off the menu, click the down arrow on the palette button, point to the border area, and then drag it away from the toolbar.

2   On the toolbar, click the arrow on the Fore Color button and select dark blue. Then click the arrow on the Back Color button, and select light gray.

The colors of all labels are set to match.

Save your changes

1   If you dragged the floating color palettes away from the toolbar, you can close them by clicking the Close button in the upper-right corner of each palette.

2   On the File menu, click Save to save your changes to the Inventory form.

Adding a Field (Bound Control)

When you want to display information from a field or add new data to a field, you use a *bound control*. A bound control is tied to a specific field in the underlying table or query. For example, the Box ID text box on the Inventory form is bound to the Box ID field in the Boxes table. In *Form view*, the control displays the box ID codes that are stored in the Box ID field.

After looking over the form you designed, Herb comes back with a request for modifications. His workers think the form would be easier to use if it displayed the box name and box size, as well as the box ID. Also, Herb says he needs a Discontinued field on the form so that the workers can mark which boxes were discontinued during the past six months. You'll add three bound controls to the Inventory form, one for each of the three fields.

Make room for a new field

The detail section of the Inventory form that you created with the Form Wizard is only big enough for its three text boxes. You need to make room for the new fields.

1   Drag the top border of the form footer bar downward to make the section taller. Drag the form window to make it larger if you need to.

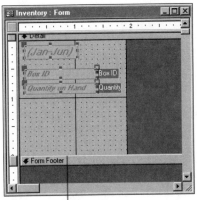

Drag the top of the Form
Footer bar downward.

Don't worry about its exact size for now; you can always adjust it again later if you need to.

You'll put a text box bound to the Box Name field right under the Box ID text box. You need to move the Quantity On Hand text box downward to make room for the new text box.

2   If all the labels are still selected, click on the form outside the labels to cancel the selection. Then drag the Quantity On Hand field to the lower portion of the detail section.

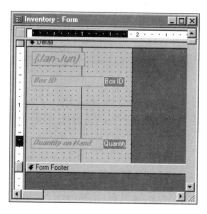

When the pointer becomes a hand icon, the Quantity On Hand label is attached to the text box—if you move one, the other moves as well.

Pointing finger

TIP To move a text box without moving its label, position the pointer over the upper-left corner of the text box. The pointer changes to a pointing finger. Now drag the text box. It moves separately from its attached label. The special, larger handle on the upper-left corner of a control is called a move handle. You can use it to move either a control or its attached label independently.

Add a field

First you'll add a text box that's bound to the Box Name field in the Boxes table. The easiest way to add a bound control to your form is to drag the field from the *field list* to the form. The field list shows the name of every field in the form's underlying table or query.

Field List

1 On the toolbar, click the Field List button.

The field list includes every field in the Boxes table, which you selected as the Inventory form's underlying table. The field list is like a floating palette—if it covers up part of your form, you can drag it to a new location.

2 From the field list, drag the Box Name field to the spot on the form where you want the field (not its label) to be.

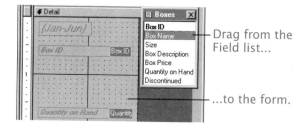

Drag from the Field list...

...to the form.

Microsoft Access creates a new text box where you drop the field, and it creates a label to the left of the field. Your new text box is bound to the Box Name field in the Boxes table.

3   Move the Quantity On Hand field upward so that it is just below the Box Name field.

4   On the toolbar, click the Form View button.

Form View

In Form view, the text box displays the name of the current box of chocolates. If you want, scroll through a few records to see the data in the text box change.

5   On the toolbar, click the button again to return to Design view.

Change the default appearance of a control

You probably noticed that the label for the Box Name control doesn't match the colors of the other labels. You can change it to light gray with dark blue text to match the other controls, but what you'd really like is for Microsoft Access to automatically give every new label on this form blue text. You can do that by changing the default properties of labels.

Fore Color

1   To change the colors of the Box Name label, click the label. Then click the arrow on the Fore Color button on the toolbar, and select dark blue; then click the arrow on the Back Color button, and select light gray.

Now you can use this label to determine how you want all new labels on this form to look.

Back Color

2   With the Box Name label selected, on the Format menu, click Set Control Defaults.

Any new label on the form will now have a light gray background and dark blue text.

Format Painter

NOTE   If you want to quickly copy the formatting of one control to another control, you can use the new Format Painter button on the toolbar. You select the control that has the format you want to copy, click the Format Painter button, and then click the control you want to copy the format to.

Add more fields

Add the Size and Discontinued fields to the form.

1   In the field list, click the Size field. Then hold down CTRL, and click the Discontinued field.

2   Drag the two fields to the detail section of the form, and drop them below the Quantity On Hand field but above the bar for the Form Footer section. The labels for the new controls are light gray with dark blue text.

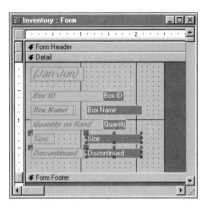

When you drop the fields on the form, Microsoft Access automatically makes the detail section taller, if necessary, to fit the two controls in the section.

3 Switch to Form view to see how your form looks. If some of the fields are hidden from view or if there is a lot of unused space in the form, click Size To Fit Form on the Window menu to view the complete form.

4 Switch back to Design view.

5 Rearrange the fields on the form so that Box ID, Box Name, and Size are on top and Quantity On Hand and Discontinued are on the bottom, with a space between the two sets of fields.

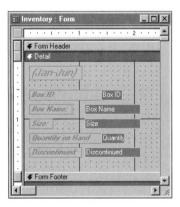

Creating a Check Box

The Discontinued field in the Boxes table has a Yes/No data type. It displays the value of Yes or No in a text box. You realize you can make your form more graphical and easier to use by replacing the Discontinued text box with a check box. That way, the person using the form can just click the check box to indicate that a box has been discontinued.

Create a check box

First you'll delete the Discontinued text box and its attached label. Then you'll replace it with a check box that's bound to the Discontinued field in the Boxes table.

1   Click the Discontinued text box to select it, and then press DELETE.

Be sure that none of the other fields are selected; otherwise, they will also be deleted. Microsoft Access deletes both the text box and its attached label.

 TIP   If you select the attached label and press DELETE, Microsoft Access deletes only the label. You can still delete the text box by selecting it and pressing DELETE.

Check Box

You can set the default control type for any field by selecting the Display Control property on the Lookup tab in Table Design view.

2   In the toolbox, click the Check Box tool.

3   From the field list, drag the Discontinued field to the lower portion of the detail section.

When you release the mouse button, Microsoft Access creates a check box that's bound to the Discontinued field.

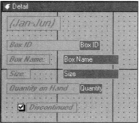

 **TIP**   If your check box's label reads something similar to "Field19" instead of "Discontinued," that means it's not bound to the Discontinued field. Delete the label and the check box, and then try again. Be sure to select the Check Box tool first, and then drag the Discontinued field from the field list.

4   Switch to Form view, and click the new check box to see how it works. Click the check box again to clear it, and then switch back to Design view.

Setting Properties

When you move a control or change its color, you're setting and changing properties of the control. You can set some properties, such as color and text size, by using tools on the toolbar. But to see and set all the properties of a control, you can use a *property sheet*.

Each control on a form has its own set of properties that determine how the control looks and operates. For example, the Control Source property of a bound control is the name of the field the control is bound to. You can bind the control to a different field just by changing its Control Source property.

Each form section also has its own set of properties. When you changed the background color of the form header section, for example, you were changing one of that section's properties.

And finally, the form as a whole has a set of properties that relate to how the entire form looks and operates. For example, if you plan to print a form, you can set its Layout For Print property to Yes. Then Microsoft Access uses printer fonts instead of screen fonts for all text and data on the form.

To display the property sheet, you can click the Properties button on the toolbar. A quick alternative method is to double-click the object with the properties you want to display (if it's not an OLE object, such as a picture or graph).

You're ready to adjust the position of the controls on the Inventory form so that they line up with each other and to use a property to further change the look of your form. First you'll set the GridX and GridY properties of the form so that the controls are easier to align horizontally and vertically. Then you'll use the grid to position the controls precisely. Finally, you'll use a Property Builder button to change the border color of a text box.

Display form properties

Make changes to the properties in the property sheet.

1   Double-click the Form selector button, which is located to the left of the horizontal ruler in the form window.

The property sheet displays the properties of the form when the form is selected.

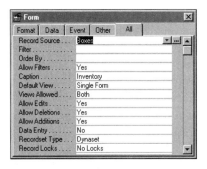

After the property sheet is open, you can display the properties of an individual control or a section of the form by clicking on the control or section.

2 Display the properties for different controls and form sections to see how the property sheet works. For example, click the Box ID text box to display its properties, and then click the label attached to this text box to display the label's properties. Click in the detail section (but not on a control) to display the section's properties.

3 After looking at a few different sets of properties, click the Form selector button to display the form's properties.

TIP For quick help on any property, click the property in the property sheet, and then press F1.

Change the grid settings

The grid marks on a form are small dots that show positions for alignment.

1 If you don't see the grid marks on your form, click Grid on the View menu.

2 In the property sheet for the form, scroll downward until you see the GridX and GridY properties.

The Form Wizard that created this form set each of these properties. These grid settings make it easy for you to move controls by very small amounts using the mouse. You'll change the fineness of the grid settings. Higher numbers indicate greater fineness.

3 Look at the ruler above the form's header. If your default unit of measurement is inches, change the GridX property to 8. If it's centimeters, change the property to 3.5.

4 Change the GridY property to 10 (or 4 for centimeters).

5 Click outside the GridY box.

The new grid settings appear on the form.

Use a Property Build button to set properties

Some of the properties on the property sheet have a Build button that assists you in setting the property. When you select a property with a builder, you'll see the Build button (with three dots on it) to the right of the property box. A builder helps you perform a task for the selected item.

To make it easier to focus on the most important piece of information in the form, you can change the Border Color and Border Width properties to make the information stand out.

1   In the Inventory form, select the Quantity On Hand text box to display its property sheet.

2   In the property sheet, click in the Border Color text box to display the Build button to the right.

Build

3   Click the Build button.

The Color dialog box opens, giving you a choice of standard or custom-designed colors.

4   Click the dark blue color, and then click OK.

5   Press ENTER to make the change.

The Border Color text box now displays the code number associated with the dark blue color that you selected for the Quantity On Hand text box.

6   To further emphasize the Quantity On Hand information, click the down arrow for the Border Width property, and select **2 pt** from the list.

The Quantity On Hand text box has a more prominent border.

Aligning Controls

Microsoft Access provides a variety of tools that help you align controls. To align controls as you add and adjust them, you can use the rulers on the top and right side of the form in Design view, the grid itself, or the Snap To Grid command. To adjust controls after you've added them, you can use the Align command on the Format menu.

Turn on Snap To Grid

It's easier to align controls to the grid when Snap To Grid is on. To see whether this command is on, you'll look at it on the Format menu.

1   Click the Format menu.

2   If Snap To Grid is not checked, click it. If there is already a check mark next to Snap To Grid, close the menu.

Align controls vertically to the grid

You'll align the controls vertically so that there's one vertical grid subdivision between controls.

1   Select the Box ID text box, and move it slightly in any direction.

Because the Snap To Grid command is on, the control moves from one grid point to another.

2   Move the Box Name text box so that there's one vertical subdivision between it and the Box ID text box. Then move the Size control so that there's one vertical subdivision between it and the Box Name text box.

3   Align the Quantity On Hand and Discontinued controls at the bottom of the detail section so that there's one subdivision of vertical space between them.

Align controls horizontally

Next you'll align the controls so that their left edges line up.

1   Click the first label (but not the text box itself), hold down SHIFT, and then click the remaining labels for all the controls on the form except the Discontinued check box.

2   On the Format menu, point to Align, and then click Left.

The left edges of the labels align.

3   Select the Box ID, Box Name, and Size text boxes (not the labels).

4   On the Format menu, point to Align, and then click Left.

The left edges of the text boxes align.

5   Align the left edges of the Quantity On Hand text box and the Discontinued check box (not the labels).

6   Switch to Form view to see how your changes look, and then switch back to Design view and save the form.

One Step Further: Formatting the Inventory Form

Your inventory form is coming together—just a few more adjustments, and then it will be nearly perfect.

Make the background for a text box invisible

You want the data in the Box ID, Box Name, and Size text boxes to appear in Form view as though they're directly on the form background, not in a box. This is a visual cue to those using the form to not change the data in these fields. You also want to make a few more changes to the other labels and controls.

1   Select the Box ID text box, and then hold down SHIFT while selecting the Box Name and Size text boxes (not the labels).

2   On the toolbar, click the arrow on the Back Color button.

3   Click the light gray color.

Back Color

4   To make the border invisible, click the arrow on the Border Color button, and then click Transparent.

The border will still be visible in Design view.

Border Color

5   To make the text more visible, click the arrow on the Fore Color button, and then click black.

Fore Color

6 Select the Quantity On Hand text box, and then change the fore color and back color to match the other controls.

7 Select all the labels, and make their borders transparent.

8 Switch to Form view to see how the form looks with data on it.

Left-align number data in a text box

Sweet Lil's boxes come in three sizes: 8 ounces, 12 ounces, and 16 ounces. By default, Microsoft Access right-aligns the numbers in a text box. You'd rather have the number in the box appear left-aligned so that it lines up with the text in the Box ID and Box Name text boxes.

1 Switch to Design view.

2 Select the Size text box.

You can change the alignment in the property sheet by using a toolbar button. The alignment buttons are available on the toolbar only when an object containing text is selected on the form. If you don't see the buttons, be sure that the Size text box is selected.

You'll use the Align Left button, but you'll see the change take place in the property sheet.

3 In the Size text box property sheet, scroll downward until you see the Text Align property.

4 On the toolbar, click the Align Left button.

Align Left

The Size text box is left-aligned, and the Text Align property box now displays Left.

5 Close the property sheet.

6 To see how a number in the box looks, switch to Form view.

Draw a line on a form

Sweet Lil's corporate style uses a heavy gray line to separate groups of fields. The gray lines on the form help group related fields visually. You'll draw a line between the first three fields and the last two fields on the Inventory form.

1 Switch the Inventory form to Design view.

2 Open the Bonbons form to see an example of the heavy gray dividing lines. Then close the Bonbons form, and select the Inventory form.

3 In the toolbox, select the Line tool.

Line

4 Below the Size field, drag across the form to create a line as wide as the form.

186

Border Width

5 On the toolbar, click the arrow on the Border Width button, and select the 2-point width. Use the Border Color palette to change the color to dark gray.

6 To make the window fit the form exactly, switch to Form view; then on the Window menu, click Size To Fit Form.

TIP If the Size To Fit Form command isn't available on the Window menu, check to see whether your form is maximized. If it is, click the Restore button in the upper-right corner of the title bar so that your form is no longer maximized, and then choose the Size To Fit Form command.

7 Save the Inventory form.

Add a ControlTip to a control

You can add your own informational ControlTips to controls so that when you point to a control, the tip is displayed. You'll add a ControlTip to the Discontinued check box.

1 Switch to Design view, and then double-click the Discontinued check box to open its property sheet.

2 Scroll down to the ControlTip Text property, and type **Click here if box has been discontinued**

3 Switch to Form view, and then point to the check box.

The new ControlTip message is displayed.

If you want to continue to the next lesson

▶ On the Inventory form, click the Close button. Or, on the File menu, click Close.

Click Yes to save your changes. This closes the form, but it does not exit Microsoft Access.

If you want to quit Microsoft Access for now

▶ In the Microsoft Access window, click the Close button. Or, on the File menu, click Exit.

Clcik Yes to save your changes. This closes the table and exits Microsoft Access.

Lesson Summary

To	Do this	Button
Create a form	In the Database window, click the Forms tab, and then click the New button. In the list box, select the table on which to base the form. Double-click the Form Wizard, and then select the fields from the table to include on your form. Select a format and title, and then click the Finish button.	
Name and save a form	On the toolbar, click the Save button. *or* On the File menu, click Save.	
Add a label to a form	Click the Toolbox button to display the toolbox. Click the Label tool in the toolbox, and then click on the form to place the label. Type the text that you want to appear in the label.	
Move a control	Move the pointer over the control until the hand icon appears. Drag the control where you want it.	
Change the size of text displayed in a control	Select the control, and be sure that the sizing handles are visible. Then change the size in the Font Size box on the toolbar.	
Resize a label so that it exactly fits its text	Select the label. On the Format menu, point to Size, and then click To Fit.	
Change the color of an object	Select the object, and then click the arrow on the Fore Color or Back Color button on the toolbar. Select the Fore Color or Back Color that you want.	
Change the width of a line	Select the line, click the arrow on the Border Width button on the toolbar, and then select a line width.	
Add a field (bound control) to a form	On the toolbar, click the Field List button to display the field list. Then drag the field from the field list to the form.	
Change the default properties of a type of control	Select a control that has the properties you want for the new default properties. On the Format menu, click Set Control Defaults.	

To	Do this	Button
Create a check box bound to a Yes/No field	Select the Check Box tool in the toolbox, and then drag the Yes/No field from the field list to the form.	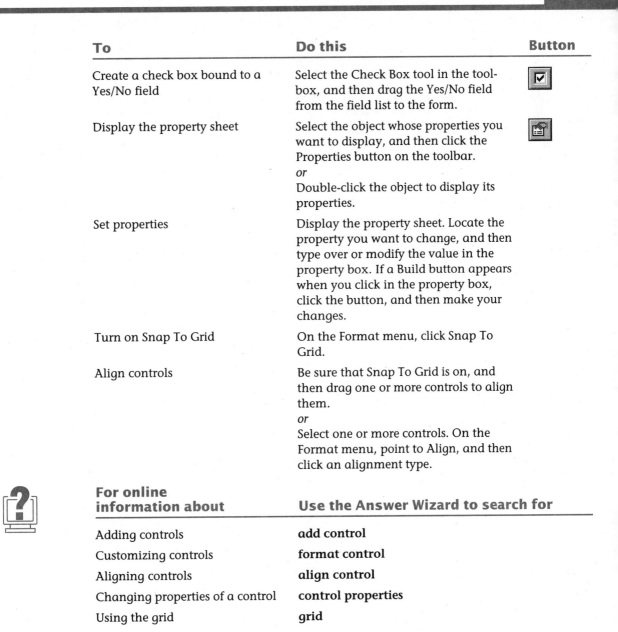
Display the property sheet	Select the object whose properties you want to display, and then click the Properties button on the toolbar. *or* Double-click the object to display its properties.	
Set properties	Display the property sheet. Locate the property you want to change, and then type over or modify the value in the property box. If a Build button appears when you click in the property box, click the button, and then make your changes.	
Turn on Snap To Grid	On the Format menu, click Snap To Grid.	
Align controls	Be sure that Snap To Grid is on, and then drag one or more controls to align them. *or* Select one or more controls. On the Format menu, point to Align, and then click an alignment type.	

For online information about	Use the Answer Wizard to search for
Adding controls	**add control**
Customizing controls	**format control**
Aligning controls	**align control**
Changing properties of a control	**control properties**
Using the grid	**grid**

Preview of the Next Lesson

In the next lesson, you'll learn how to add pictures to your form's design and how to add a control bound to a field that contains pictures or other OLE objects.

Using Pictures and Other Objects

Estimated time
20 min.

In this lesson you will learn how to:

- Add a picture to a form.
- Add a control (object frame) that displays an object from a record.
- Make an object that's stored in a table fit in the object's frame.

A picture might be worth a thousand words—but only if it's where people can see it. You can put pictures, graphs, and other objects created in other programs on your Microsoft Access forms and reports. For example, you can put your company's logo on a report next to a graph showing company sales. In addition, you can store objects in tables in your database and display the objects on a form similar to the other data in the table.

In this lesson, you'll learn how to put a picture on a form, and you'll learn how to create a control that displays objects stored in a table.

Understanding OLE

An OLE object is any piece of information created with a Windows-based program that supports linking and embedding. With the OLE features in Microsoft Access, you can place OLE objects—such as pictures, sounds, and graphs—on your forms and reports, and you can store objects as data in your tables. In addition, OLE makes it easy to edit these objects directly from the form or report.

When you place an object on a form or report, it's displayed in a control called an object frame. Microsoft Access provides two kinds of object frames—unbound and bound. A *bound object frame* displays a picture, graph, or any OLE object that is stored in a table in a Microsoft Access database. Unlike a picture created and stored in Microsoft Paint, an unbound object frame is not bound to a table.

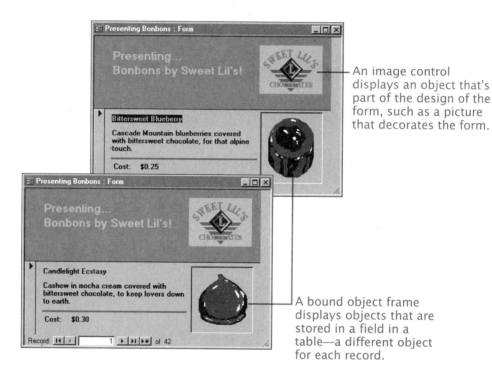

An image control displays an object that's part of the design of the form, such as a picture that decorates the form.

A bound object frame displays objects that are stored in a field in a table—a different object for each record.

You can either *embed* or *link* an object in an object frame. When you embed an object, Microsoft Access stores the object in your database file. You can easily modify the object from within Microsoft Access. If the object came from another file, only the embedded object in your database is changed, not the object in the original file.

On the other hand, when you link an object, Microsoft Access doesn't put the object in the object frame; instead, it creates a link to the object's source file (the file in which the object was created) in the frame. You can still look at the object and make changes to it on the form or report, but your changes are saved in the object's source file, not in your database file.

In this lesson, you'll create an image control and embed a picture in it. You'll also create a bound object frame that displays pictures stored in the Bonbons table. You won't be linking any objects in this lesson.

Start the lesson

 If Microsoft Access isn't already started, start it and open the Sweet Lil's database. If the Microsoft Access window doesn't fill your screen, maximize the window.

Adding a Picture to a Form

An outside vendor wants to package Sweet Lil's bonbons in his own products, and it's your job to present the bonbons to him in their best light. In your presentation to the vendor, you'll use an online form that displays information about each of Sweet Lil's bonbons. The Sweet Lil's database already has a form called Presenting Bonbons with some of the right data on it, but the form could use a little more visual appeal.

Open a form in Design view

You'll start by adding Sweet Lil's logo to the form header of the Presenting Bonbons form. To add a picture to the design of the form, you must be working in Design view.

1   In the Database window, click the Forms tab.

2   Select the Presenting Bonbons form, and then click the Design button.

The form opens in Design view.

3   If the form window isn't large enough to display all of the detail section, resize it to make it bigger.

Add a picture

If the toolbox isn't displayed, click Toolbox on the View menu.

The Sweet Lil's logo is in a Microsoft Paint file named Sweet Lil's Logo. The Sweet Lil's Logo file was copied to your Practice folder when you copied the practice files to your hard disk. You'll add an image control (a new and faster version of an unbound object frame) to the form header of the Presenting Bonbons form, and then embed the logo in the frame.

Image

1   In the toolbox, click the Image tool to create an image control on the form.

2   Click in the form header section, to the right of the title "Presenting...Bonbons by Sweet Lil's!"

The Insert Picture dialog box opens so that you can insert the picture file you want.

3   In the Insert Picture dialog box, click the Look In Favorites button. Then double-click the Access SBS Practice folder, and double-click Sweet Lil's Logo.

The logo is inserted in the form header section of the form. You can drag the control to reposition it if you need to.

193

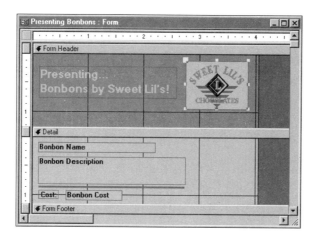

If you want to resize the image, you can drag the sizing handles on the image control frame and then use the image control's property sheet to fit the picture into the new frame margins. Double-click the image; then on the property sheet, click in the Size Mode box, and select Clip, Stretch, or Zoom. Clip displays the picture at actual size; Stretch sizes the picture to fit within the margins (and may distort the picture); Zoom sizes the picture to fit within the height or width of the margins without distorting the picture.

Look at the picture in Form view

The logo will appear on the form of each record.

Form View

1   Switch to Form view to see how the logo looks with a record of data.

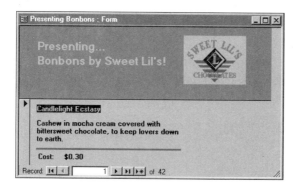

2   Move from record to record on the form.

Because the logo is placed in the header section of the form, it appears on the form background for every record.

3   Switch back to Design view.

Double-clicking the image displays the control's property sheet rather than starting Microsoft Paint, because the picture is an image control instead of an unbound object. If you want to edit the image, you open Microsoft Paint, edit the picture file, and then replace the old image in the form with the new image.

Adding a Control That Displays a Picture from a Record

The Bonbons table includes a field named Picture that contains pictures of Sweet Lil's bonbons. You'll add a control to the detail section of the Presenting Bonbons form that displays the pictures in Form view.

Add a bound object frame to a form

Your control will be bound to the Picture field, so you'll use the Bound Object Frame tool.

Bound Object Frame

1   In the toolbox, select the Bound Object Frame tool.

TIP   Here's an easy way to remember which tool is for the bound object frame and which is for the unbound object frame. The picture on the tool for the bound object frame includes some letters at the top, similar to an attached label. You can think of those letters as the name of the field that the control is bound to. When you create a bound object frame, Microsoft Access adds an attached label to the frame, just as it does when you create a text box.

2   Drag the pointer to create a square-shaped control that fits in the right side of the detail section.

When you release the mouse button, Microsoft Access creates a bound object frame with an attached label. You don't need the label, so you'll delete it.

3   Click the attached label, and then press DELETE.

Bind the object frame to the Picture field

In Lesson 11, you learned how to create a control that's bound to a field by dragging the field from the field list to the form. Now you'll learn another way to bind a control to a field—by setting the Control Source property of the control.

1   If the property sheet isn't displayed, double-click the new bound object frame to display its properties. If the property sheet is displayed but shows the properties for another control, click the bound object frame.

You will bind the object frame to the Picture field, which contains the pictures of the bonbons.

2   In the property sheet, select the Control Source box, click the down arrow, and then select Picture from the list of fields.

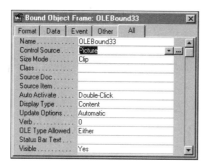

Look at the data

Do you know why a picture of a bonbon didn't appear in the bound object frame after you bound it to the Picture field? The answer is clear when you think about which view of the form shows the data from the table. You're looking at the form in Design view, but the pictures of bonbons aren't part of the design of the form. They're part of the data in the Bonbons table.

Don't be concerned if your picture does not fit perfectly in the frame. You'll fix it in the next exercise.

1   Switch to Form view, and if necessary, move to the first record.

The picture for Candlelight Ecstasy appears as the first bonbon in the table.

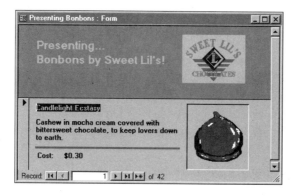

2   Move to the next record in the table.

Now the control displays the picture for Bittersweet Blueberry.

Edit the picture

You use the same method to modify a picture in a bound control as in an unbound control—except that you do it in Form view, where the data is displayed, rather than in Design view.

For steps on adding a new bonbon, including its picture, to the Bonbons table, see Lesson 2, "Getting the Best View of Your Data."

1   In Form view, double-click the picture of the Bittersweet Blueberry bonbon.

Microsoft Paint starts and displays a border around the picture to indicate that you can edit within the border. If you want, you can use Microsoft Paint to change the picture, but you don't have to make changes to continue with this lesson.

2   When you're finished looking at or editing the picture, click the form outside of the picture.

Microsoft Paint closes. If you update the picture, your changes are saved in the Bonbons table.

3   Look at a few more records, and then switch back to Design view.

Only the first five bonbons and a few bonbons that appear later in the table have pictures. In the other records, the Picture field is empty.

Making an Object from a Table Fit in a Frame

If the pictures of bonbons don't fit in your bound object frame exactly, you might see an empty white area on the edge of the frame (indicating that the frame is too big), or the frame might cut off a portion of the picture (indicating that it's too small).

With an image control, such as the logo in the form header, you can choose properties on the property sheet to fit the picture exactly to the frame. You size bound object frames the same way.

To choose the best way to display an object in its bound object frame, you set the frame's Size Mode property. The Size Mode property has three possible settings:

■ *Clip* displays as much of the object as will fit in the frame with no changes to the size of the object and no distortions. This is the default setting. Part of the picture may be cut off if it's too large for the frame.

■ *Stretch* enlarges or shrinks the object to fit the size of the frame. This might distort the proportions of the object, especially if its size is quite different from the frame's size.

■ *Zoom* enlarges or shrinks the object to fit the frame as well as it can without changing the proportions of the object.

Scale the picture to fit the control

To fit the pictures exactly, set the Width and Height properties of the bound object frame to 1.15 inches.

Because your frame is close to the same size as the pictures in the Bonbons table, you can set the Size Mode property to Stretch; each picture will then fit the frame with a minimum of distortion.

1   In Design view, set the Size Mode property of the bound object frame to Stretch.

2   Switch to Form view.

Microsoft Access scales the picture so that it fits in the frame perfectly.

3   Switch back to Design view.

Give the object frame a raised appearance

Give the object frame for the Picture field one more visual touch.

Special Effect

The Special Effect button will change depending on what effect is currently selected for the control.

Raised

1   With the object frame selected, on the toolbar, click the arrow on the Special Effect button.

2   On the palette of special effect buttons, click the Raised button.

3   Switch to Form view to see how the form looks now.

4   To size the form's window so that it fits the form, click Size To Fit Form on the Window menu.

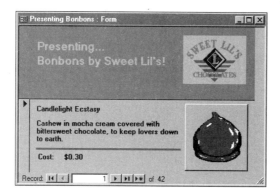

The form looks great—you're ready for your presentation.

5   Save the Presenting Bonbons form, and then close it.

One Step Further: Creating and Adding an Original Picture

So far, all the examples in this lesson use pictures that were created and saved before you put them on your form. You can also create an object at the same time you embed it. You'll embed your own drawing of a bonbon in the Picture field in the Bonbons table.

Add your own bonbon picture

Pictures of bonbons are stored in the Bonbons table. You can use the Presenting Bonbons form to add your own picture of a bonbon to the table.

1   Open the Presenting Bonbons form in Form view. Go to a record that doesn't have a picture (such as the sixth record).

2   Click the empty Picture field with the right mouse button, and then click Insert Object.

198

3   Be sure that the Create New option is selected. Then in the list box, double-click Bitmap Image.

4   Paint your picture of a bonbon, or just put a piece of sample text in a box (for example, **Delicious!**). Then click in the form (outside the picture frame) to close Microsoft Paint and return to Microsoft Access.

Your picture or text appears in the object frame.

TIP   Because the control's Size Mode property is set to Stretch, the entire Microsoft Paint work area is scaled to fit in the control. For that reason, your picture might appear very small. Either change the Size Mode property to Clip before choosing Insert Object or paint a larger picture.

5   Save your changes.

The picture you drew in the Bonbons table is saved.

If you want to continue to the next lesson

➤ On the Presenting Bonbons form, click the Close button. Or, on the File menu, click Close.

This closes the form, but it does not exit Microsoft Access.

If you want to quit Microsoft Access for now

➤ In the Microsoft Access window, click the Close button. Or, on the File menu, click Exit.

This closes the table and exits Microsoft Access.

Lesson Summary

To	Do this	Button
Add an image control to a form or report	In Design view, select the Image tool in the toolbox. Click where you want the image on the form. In the Insert Picture dialog box, double-click the picture file you want.	
Size an image control to fit the object it contains	In Design view, display the control's property sheet. In the Size Mode box, select Clip, Stretch, or Zoom.	

199

To	Do this	Button
Add a bound object frame to a form or report	In Design view, select the Bound Object Frame tool in the toolbox. Draw an object frame on the form. Set the Control Source property of the object frame to the name of the field that contains the objects. To view, edit, or add objects, switch to Form view.	
Modify a Microsoft Paint picture on a form or report	For an image control, double-click the object in Design view. For a bound object (stored in a table), double-click the object in Form view. Make your changes, and then click on the form outside the picture frame.	
Scale an object so that it fits in a bound object frame	In Design view, set the Size Mode property of the bound object frame to Stretch.	

For online information about	Use the Answer Wizard to search for
Adding a bound frame to a form	**bound frame**
Adding an image control to a form	**image control**
Fit objects in a frame	**fit frame**

Preview of the Next Lesson

In the next lesson, you'll learn how to create a form that shows information from two tables at the same time. The form will show information about both the customer and each order the customer has placed.

Showing Related Records on a Form

Estimated time
20 min.

In this lesson you will learn how to:

- Create a form with a subform.
- Create a command button that opens a form.

Arranging and presenting data efficiently are keys to making a database easy to use. A customer's phone number is in one table; the orders that the customer placed are in another. When you call the customer, you want to see a list of the customer's orders along with the customer's name and number.

You can design your forms to display data in any way that it is most useful to you. In this lesson, you'll learn how to create a form that shows one record at the top (such as a customer's record) and related records in a subform at the bottom (such as a record for each order the customer placed). You'll also learn how to create a command button that opens another form with information that you need.

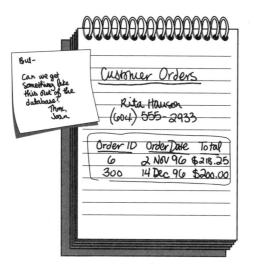

Creating Two Forms That Work Together

You might want to work with a form that requires information from more than one table, or from a table and a query. To do that, you use a form with a subform. A subform is a form within a form. By using a subform, you can combine information so that you don't have to switch back and forth between separate tables or forms.

In most cases, the subform is linked to the main form, so it shows records that are related to the record on the main form. For example, the Boxes form in the Sweet Lil's database shows information about a box of bonbons. The subform, which lists the bonbons in the box, is linked to the main form.

The main form shows the records for a single box.

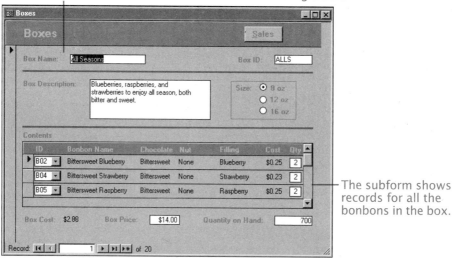

The subform shows records for all the bonbons in the box.

A subform is saved as a separate form in the database. The form that appears as the subform on the Boxes form is named Boxes Subform. If you open this form separately, apart from the Boxes form, it shows all the bonbons in the database.

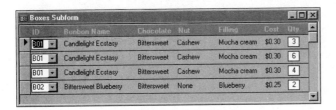

You can also start Microsoft Access and open the Sweet Lil's database in a single step. Click the Start button, point to Documents, and then click Sweet Lil's.

In this lesson, you'll create a form that shows customer information on the main form— the customer's name and phone number—and displays a list of the customer's orders on a subform. If one customer placed ten orders, you'll see all ten orders listed under the customer's name.

Start the lesson

> If Microsoft Access isn't started yet, start it and open the Sweet Lil's database. If the Microsoft Access window doesn't fill your screen, maximize the window.

Creating a Form with a Subform

The easiest way to create a form with a subform is to use the Form Wizard. The Form Wizard creates both forms and makes them work together. It can even link the two forms automatically as long as both of these conditions are met:

■ The main form is based on a table or query.

For details about creating relationships between tables, see Lesson 8, "Relating Tables."

■ The subform is based on a table that's related to the main form's table; or, the subform is based on a table or query that contains a field with the same name and data type as the primary key of the main form's table.

In the example you create in this lesson, the main form is based on the Customers table, so the first condition is met. The primary key of the Customers table is the Customer ID field.

The subform is based on a query named Orders With Subtotals that also includes a Customer ID field, so the second condition is met. This query contains information about a customer's orders that you want to display on the subform.

Microsoft Access uses the Customer ID fields in the underlying table and query to link the main form and subform automatically.

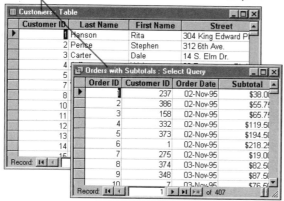

 NOTE If the two conditions for automatically linking a main form and a subform are not met, you can still link the two forms yourself. Both the underlying table or query for the main form and the underlying table or query for the subform must still contain *linking fields*—fields that have the same value for linking records.

Start the Form Wizard

When you use a Form Wizard to create a form with a subform, you need to select the underlying table or query for both the main form and the subform, and the relationship between the two needs to be set up before you create the forms. In this case, the Customers table has been joined to the Orders With Subtotals query in the Relationships window (see Lesson 8, "Relating Tables," for details about the Relationships window).

1   In the Database window, click the Forms tab to display the list of forms, and then click the New button.

    The New Form dialog box appears.

2   Double-click Form Wizard.

    The Form Wizard opens.

3   In the Tables/Queries list box, select Table: Customers.

4   In the list of Available Fields, double-click First Name, Last Name, State/Province, and Phone.

5   In the Tables/Queries list box, select Query: Orders With Subtotals.

6   In the list of Available Fields, double-click Order ID, Order Date, and Subtotal, and then click Next.

7 When the Wizard asks which table or query you want to view by, click By Customers.

8 Select the Form With Subform option, and then click Next.

9 Select Datasheet as the layout for your subform, and then click Next.

10 Select the Standard style for the form, and then click Next.

11 Change the title of the form to **Customers and Orders**, and then click the Finish button.

Mirosoft Access saves both the main form and the subform. You can also change the name of the subform, if you want to. Microsoft Access creates the Customers And Orders form, and the form opens.

To resize the columns in the subform, double-click the column header borders while the main form is open in Form view.

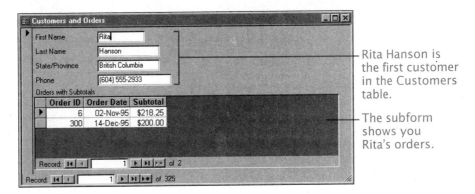

Rita Hanson is the first customer in the Customers table.

The subform shows you Rita's orders.

See how the form works

The subform is automatically linked to the main form. To see how this works, look at some of the other customer records.

1 Go to the next customer record, using the navigation buttons at the bottom of the Form window.

The records in the subform change to display the current customer's orders.

2 Switch to Design view.

In Design view, you can see the controls on the main form and one large control for the subform. The subform control has properties that link the records on the subform to the appropriate record on the main form.

3 If the property sheet isn't displayed, click the Properties button on the toolbar to display it.

Properties

4 Select the control for the subform to display its properties.

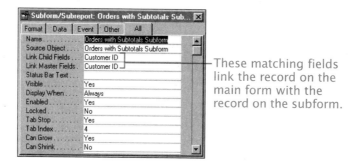

These matching fields link the record on the main form with the record on the subform.

5 Close the properties sheet.

A subform doesn't have to be seen in Design view. To see and modify the subform itself, you'll need to open the subform in Design view.

6 Select the Orders With Subtotals Subform in the Sweet Lil's database window, and click Design to open the form in Design view.

The Form Wizard put a text box on the subform for each field you selected from the subform's underlying query.

7 Close the subform.

8 Save and close the main form.

Creating a Command Button to Open a Form

You can add a command button to a form to automatically open another form that contains information you want to check.

The Operations department wants a fast way to tell what the shipping charge is for a particular order. You use the Command Button Wizard to add a button to the Customers And Orders form. By using the button, you can open the Shipping form and look up the cost of each shipper to a particular destination.

Create an Open Form command button with a Wizard

The Customers And Orders form contains all the information about what each customer has ordered.

1 Open the Customers And Orders form in Design view.

2 In the toolbox, click the Command Button tool.

Command Button

3 Click the location on the form where you want to place the upper-left corner of the button (such as next to the First Name text box).

The first Command Button Wizard dialog box appears.

4 In the Categories box, select Form Operations.

5 In the Actions box, select Open Form, and then click the Next button.

Choose a form to open

The Shipping form has the details about what shippers charge for each destination.

You created the Shipping form in Lesson 7.

1 Select the Shipping form, and then click Next.

2 Select the "Open the form and find specific data to display" option, and then click Next.

3 To show which fields contain matching data, select the State/Province field from the Customers And Orders table, select the Ship State/Province field from the Shipping table, and then click the double-arrow button. Click Next.

4 Select the Text option, and then select the text "Open Form." Type **Ship Charge** and then click Next.

5 Name the button **Ship Charge** and then click the Finish button.

The Customers And Orders form appears in Design view, including the new Ship Charge command button.

Use the command button

The Ship Charge command button is ready to use.

1 Switch to Form view.

2 Click the Ship Charge command button to open the Shipping form.

The Shipping form opens, showing the state or province destination that matches the record selected on the Customers And Orders form.

3 Select another record on the Customers And Orders form.

4 Click the Ship Charge command button.

The record on the Shipping form changes to show the shipping charge for the new destination.

5 Save the Customers And Orders form, and then close both the Customers And Orders form and the Shipping form.

One Step Further: Adding Calculated Controls to a Form

The First Name and Last Name text boxes on the Customers And Orders form are bound to the First Name and Last Name fields in the Customers table. But suppose you want to show a customer's first name and last name together in one text box.

For more information about expressions, see the Appendix, "Using Expressions."

To do that, you use a *calculated control*. A calculated control is tied to an expression instead of a field. The expression can combine text values from more than one field in the underlying table or query, or it can perform calculations on values from the fields.

To tie a text box to an expression, you type the expression in the text box in Design view. Always start the expression with an equal sign (=).

207

Add and delete controls

You'll replace the First Name and Last Name text boxes on the Customers And Orders form with one text box that shows both names.

1   Open the Customers And Orders form in Design view.

2   Select the First Name and Last Name controls at the same time by holding down SHIFT and then clicking each text box.

3   Press DELETE to delete the First Name and Last Name text boxes and their labels.

Text Box

4   In the toolbox, click the Text Box tool to add an unbound text box to the form.

5   Click in the Detail section where you want the upper-left corner of the text box (not its attached label) to be.

A text box appears that is not bound to any field in the Customers table. It has a generic label such as "Text28."

Tie a text box to an expression

A text box that is bound to a field displays the field name in Design view. To bind a text box to an expression instead, you type the expression in the box. You'll use the "&" operator in the expression to display one text value followed by another.

1   Move the pointer over the text box. When the pointer turns into a vertical line, click in the text box.

Text28: ┌────────────┐ Click in the text box to get an insertion point.

The "&" operator is also known as the "concatenation" operator.

2   Type =[**First Name**] & " " & [**Last Name**] in the text box, and then press ENTER.

Be sure to start the expression with an equal sign, and put a space between the two quotation marks in the expression so that there's a space between the first name and last name.

This expression tells Microsoft Access to display the value in the First Name field...

=[First Name]&" "&[Last Name]

    ...followed   ...followed by the value
    by a space...   in the Last Name field.

In an expression, you place brackets around field names and double quotation marks around a space or other text characters.

3   Switch to Form view and see the results.

The full name appears in the text box.

4   Switch back to Design view.

Enhance the appearance of the form

When you added the text box to the form, Microsoft Access gave it a default label, such as Text28. You'll replace the text in the label with something more descriptive.

1   Click the text box's attached label to select it, and then position the pointer over the label until it turns into a vertical line.

2   Double-click the generic label to select the text.

3   Replace the text in the label with **Customer Name**

The size of the label adjusts to fit the new text.

4   Switch to Form view. On the Window menu, click Size To Fit Form so that the window fits the form.

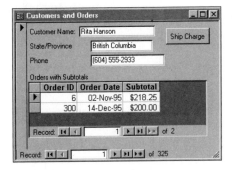

5   Save the form.

If you want to continue to the next lesson

➤   On the Customers And Orders form, click the Close button. Or, on the File menu, click Close.

This closes the form, but it does not exit Microsoft Access.

If you want to quit Microsoft Access for now

➤   In the Microsoft Access window, click the Close button. Or, on the File menu, click Exit.

This closes the table and exits Microsoft Access.

Lesson Summary

To	Do this	Button
Create a form with a subform	In the Database window, click the Forms tab, and then click the New button. Double-click Form Wizard, and then select the first table or query that contains the data you want on the main form. Add the fields you want from that table/query. Then click the second table or query you want on the form, and add the fields you want. Answer the questions in the Form Wizard dialog boxes to finish the form.	
Create a command button to open a form	Click the Command Button button in the toolbox. Click on the form to position the button. In the Categories box, select Form Operations, and then select Open Form from the list of actions. Then follow the directions in the Button Wizard dialog boxes.	
Use a command button on a form	In Form view, click the command button.	

For online information about	Use the Answer Wizard to search for
Creating forms with subforms	**subforms**
Creating a command button	**command button**

Preview of the Next Lesson

In the next lesson, you'll learn how to make your forms easier to use by providing choices in lists and option groups.

Making Data Entry Easy and Accurate

Estimated time
40 min.

In this lesson you will learn how to:

- Create a combo box control.
- Base a combo box on a query.
- Change the tab order of controls on a form.
- Set an initial (default) value for a control.
- Require data in a field.
- Validate data entered in a control.

The information you get from your database is only as good as the data you put into it. Forms are where most information is added into your database. Ensuring that the entries on a form are accurate is essential if you are to get the information you need from your database. By making forms easy to use and by preventing certain types of data from being changed, you can help to make data entry go faster and reduce the possibility of errors.

When looking up customer information on a form, you might find it easier and friendlier to identify the customer by a name rather than by a number. If you can pick the name from a list instead of typing it, that's even more convenient and ensures that the value entered in the table is correct. But Microsoft Access can find a customer's information faster if you give it the customer's ID number instead of the name. How do you design your form so that it is easy to use, finds information as quickly as possible, and guarantees that the data you enter is accurate?

The answer is to design a list box or combo box on your form that lets you select a name but that tells Microsoft Access the ID number associated with the name.

In Lesson 8, you used the Lookup Wizard to create a lookup field in the Orders table. One of the tasks the Lookup Wizard performed was to create a default combo box control type for that field, so that whenever you placed the field in a form, a combo box would be automatically created. In this lesson, you'll learn how to create a combo box that is not stored as the default control type in a table, but the combo box is a specific control on a specific form. Your combo box will allow you to select a customer's name from a list, and then it will store the customer ID in a field.

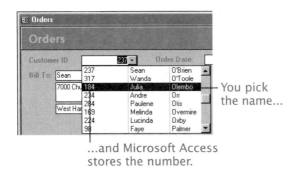

You pick the name...

...and Microsoft Access stores the number.

Even with forms that allow you to select items from a list, there are still ways that errors can be made. When writing today's date, you might accidentally put down the previous year instead of this year. When viewing data on a form, you could inadvertently change or erase a value in a field. How do you protect your data from everyday mistakes such as these?

In this lesson, you'll learn how to display a value such as today's date automatically so that you don't have to type it yourself. You'll learn how to design a control so that it automatically displays a message if you enter invalid data in it. You'll also learn how to set a property so that data is required in a field.

How Controls and Properties Protect Your Data

Choosing data from a list in a combo box or a list box makes data entry fast and accurate. By changing the properties of a table or form to limit the information that can be entered into a field, you can also make entering information easy and safe from error.

Microsoft Access has two types of controls that provide a list of choices you can scroll: list boxes and combo boxes. Because looking up a value in a list is often easier and quicker than remembering the value you want, these controls can make your forms easier to use and can prevent mistakes.

A list box is a simple list of values that you can select from.

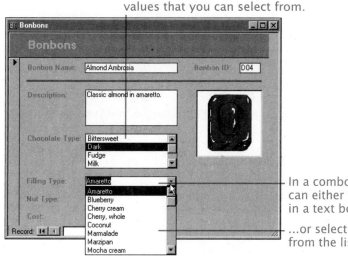

In a combo box, you can either type a value in a text box...

...or select a value from the list.

The list in a list box or combo box consists of a number of rows of data. Each row can have one or more columns. You specify which column contains the data you want stored in the field, and you can use other columns to display data, such as full names, that help you pick the right row. A list can be based on a table or a query.

To further protect your data, you can give a control a default value, which appears automatically in a field.

In addition to setting a default property, you can set properties that will:

- Describe what data is correct for a control by setting the control's Validation Rule property.

You can also start Microsoft Access and open the Sweet Lil's database in a single step. Click the Start button, point to Documents, and then click Sweet Lil's.

- Display a message that tells you how to fix an incorrect entry by setting the control's Validation Text property.

- Prevent changes from being made to data on a form by setting the form's Allow Edits property.

Start the lesson

➤ If Microsoft Access isn't already started, start it and open the Sweet Lil's database. If the Microsoft Access window doesn't fill your screen, maximize the window.

Creating a Combo Box

When operators take new telephone orders for Sweet Lil's chocolates, speed and accuracy are their top priorities. To make their job easier, you plan to make several enhancements to the on-line form they use.

Currently, operators enter the ID number of the customer placing the order in a text box on the Orders form. You'll replace the text box with a combo box that shows a list of customer names as well as their ID numbers, so that you can select the ID instead of typing it.

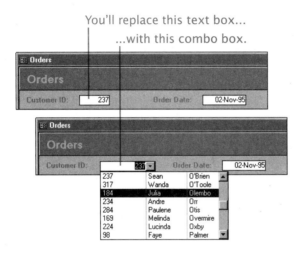

In many cases, the best way to define the list is to create a separate query that selects and arranges the data just the way you want it to appear in the list. Then you can tell Microsoft Access to use the fields in the query as columns in the list.

 TIP If you want to change the text box into a label, list box, or simple combo box, you can use the new Control Morphing feature. Select the control you want to change; then on the Format menu, point to Change To, and click a new control type.

Look at the Customer List query

In this case, you want the list to show the last name, first name, and ID number of each of Sweet Lil's customers. You could create a new query that includes these fields, but the database already contains a query named Customer List that has exactly the data you want. Before creating your combo box, take a look at the Customer List query you'll use to define the rows that will be displayed in the combo box's list.

1   In the Database window, click the Queries tab, and then open the Customer List query in Design view.

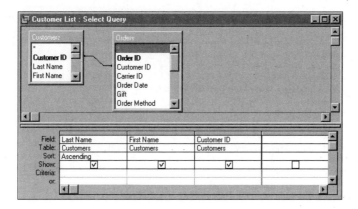

As you can see, this query is based on the Customers table and the Orders table. The Customer ID field links the two tables.

2   Look at the Customer List query in Datasheet view to see how the information appears.

3   Close the Customer List query.

Delete a text box

Before adding the combo box, make room for it by deleting the Customer ID text box and its label.

1   Click the Forms tab, and then open the Orders form in Design view.

2   If the Orders form window is too small for you to see all its controls, resize the window to make it larger.

3   Click the Customer ID text box, and then press DELETE.

The Customer ID text box and its label are deleted.

Create a combo box bound control

Your combo box on the Orders form will be bound to the Customer ID field in the Customer List query. When an operator selects a customer from the combo box list on the form, Microsoft Access will store the customer's ID number in the bound field in the table.

To create a bound combo box, you click the Combo Box tool in the toolbox and then drag the field you want from the field list to the form. The Combo Box Wizard will guide you through the creation process.

Toolbox

Field List

Combo Box

1   Be sure that the toolbox and the field list are visible. If the toolbox isn't visible, click Toolbox on the toolbar. If the field list isn't visible, click the Field List button on the toolbar.

2   In the toolbox, click the Combo Box tool.

Now when you drag the Customer ID field from the field list, Microsoft Access creates a combo box that's bound to the field.

3   Drag the Customer ID field from the field list to just above the First Name field on the form.

When you release the mouse button, the first Combo Box Wizard dialog box appears.

Create a combo box list

The Combo Box Wizard guides you through the creation of the combo box list for your form.

1   In the first Combo Box Wizard dialog box, be sure the option is selected that will look up values in a table or query, and then click Next.

2   In the View area, select the Queries option button, and then select the Customer List query. Click Next.

3   On the Available Fields list, double-click the Customer ID, Last Name, and First Name fields for the columns in your combo box, and then click Next.

4   Double-click the right edge of each column header to adjust the column width to its best fit. Click Next.

5   Select Customer ID as the column that contains the data you want to store in your table, and then click Next.

6   Be sure that the option to store the value in the Customer ID field is selected, and then click Next.

7   Customer ID automatically appears as the choice for the label for your combo box. This is the label you want, so click the Finish button to complete the combo box.

The Orders form has a combo box bound to the Customer ID field.

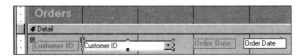

Use the combo box

You can immediately see how using the combo box makes looking up a customer's ID easy.

1   Switch to Form view.

2   Click the down arrow on the combo box, and select any name from the list.

The customer ID number appears in the Customer ID field. Now when an employee takes a new order, all he or she has to do is select the customer's name, and all customer information is filled in automatically.

Place a control in the correct tab order

When you switched to Form view, the Order Date field was automatically selected. To make the Customer ID field selected whenever you open the form, you can change the *tab order* of the Orders form. The tab order of a form is the order in which the insertion point moves through fields when you tab from field to field in Form view.

When you create a new control, Microsoft Access puts the new control last in the tab order of the form, regardless of where you place the control on the form. You'll edit the tab order of the form so that the new Customer ID combo box you just created is first in the tab order, not last.

1   Switch to Design view, and then select the Customer ID combo box control if it is not already selected.

2   On the View menu, click Tab Order.

The Tab Order dialog box appears.

3   Scroll downward in the list of controls until you see the Customer ID control, which is last in the list.

4   Click once in the left column to select the Customer ID control, and then drag it to the top of the list.

5   Click OK.

Now your new control is first in the tab order, where it belongs.

6   Switch to Form view to test the tab order.

7   Save the Orders form.

Setting an Initial (Default) Value for a Control

Customer orders are the heart of Sweet Lil's business—a mistake on an order can mean lost revenue and lost customers. You plan to enhance the Orders form so that it will help ensure that the data on the form is correct. You'll give the form's Order Date text box a default value so that the operators don't have to type the date themselves.

Today's date appears automatically...

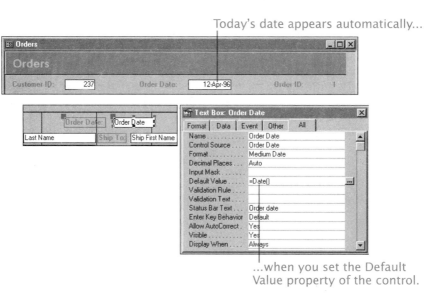

...when you set the Default Value property of the control.

You can set the Default Value property either to an expression or to a constant value, such as text or a number. In this case, you'll set it equal to an expression that includes the Date function. The Date function is a small program that retrieves the current date from the system clock in your computer.

Display today's date in a text box

Enter the expression in the property sheet of the Orders form.

Properties

1 Switch to Design view for the Orders form.

2 If the property sheet isn't displayed, click the Properties button on the toolbar. Then click the Order Date text box to display its properties.

3 In the Default Value property box, type the expression =**Date( )**

4 Switch to Form view.

Since Microsoft Access enters the default value when you start a new record, you'll go to a new record to see your property setting work.

5 Click the New Record navigation button at the bottom of the form to move to a new blank record.

A new record appears with today's date in the Order Date text box.

Validating Data Entered in a Control

You've seen how to make data entry easier and more accurate by setting default values. You can also protect your data by adding a validation rule to a control. A validation rule checks the data that you enter in the control against a rule that you define. You can create an error message that automatically appears if the data doesn't meet the rule's requirements, so incorrect data won't be saved in your table.

For example, operators enter the expiration date of the customer's credit card in the Expiration Date text box on the Orders form. If the date entered has passed, you can display a message alerting the operator that the card has expired. You do this by setting a validation rule that requires the date entered to be greater than or equal to today's date. You'll also write an error message that tells the operator what to do if the card has expired.

Set the Validation Rule and Validation Text properties

Make changes to the Order form's property sheet.

1   Switch to Design view for the Orders form.

2   Display the properties of the Expiration Date text box.

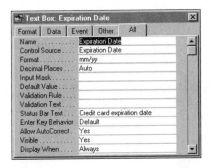

3   In the Validation Rule property box, type the expression >=**Date()**

4   Click in the Validation Text property box. Because the message you will type is long, press SHIFT+F2 to display the Zoom window so that you can see all your text as you type.

5   Type the following message:

Credit card has expired! Click the OK button, and then press Esc. Pick a different card or cancel the order.

Your validation text message can be up to 255 characters long.

6   Click OK to close the Zoom window.

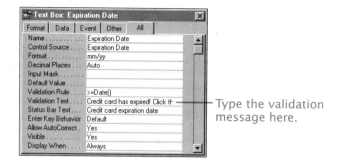

Type the validation message here.

Test your validations

Now try to enter an expired date and see what happens.

1   Switch to Form view, and move to the last record.

2   In the Expiration Date text box, change the value to **11/93**

3   Press TAB.

Your error message appears.

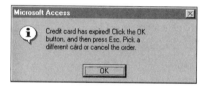

4   Click the OK button to clear the message.

5   On the Edit menu, click the Undo command to replace 11/93 with the original value in the text box.

Now you can enter a different credit card or cancel the order.

6   Save and close the Orders form.

Requiring Data Entry in a Field

Setting properties on a form makes forms easier to use and more accurate, but they control only the individual form where you made the settings. You might want the data in a field always to follow certain rules, no matter what form uses it. To do this, you can set global properties in the table that contains the field you want to affect.

If you had set the Validation Rule and Validation Text properties on the Orders table instead of on the Orders form, all forms containing the Expiration Date field would contain the same validation rules. You can still change or delete the validation rule on an individual form if you want.

The Required property is another field property you can set in a table that affects all forms using that field. If the Required property is set to Yes, you *must* enter a value in that field or any control bound to that field.

For example, when you use the Subscription form, you might want to require that a customer's address always contains a postal code so that shipping isn't delayed.

Set the Required property

The Subscription form is based on the Customers table, so you will set the Required property of the Customers table. While you're changing the design of the Customers table, you can't open the Subscription form in Form view; however, you can open it in Design view.

1 In the Database window, click the Tables tab, and open the Customers table in Design view.

2 Click in the Postal Code field.

3 In the Field Properties section, change the Required field to **Yes**

From now on, you cannot save a record with a *null value*, meaning that this field must contain information.

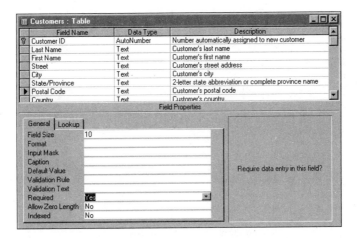

4 Close the Customers table.

5 Click the Yes button to save the changes.

A message appears asking if you want to check the existing data to be sure it follows the new validation rule. If you don't check the data, you could have records that have null values in this field.

6 Click the Yes button to test the existing data with the new rule.

If any records violate the rule, another message box appears to warn you.

Test the Required property

Try to enter a record in a form, without a postal code.

1   In the Database window, click the Forms tab, and then double-click the Subscription form to open it in Form view.

2   Enter the following record:

Matthew Wilson
1876 Parker Lane
Wilshire, MD

3   Leave the Postal Code field blank, and tab to the next field.

4   Enter **US** and then select the option boxes for 6 months and Renewal.

5   Try to tab to a new record.

A message appears telling you that this field cannot contain a null value, which means that it cannot be empty.

6   Click the OK button.

7   Enter a postal code of **17634** for the current record.

8   Close the form.

One Step Further: Changing the Editing Properties of a Form

Besides being able to protect your data from incorrect entries, you can set properties of forms so that data cannot be entered at all. To do this, you disallow editing of the form by changing the Allow Edits property to No.

Disallow edits in a form

The Presenting Bonbons form in the Sweet Lil's database is used in presentations of Sweet Lil's product line to outside vendors. To prevent inadvertent changes to the data, you'll disallow edits so that it is not possible to make any changes to data on the form.

Properties

You will be able to open the picture object in Microsoft Paint, but edits to the image cannot be saved.

1   Open the Presenting Bonbons form in Design view.

2   If the property sheet isn't visible, click the Properties button on the toolbar.

3   To display the form's property sheet, click the Form selector button, which is located to the left of the horizontal ruler in the form window.

4   Set the form's Allow Edits, Allow Deletions, Allow Additions, and Data Entry properties to No.

5   Switch to Form view, and try to change data on the form, such as the bonbon name or the cost.

You can't edit, add, or delete records now.

If you want to continue to the next lesson

➤ On the Presenting Bonbons form, click the Close button. Or, on the File menu, click Close.

Click No to not save changes to the form. This closes the form, but it does not exit Microsoft Access.

If you want to quit Microsoft Access for now

➤ In the Microsoft Access window, click the Close button. Or, on the File menu, click Exit.

Click No to not save changes to the form. This closes the form and exits Microsoft Access.

Lesson Summary

To	Do this	Button
Use a Wizard to create a combo box bound to a field	In the form's Design view, click the Combo Box tool in the toolbox. Then drag the field from the field list to the form. Answer the questions in the Wizard dialog boxes.	
Use a combo box on a form	In Form view, click the down arrow on the combo box, and select from the list.	
Put a control in the correct tab order	In a form's Design view, on the View menu, click Tab Order. Drag the fields into the order you want.	
Display today's date in a text box for new records	In the form's Design view, set the text box's Default Value property to this expression: =Date( )	
Set an initial (default) value for a control	In the form's Design view, set the control's Default Value property. You can set the property to text, a number, or an expression.	
Check the value entered in a control, and then display a message if it's incorrect	In the form's Design view, set the control's Validation Rule and Validation Text properties.	
Require data to be entered in a field	In the table's Design view, set the Required property to Yes.	

For online information about	Use the Answer Wizard to search for
Creating combo boxes	**combo box**
Setting default values for controls on a form	**control default**
Setting validation rules for controls on a form	**control validation**
Requiring that data is entered in a field	**require data entry**

Preview of the Next Lessons

In Part 5, you'll learn how to use a Report Wizard to create a quick report. You'll also learn how to modify the report in Design view to show groups of records. You'll create a report that includes groups and subtotals for each group. Then you'll customize the report by adding descriptive text for each group, calculating a percentage for each group, and changing the sort order.

Review & Practice

In the lessons in Part 4, you learned to customize forms with controls, such as buttons and pictures. You created a combo box to make data entry easier, and you learned how to ensure the accuracy of your data. The Review & Practice section that follows gives you a chance to practice some of the ways you can customize your forms.

Review & Practice

You will review and practice how to:

Estimated time
30 min.

- Add a label to a form.
- Add a bound control to a form.
- Add a picture to a form.
- Create a form with a subform.
- Create a command button.
- Create a combo box on a form.
- Set properties to protect your data.

Now that you know how to add controls to a form, you can make other forms in the Sweet Lil's database easier to use, and at the same time ensure the accuracy of the data that goes on them.

Scenario

Word has traveled throughout Sweet Lil's about the capability of making forms more usable. Several departments have realized that when forms are easier to use, information can be entered and retrieved more quickly. In addition, easy-to-read forms are good presentation tools for company meetings and for customers. You agree to enhance several forms to improve company communications.

Step 1:   Add a Label to a Form

The Marketing department would like to make it easy to identify and work with data that is collected on a form. Add a label to the Boxes Sales form to make it more descriptive, and change a color on the form to make it better looking.

1 Open the Box Sales form in Design view.

2 Use the Label tool from the toolbox to create a label control in the header section of the form.

3 Type **4th Quarter** in the label.

4 Use the Fore Color to change the foreground color to light gray to match the form's title. (Hint: Try using the Format Painter to copy the Box Sales Label format in one step.)

5 Resize the label so that the text is easy to read.

For more information on	See
Adding a label to a form	Lesson 11
Changing the size of a control	Lesson 11
Using the Fore Color button	Lesson 11

Step 2:   Add a Bound Control to a Form

It would be convenient to see the box size as you enter data about Sweet Lil's bonbons. You add a bound control to the Boxes Sales form to easily see the weight of each box of candy. You then make the new bound control match the format of the others on the form. You also change the field's name so that if you ever refer to it in another form or query it has a logical name.

1 Make room on the Boxes Sales form to place a new field just below the box name field and above the gray line that separates the main form and the subform.

2 Drag a field from the Field List to create a bound control for the size of the box.

3 Because the largest size box is 12 ounces, resize the new Size text box so that it is an appropriate size for up to two digits.

4 Change the Caption property of the Size label to **Box Size:**

5 Switch to Form view to check your enhancements. If necessary, adjust the label size.

6 In Design view, select the Box Size label, and change its Fore Color property to dark blue.

7 Change the label's Name property to **Box Size** instead of the default field number.

8 Close the Boxes Sales form, and save your changes.

For more information on	See
Adding a bound control to a form	Lesson 11
Setting the properties of a control	Lesson 11

Step 3: *Add a Picture to a Form*

The Human Resources department has learned that you can add pictures to forms in the Sweet Lil's database. They plan to add employees' photographs in the future; but for now, they want to upgrade the Employees form with the company logo.

1 Open the Employees form in Design view.

2 Use the Image tool in the toolbox to create an image control in the form header section.

3 Insert the Sweet Lil's Logo file from the Practice folder into the control.

4 Look at the picture in the control in Form view.

5 Return to Design view, and set the control's Name property to Company Logo.

6 Close the form, and save your changes.

For more information on	See
Adding a picture to a form	Lesson 12
Sizing an embedded object	Lesson 12

Step 4: *Create a Form with a Subform*

The Shipping department would like to be able to see at a glance what a carrier charges for a particular destination.

Create a form with a subform to check the list of charges for each shipper.

1 Use the Form Wizard to create a main form based on the Carriers table, with a subform based on the Shipping table.

2 Add the Carrier ID, Carrier Name, and Air Delivery fields to the main form.

3 Add the Ship State/Province and Shipping Charge fields to the subform.

4 Name the main form **Carriers Charges** and the subform **Ship Charge Subform**.

5 Close the form.

For more information on	See
How two forms work together	Lesson 13
Creating a form with a subform	Lesson 13

Step 5: *Create a Command Button*

The Presenting Bonbons form is being well received as a tool to show bonbons to vendors. But some people immediately want more information about each bonbon. You create a command button on the Presenting Bonbons form to open the Bonbons form.

1 Open the Presenting Bonbons form in Design view.
2 Create a command button on the Presenting Bonbons form using the Command Button tool in the toolbox.
3 Set the command button to open the Bonbons form with specific data in it.
4 Select the Bonbon Name field as the field that contains matching data.
5 Type **Bonbon Details** as the text on the button. Give the same name to the button.
6 Switch to the Form view of the Presenting Bonbons form to try the new button.
7 Close both forms, and save your changes to the Presenting Bonbon forms.

For more information on	See
Creating a command button	Lesson 13

Step 6: *Create a Combo Box on a Form*

The Orders Subform contains a text box in which operators type the ID code of the box the customer wants. The control is bound to the Box ID field in the Order Details table. It would be easier for operators if they could select the code from the list and if they could see the full name of the box. The Box List query displays fields the way you would like the combo box to appear.

1 Open the Orders Subform form in Design view.
2 Delete the Box ID text box in the detail section.
3 Use the Combo Box tool in the toolbox to replace it with a combo box bound to the Box ID field.
4 Define the list so that it displays the values from the Box List query.
5 Delete your new combo box's attached label, and resize the combo box so that it fits in the space.
6 Set the tab order of the subform so that the Box ID combo box is first.
7 Close the Orders Subform, and save your changes.
8 Open the Orders form, and test the combo box. Then close the Orders form.

For more information on	See
Creating a combo box on a form	Lesson 14
Setting the tab order of a form	Lesson 14

Step 7: *Set Properties to Protect Your Data*

You want to create a number of different order forms, all feeding data to the Orders table. You want the current date to appear on every form, and you want to be sure that a credit card's expiration date must be a future date.

1   Open the Orders table in Design view to set default values affecting the Order Date control.

2   Set the Default Value property of the Order Date field so that the field's default value is today's date.

3   Select the Expiration Date field, and then set its Validation Rule property so that the date entered into this field cannot be a date in the past.

4   Type a message for the Validation Text property to inform the person entering the data that the expiration date is invalid and to instruct them what to do.

5   Save the Orders table.

For more information on	See
Setting default values for a control	Lesson 14
Validating data entered in a control	Lesson 14

If you want to continue to the next lesson

➤ On the Orders table, click the Close button. Or, on the File menu, click Close.

This closes the form, but it does not exit Microsoft Access.

If you want to quit Microsoft Access for now

➤ In the Microsoft Access window, click the Close button. Or, on the File menu, click Exit.

This closes the table and exits Microsoft Access.

Part

5

Customizing Your Reports

Creating a Quick Detail Report

Estimated time
30 min.

In this lesson you will learn how to:

- Use a Report Wizard to create a detail report.
- Preview and print a report.
- Understand and change the design of a report.
- Show groups of records by hiding duplicates.

How do you get a quick report that shows off your data in print? You might want a sales report to take to a meeting right away or an attractive list of products for a prospective customer. Ideally, you'd like to create a great-looking report in a few minutes—a report that looks like it was designed by a professional.

A Report Wizard can do most of the work for you. As you have done with other wizards, you can answer a series of questions to build a professional-looking report. You can use the report as is, or you might want to touch it up and add a few custom details.

In this lesson, you'll learn how to create a simple detail report with a Report Wizard. You'll preview the report and then switch to Design view to make a few changes.

What Is a Detail Report?

Although you can print a table or query directly, you can take a little more time and create a report that presents your information in an easier-to-read, more professional-looking format. A *detail report* displays the same essential information you see when you print a table or query, but it contains additional elements, such as *report headers*, *page headers*, and *page footers*.

The query displays the raw data...

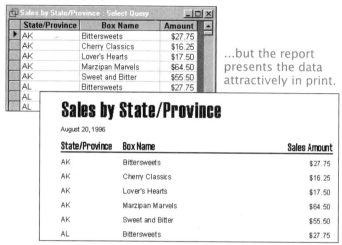

...but the report presents the data attractively in print.

In this lesson, you'll create a detail report. In the following lesson, you'll learn how to create a grouped report, which combines your data into groups and calculates totals or other information for each group.

You can also start Microsoft Access and open the Sweet Lil's database in a single step. Click the Start button, point to Documents, and then click Sweet Lil's.

As you learned in Lesson 5, the fastest way to create a report is with a Report Wizard. A Report Wizard places fields on the report and presents the data in one of several presentation styles. After you've created the report, you can customize it.

Start the lesson

> If Microsoft Access isn't started yet, start it and open the Sweet Lil's database. If the Microsoft Access window doesn't fill your screen, maximize the window.

Creating a Detail Report

Sweet Lil's is planning new advertisements that promote the most popular boxes of bonbons. At a meeting with other people from the Marketing department, you plan to hand out a report that shows sales by state or province. You don't need anything elaborate—just an easy-to-create, easy-to-read report.

Decide which Report Wizard to use

The two reports in the following illustration show the differences between a Single-Column and a Tabular report. The Single-Column report displays the data in one long column, while the Tabular report uses a more compact format and presents the data in a table.

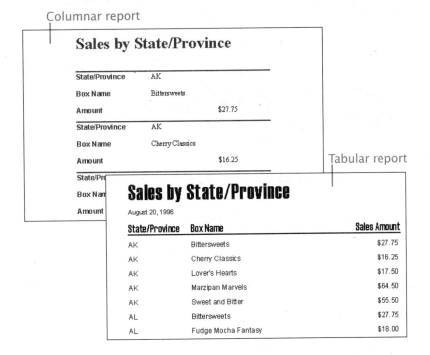

Columnar report

Tabular report

Begin a new report

The Sales By State/Province query in the Sweet Lil's database contains the records you need for this report.

1 In the Database window, click the Reports tab, and then click the New button.

The New Report dialog box appears.

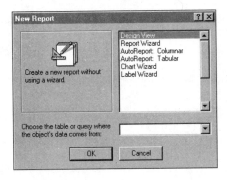

2   Select AutoReport: Tabular in the list of wizards.

3   In the list box in the lower portion of the dialog box, where you are asked to choose a table or query, select the Sales By State/Province query.

4   Click OK.

The AutoReport Wizard creates a tabular report for you, and the new report appears in Print Preview.

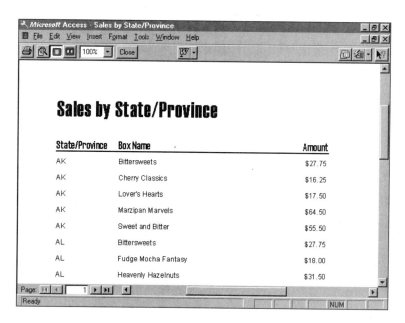

5   Check which view you have of your report by clicking the File menu and looking at the list.

Print Preview has a bullet mark next to it.

 NOTE   The look of the text in your report might differ from that in the illustration, depending on the printer that is selected and the current default report AutoFormat. Later in this lesson, you'll learn how to change the default AutoFormat.

6   On the File menu, click Save, and name the report **Sales by State/Province**

Previewing and Printing a Report

By previewing your report, you can make sure you've designed it the way you want before you print it. After you create the Sales By State/Province report, the report is magnified.

Change the picture size in Print Preview

Use the magnifying-glass pointer to switch between viewing data in a magnified view and seeing the layout of the entire page.

1   To see the whole page, click anywhere on the report.

A reduced view appears so that you can see the whole page.

2   To return to a magnified view, click the report again.

The spot where you click the magnifying-glass pointer will be in the center of the screen in magnified view.

Move from page to page

Move around the report to see how the information is laid out.

➤   Use the navigation buttons at the bottom of the window to page through your report.

Print the report

If your system is set up for printing, try printing the report now. Because this is a long report, you will print a sample page to view the report.

1   On the File menu, click Print.

2   Click the Pages option.

3   To print only the first page, type **1** in the From box, and type **1** again in the To box.

4   Click OK.

Exploring the Design of the Report

As you preview the report, you can see how Microsoft Access displays the records from your query along with added information that makes the report easier to read. If you page through this report, you'll see:

■ A *report header* at the top of the first page of the report that includes the title of the report.

■ A *page header* at the top of every page of the report that displays the heading for each column of data.

■ The *detail* section, between the page header and the page footer, displays the records from the Sales By State/Province query, which you selected as the report's underlying query when you created the report.

■ A *page footer* at the bottom of every page of the report. In this case, the page footer shows the page number, total pages, and the date the report was printed.

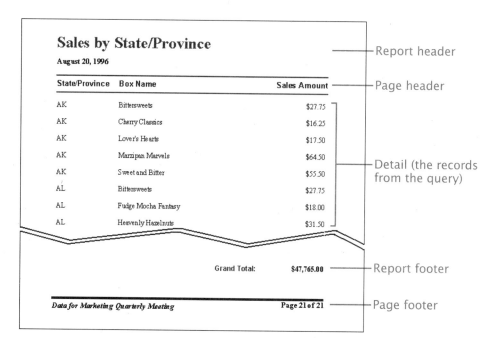

Return to Design view

Design view is a blueprint for the report.

1   When you have finished previewing or printing the report, click the Close button on the toolbar.

    The report appears in Design view.

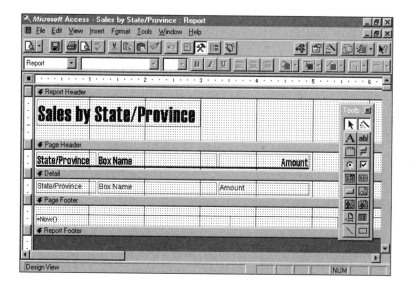

2 If the Report window is too small for you to see all the controls, resize the window to make it larger.

In Design view, the different sections represent the elements you saw in Print Preview. The report design shows how to display each element when you preview or print the report. The detail section in Design view shows how the records from the underlying table or query should look. When you look at the report in Print Preview, you'll see many records, each formatted as shown in Design view.

 NOTE When you have the report open in Design view, you can print by clicking Print on the File menu. You can also print a report from the Database window without opening the report. First select the report from the list on the Reports tab, and then click the Print button.

Move the design tools out of the way

When you switch to Design view, the toolbox might cover up part of the report. You'll use the toolbox to customize your report. For now, though, you might want to move it so that you can see the report better.

Toolbox

➤ If the toolbox is not visible, click the Toolbox button on the toolbar.

Drag the title bar of the toolbox to move it to a more convenient location.

Identify the elements created by the Report Wizard

These are some of the tasks a Report Wizard does for you:

- ■ Creates the sections on your report.
- ■ Places the data and other information in the appropriate sections.
- ■ Aligns the columns and adds some decorative lines to create an attractive report.
- ■ Selects fonts and font sizes for all the text on the report.
- ■ Adds today's date to the report header or footer, depending on the default style.

You can build a report from scratch that contains all of these elements. But you can often save hours if you start with a Report Wizard and then customize the report after the Report Wizard creates it.

When you created the Sales By State/Province report, the AutoReport Wizard did a lot of work behind the scenes.

➤ Based on the above list, find each item on your report that the Report Wizard created for you automatically.

239

Customizing the Design of a Report

It took only a short time to create this report, and it attractively presents the data you need for your meeting. There are a few minor things, however, you'd like to change. Working in Design view, you'll:

■ Change the text in the Amount label so it's more descriptive, and move the date text box into the report header.

■ Add some information, including a grand total, to the page footer and report footer.

Change the label in the page header

1   In the Page Header section, select the Amount label.

2   Move the pointer to the left of the word "Amount" so that the pointer appears as a vertical line, and then press the mouse button.

3   Type **Sales** followed by a space, and then press ENTER.

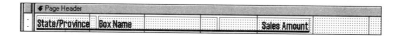

Move labels

1   Select the label that contains the expression =Now() in the Page Footer section, and drag it to the Report Header section, just below the Sales By State/Province report title.

2   Click the Report View button on the toolbar to see how your changes will look on the printed report.

Report View

The report printing date appears in the Report Header on the first page.

Add more information to the page footer

To help other Marketing personnel understand the purpose of the report, you'll add a footer to each page of the report.

1   On the toolbar, click the Close button to switch to Design view.

A

Label

2   In the toolbox, click the Label tool.

3   Click in the left-hand side of the Page Footer section to add the label.

4   In the new label, type **Data for Marketing Quarterly Meeting** and then press ENTER.

The label appears in the same font as the labels in the Page Header—the default font style for labels in this report. You want the label to be the same font as the page numbers in the page footer, but in italic.

Format Painter

5   Select the text box that contains the page numbers. On the toolbar, click the Format Painter button, and then click the new label.

Italic

6   Select the new label, and then click the Italic button on the toolbar to make the text italic. On the toolbar, click the Align Left button to make the text left-aligned.

Add a grand total to the report footer

You'll add a grand total to the Report Footer, which will appear on the last page.

Align Left

1   In the toolbox, click the Text Box button, and then click in the right side of the Report Footer.

A new text box and label are pasted in the Report Footer, and a grid area appears in the Report Footer area to encompass the new text box.

Text Box

2   Click in the new label, and then type **Grand Total** and press ENTER.

3   Double-click the new text box.

The property sheet for the text box appears.

4   In the Control Source box, type **=sum([amount])**

5   In the Format box, click the down arrow, and select Currency. Then close the Property sheet.

Bold

6   While the text box is selected, click the Bold button on the toolbar so that the grand total will be bold type.

7   On the toolbar, click the Print Preview button to view the report.

You'll see the page footer at the bottom of every page, and the new grand total at the bottom of the last page.

Hiding Duplicates to Show Groups of Records

What's wrong with the report? When you look down the left side, you see the name of the state or province repeated over and over. You only need to see each name once for each group. In Lesson 16, you'll learn how to create a grouped report, which will solve this problem. But for the report you're working on now, there's another quick way to fix this.

As the report is now, Microsoft Access displays data for the State/Province field even if this field contains duplicate values. You can change the Hide Duplicates property for the State/Province text box so that duplicate values are shown only once.

Hide the duplicate values

Close

1 On the toolbar, click the Close button to switch to Design view.

2 In the detail section, double-click the State/Province text box.

3 In the property sheet, change the setting of the Hide Duplicates property to Yes, and then close the property sheet.

4 On the toolbar, click the Report View button to switch to print preview.

Report View

State/Province	Box Name	Sales Amount
	Sales by State/Province	
	August 20, 1996	
AK	Bittersweets	$27.75
	Cherry Classics	$16.25
	Lover's Hearts	$17.50
	Marzipan Marvels	$64.50
	Sweet and Bitter	$55.50
AL	Bittersweets	$27.75
	Fudge Mocha Fantasy	$18.00
	Heavenly Hazelnuts	$31.50
	Island Collection	$70.00
	Lover's Hearts	$17.50
Alberta	Bittersweets	$166.50

Each state or province appears only once on the report.

5 Save the report and close it.

One Step Further: Creating a Custom AutoReport

An international gourmet food company is interested in ordering large quantities of individual bonbons from Sweet Lil's. The international company's representative wants a report that shows all of Sweet Lil's bonbons categorized by chocolate type. Because the representative wants it immediately, you want to make a report as fast as possible.

In Lesson 10, you used the AutoReport Wizard to create a report based on a query. You can create this new report even more quickly by using the AutoReport button on the toolbar, and then you can customize the AutoReport feature to create the type of report you use most often.

Create a report with the AutoReport button

New Object

1 In the Database window, select the Chocolate Types query.

2 On the toolbar, click the arrow on the New Object button, and then click AutoReport.

A report based on the Chocolate Types query is created automatically and appears in Print Preview.

3 Click the report to see a whole page at once.

The report style is inappropriate for distribution outside the company. You would like a slightly different look for the report.

4 Switch to Design view by clicking the Close button so that you can change the format using AutoFormat.

Change the default format of an AutoReport

You can set a default format so that the AutoReport is in the style you want.

AutoFormat

1 On the toolbar, click the AutoFormat button.

The AutoFormat dialog box appears.

2 On the list of Report AutoFormats, select Bold, and then click OK.

The report is formatted in the Bold style.

3 Switch to Print Preview.

Your report appears in Bold style. All new reports you create with AutoReport will be in the Bold style unless you change the AutoFormat again.

4 Save the report with the name **Chocolate Types**

Customize your report

To further improve the appearance of the report, you adjust it so that each type of chocolate appears only once.

1 On the toolbar, click the Close button to switch to the Design view of the Chocolate Types report.

2 In the detail section, select the Chocolate Type text box.

3 In the property sheet, change the setting of the Hide Duplicates property to Yes.

4 Switch to Print Preview to see your changes.

5 Save the report.

243

If you want to continue to the next lesson

▶ On the Chocolate Types report, click the Close button. Or, on the File menu, click Close.

This closes the report, but it does not exit Microsoft Access.

If you want to quit Microsoft Access for now

▶ In the Microsoft Access window, click the Close button. Or, on the File menu, click Exit.

This closes the table and exits Microsoft Access.

Lesson Summary

To	Do this	Button
Create a quick detail report using the AutoReport Wizard	Click the Reports tab, and then click the New button. Select the underlying table or query, and then click the AutoReport: Tabular or AutoReport: Columnar wizard.	
Preview a report	In the Database window, double-click the report. *or* In Design view, click the Report View button on the toolbar.	
View the design of a report	In the Database window, click the report, and then click the Design button.	
Print a report	In the Database window or in Print Preview, click the Print button on the toolbar. *or* In Design view, click Print on the File menu.	
Hide duplicates in the detail section	In Design view, select the control for which you want to hide duplicates. In the property sheet for this control, set the Hide Duplicates property to Yes.	

For online information about	Use the Answer Wizard to search for
Creating a report	**create report**
Customizing a report	**customize report**

Preview of the Next Lesson

In the next lesson, you'll learn how to create a report that includes groups and subtotals for each group. Then you'll customize the report by adding descriptive text for each group, calculating a percentage for each group, and changing the sort order.

Lesson

16

Creating a Grouped Report

In this lesson you will learn how to:

Estimated time
30 min.

- Create a grouped report.
- Customize the group header.
- Use an expression in the group footer.
- Change the sort order.
- Print groups together.
- Add customized page numbering.

Your data becomes more meaningful when it's grouped or divided into categories. When you're looking at regional sales patterns, for example, you don't want to see just a long list of sales data—what you'd rather see is a list of sales for each region. What would be even better is a list of sales with a subtotal for each region so that you can see at a glance where your sales are strongest.

Using Report Wizards, you can design grouped reports that make your data easier to understand. In this lesson, you'll create a report that groups your data and automatically calculates subtotals for each group. Then you'll create another grouped report that calculates a percentage, and you'll change the sort order of that report and add customized page numbering.

What Are Groups and Totals?

A *group* is a collection of similar records. By creating a grouped report, you can often improve your reader's understanding of the data in the report. That's because a grouped report not only displays similar records together but also shows introductory and summary information for each group.

In the following report, the records are grouped by state or province. The records for the state of Alaska (AK), for example, make up the first group.

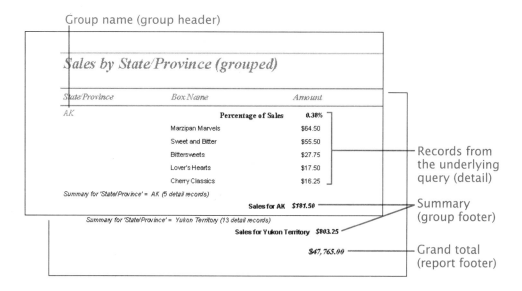

Group name (group header)

Sales by State/Province (grouped)

State/Province	Box Name	Amount
AK	Percentage of Sales	0.38%
	Marzipan Marvels	$64.50
	Sweet and Bitter	$55.50
	Bittersweets	$27.75
	Lover's Hearts	$17.50
	Cherry Classics	$16.25

Summary for 'State/Province' = AK (5 detail records)

Sales for AK $181.50

Summary for 'State/Province' = Yukon Territory (13 detail records)

Sales for Yukon Territory $803.25

$47,765.00

Records from the underlying query (detail)

Summary (group footer)

Grand total (report footer)

The group header (AK, in this case) identifies or introduces the group. The detail section, the body of the group, displays the appropriate records from the underlying query. The group footer summarizes the data for the group, showing the total sales for Alaska. The report footer at the very end of the report includes the grand total for the sales from all states and provinces.

In this lesson, you'll use the Groups/Totals Report Wizard to create grouped reports. This Report Wizard is a real time-saver. It asks how you want to group records in your report, and then it adds the group header and group footer sections for you. It even adds the expressions that perform the subtotal and total calculations.

Start the lesson

You can also start Microsoft Access and open the Sweet Lil's database in a single step. Click the Start button, point to Documents, and then click Sweet Lil's.

▶ If Microsoft Access isn't started yet, start it and open the Sweet Lil's database. If the Microsoft Access window doesn't fill your screen, maximize the window.

Creating a Grouped Report

Sweet Lil's new Marketing manager plans to expand sales through a mail order campaign. You'll start this process by sending a mail order advertisement only to people in the states and provinces where your products have been most successful.

What you'd like to see is a report that shows the total sales for each state and province so that you can decide where to send the advertisement. The quick detail report you created in Lesson 15 shows a list of sales, but it doesn't show you the totals for each state and province.

To get the report you want, you'll create a new report using the Report Wizard. In this report, you want to see sales totals for each state and province, so you'll choose State/Province as the field to group by. You'll choose options that calculate both a sum and a percentage of the total for each state or province. The Sales By State/Province query in the Sweet Lil's database provides the records you need.

Begin a new report

Create a new report based on a query.

1 In the Database window, click the Reports tab, and then click the New button.

2 In the list of wizards, select Report Wizard.

3 In the list box of tables and queries, select Sales By State/Province, and click OK.

Enter information in the Report Wizard dialog boxes

Now that you've selected a Report Wizard, you'll go through a series of dialog boxes. Each of the following steps shows you how to enter information in one dialog box.

1 Add all three available fields to the report, and then click Next.

2 When you're asked if you want to add any grouping levels, double-click the State/Province field, and then click Next.

Sort

3 In the next dialog box, you're asked what sort order and summary information you want for your details. In the first list box, select Box Name. The Sort button next to the list box shows that the box names will be sorted in alphabetical order, from A to Z.

If you wanted to sort box names from Z to A, you would click the Sort button.

4 Click the Summary Options button at the bottom of the dialog box.

The Summary Options dialog box appears, showing data fields that can be summarized (in this case, only the Amount field can be summarized).

5   Click the Sum check box for the Amount field, click the check box for Calculate Percent Of Total For Sums, and be sure that the Detail And Summary option button is selected. Then click OK, and click Next on the Report Wizard dialog box.

6   When you're asked how you want to lay out your report, be sure that the Stepped option is selected and the Orientation option is Portrait. Click Next.

7   When you're asked what style you would like, select Corporate, and then click Next.

8   Change the title of the report to **Sales by State/Province (grouped)** and click Finish.

The Report Wizard creates your grouped report.

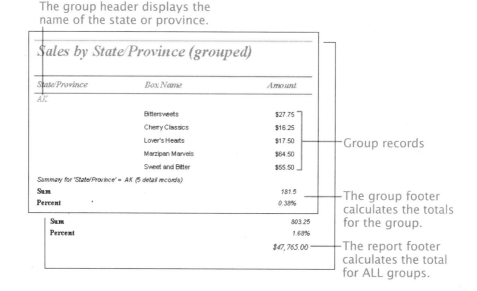

The group header displays the name of the state or province.

Group records

The group footer calculates the totals for the group.

The report footer calculates the total for ALL groups.

Check the report in Design view

Switch to Design view to compare the two views.

1   Because you have just created this report with a Report Wizard, click the Close button on the toolbar to switch to Design view.

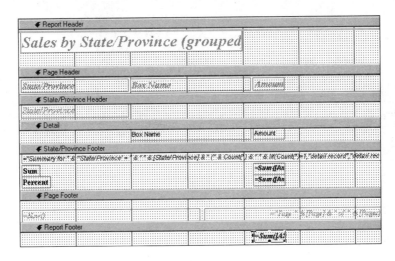

2   If the Report window is too small, resize it so that you can see more of the controls
    on the report. You might need to move the toolbox or property sheet out of the way
    for a better view of the report.

The Report Wizard has added these elements to your report:

■ **An expression that displays the current date** At the bottom of each page,
  today's date appears in the page footer.

■ **A group header and a group footer** The Report Wizard has added a group
  header and a group footer for the State/Province group. In Design view, they're
  identified as the State/Province Header and the State/Province Footer. In more
  complex reports, you might have several group headers with different names.

■ **Expressions that calculate totals** The expression for totals in the State/
  Province footer is exactly the same as the expression in the report footer:
  =Sum([Amount]). When you place an expression in the State/Province footer
  or the State/Province header, it performs calculations for the records in each
  State/Province group. When you place an expression in the report footer or
  the report header, it calculates a value for all records in the report.

■ **An expression that adds percentages** In the State/Province Footer, the
  Report Wizard has added the expression =Sum([Amount])/([Amount Grand
  Total Sum]), which calculates the percentage of the grand total for each State/
  Province group.

■ **An expression that adds page numbers** At the bottom of each page, the
  current page number and total number of pages appear automatically in the
  page footer.

Customizing the Group Header

Now you can skim through your report easily and find the figures you're interested in. For your mail order campaign, you'll choose only those states and provinces with the highest percentages of sales.

You'd like to see at a glance what percentage of total sales is brought in by each state and province, and you'd like to display this information next to the name of the state or province.

Move a text box

Move the text box with the percentage expression to the group header for better visibility.

1 Drag the text box with the expression =Sum([Amount])/([Amount Grand Total Sum]) into the State/Province header, and place it above the Amount text box of the Detail section.

2 Drag the Percent label from the State/Province Footer up to the State/Province Header, and place it to the left of the percentage text box. Then change the text in the label to **Percentage of Sales**

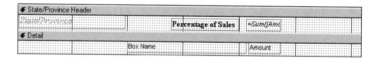

3 Switch to Print Preview to review your work.

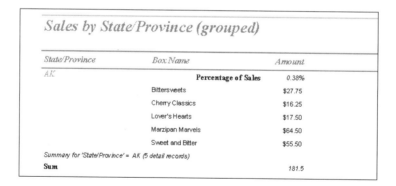

Using an Expression in the Group Footer

You'd like to make it easier to skim the report and find the total sales figure for each state or province, so you'll add some text to identify each sales total. For example, to the left of the Alaska total, you'd like to see "Sales for AK" instead of "Sum."

To add this text, you'll use a text box with an expression so that the appropriate name for each state or province is filled in automatically.

The toolbox includes both a Label tool and a Text Box tool. Because you're adding descriptive text, you might think you'd use a label. But a label can contain only words, while a text box can contain an expression that performs a task for you.

Add a text box in the State/Province footer

ab|

Text Box

1   Switch to Design view by closing the Print Preview window.

2   In the toolbox, click the Text Box tool.

3   Click near the middle of the State/Province footer to add the text box.

4   Click in the text box you've just added to place the insertion point, and then type the following expression: =**"Sales for "** & **[State/Province]**

For more information on expressions, see the Appendix, "Using Expressions."

Be sure to start the expression with the equal sign (=), and leave a space before the second quotation mark. If you don't leave a space, your label will contain text like this: Sales forAK.

The words in the quotation marks will appear on your report exactly as you type them. The & symbol means "followed by." The information in brackets is taken from the State/Province field and will change for each location.

5   Press ENTER.

6   Select and delete the original Sum label and the label attached to the new text box.

7   Make the text box wide enough to accommodate long state or province names, and move it so that it's roughly in the following position.

Change the format of the text box

B

Bold

Now you'll emphasize the text box with bold text.

1   Select the text box, and then click the Bold button on the toolbar.

[Report View icon]

Report View

2   Click the Report View button to see the report.

3   Save the report.

Changing the Sort Order

In the advertisement you send to a particular state or province, you want to feature boxes of bonbons that are best-sellers in that region.

When you originally created your report, you grouped by the State/Province field and then sorted by the Box Name field. Now you'd like to change the sort order. Within each state or province, you'd like to see a list of boxes starting with the box that brought in the most money and ending with the one that brought in the least. In other words, you want to sort by the Amount field rather than by the Box Name field, and you want to sort in descending order.

When you create reports with a Report Wizard, you're asked about how you want to group and sort your data. If you decide to change sorting or grouping after you've created a report, you don't have to start from scratch and run the Report Wizard again. Instead, you can use the Sorting And Grouping box to make the changes.

Open the Sorting And Grouping box

Sorting And Grouping

1   Switch to Design view for the Sales By State/Province (grouped) report.

2   On the toolbar, click the Sorting And Grouping button.

The Sorting And Grouping box appears.

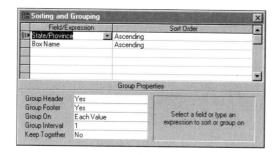

You can see the settings that were established when you answered the Report Wizard's questions.

The Field/Expression column shows fields that are used either for grouping and sorting or for sorting only. To the left of the State/Province field is the Grouping icon, which tells you that this field is used for grouping and sorting. The Box Name field doesn't have this icon, so you can tell it is used solely for sorting.

Change the sort order

Using the Sorting And Grouping box, you'll specify Amount instead of Box Name as the second field to group by.

1   In the Field/Expression column, click the Box Name cell, and then click the arrow to display a list of fields.

2   Select the Amount field from the list.

The Amount field replaces the Box Name field.

3   Click the Sort Order cell to the right of the Amount field, and then click the arrow.

4   Select Descending from the list.

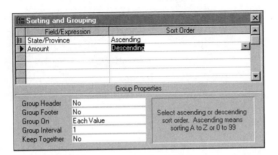

By selecting Descending, you're asking Microsoft Access to display the box sales for each State or Province starting with the highest amount and working down to the lowest.

5   Close the Sorting And Grouping box, and then switch to Print Preview.

Your report should now show the boxes listed in descending order of sales.

Sales by State/Province (grouped)

State/Province	Box Name	Amount
AK	**Percentage of Sales**	0.38%
	Marzipan Marvels	$64.50
	Sweet and Bitter	$55.50
	Bittersweets	$27.75
	Lover's Hearts	$17.50
	Cherry Classics	$16.25

Summary for 'State/Province' = AK (5 detail records)

Sales for AK   *181.5*

Printing Groups Together

Some of the groups in the report begin on one page and finish on another. You can avoid a page break in the middle of a group by setting the Keep Together property in the Sorting And Grouping box.

1   In Design view, click the Sorting And Grouping button on the toolbar.

2   In the Keep Together property box, click the down arrow, and select Whole Group from the list.

3   Close the Sorting And Grouping box, and then preview the report.

A complete group now appears on the same page, except where the group itself is bigger than a full page.

Adding Custom Page Numbers

When you created the Sales By State/Province (grouped) report with the Report Wizard, a text box containing an expression for a page number and total pages was automatically added to the design of your report. You can change the style of page numbering easily by using the new Page Numbers dialog box. You will delete the page number that the Report Wizard created for you and then insert a new page number text box in the center of the page footer, with no number on the first page.

Create a new text box

1   Switch to Design view.

2   Select the text box in the page footer containing the page number expression, and then press DELETE.

3   On the Insert menu, click Page Number.

    The Page Numbers dialog box appears.

4   Select the Page N Of M option, the Bottom Of Page option, and Center in the Alignment list box.

5   Click the Show Number On First Page check box to clear it, and then click OK.

    The new text box appears in the center of the Page Footer section. You can move it to a better position if you want to.

6   Preview your report, and examine the new footer.

7   When you have finished previewing it, save and close the Sales By State/Province (grouped) report.

One Step Further: Sorting and Grouping Properties

For quick identification of listings in a report, you can group items by the first letter of their names and print the letter in a group header. First you'll create a quick report based on the Customer List query, and then you'll change the properties in the Sorting And Grouping box to add a letter at the beginning of each alphabetic group of customer last names.

Create a new report

1   In the Database window, select the Customer List query without opening it.

New Object

2   On the toolbar, click the down arrow on the New Object button, and select AutoReport.

3   Switch to Design view.

Set the Sorting and Grouping properties

*Sorting And
Grouping*

1 On the toolbar, click the Sorting And Grouping button.

The Sorting and Grouping dialog box appears.

2 Click the first cell of the Field/Expression column, and then select Last Name from the list to set the letter at the top of each alphabetic group.

3 Click the second cell of the Field/Expression column, and then select Last Name from the list to set the actual sorting in the group.

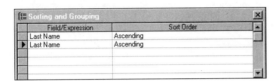

4 Set the properties in the Sorting And Grouping box to match those in the following table. When you have finished, close the Sorting And Grouping dialog box.

Field/ Expression	Sort Order	Group Header	Group Footer	Group On	Group Interval	Keep Together
Last Name	Ascending	Yes	No	Prefix Characters	1	With First Detail
Last Name	Ascending	No	No	Each Value	1	No

By choosing Prefix Characters for the Group On property, and 1 for the Group Interval, you will see only the first letter of each group's last name. By choosing With First Detail for the Keep Together property, a group will not be restricted to one page but will be allowed to run over a page break.

Use an expression in the group header

Now that you have set the properties, you need to create a text box and an expression to display the result.

Center

1 Create a text box for the Last Name Header of the report and delete the attached label.

2 Position the text box in the center of the header, and then click the Center-Align Text button on the toolbar to center the text within the text box.

3 To print only the first letter of the name at the beginning of each new group, enter the expression =**Left([Last Name],1)** in the text box, and then press ENTER.

The Left function with the number 1 extracts one character from the Last Name field, beginning on the left. In this case, you will see the one letter that begins all the last names of each group.

257

4 On the toolbar, use the Back Color button to set the back color of the text box to light gray. Use the Fore Color button to set the text to dark blue.

5 Preview the report, and then save it with the name **Customer List (grouped)**

If you want to continue to the next lesson

➤ On the Customer List (grouped) report, click the Close button. Or, on the File menu, click Close.

This closes the report, but it does not exit Microsoft Access.

If you want to quit Microsoft Access for now

➤ In the Microsoft Access window, click the Close button. Or, on the File menu, click Exit.

This closes the table and exits Microsoft Access.

Lesson Summary

To	Do this	Button
Create a grouped report	In the Database window, click the Reports tab, and then click the New button. Select a table or query, select Report Wizard, and then click OK. To create the report, answer the questions in the dialog boxes.	
Change the sort order in a report	Display your report in Design view. On the toolbar, click the Sorting And Grouping button. In the Field/Expression column, select the field for which you want to change the sort order. Then select Ascending or Descending in the Sort Order cell for this field.	
Print groups together	Display your report in Design view. On the toolbar, click the Sorting And Grouping button. Set the Keep Together property to Whole Group.	
Add custom page numbers	Display your report in Design view. On the Insert menu, click Page Numbers. In the Page Numbers dialog box, select the options you want, and then click OK.	

For online information about	Use the Answer Wizard to Search for
Creating grouped reports	**grouped reports**
Changing the sorting and grouping order in a report	**change sorting and grouping**
Adding custom page numbers	**page numbers**

Review & Practice

In the lessons in Part 5, you learned to customize reports. By using the Groups/Total Report Wizard, you were able to organize the information on the reports in meaningful ways. You tailored the design of the reports and changed the sort order to be more useful. The Review & Practice section that follows gives you a chance to practice some of these methods.

Review & Practice

In this review you will practice how to:

Estimated time
20 min.

- Create a detail report and hide duplicate entries.
- Create a grouped report.
- Use an expression to describe group totals.
- Change the sort order.
- Print groups together.
- Add custom page numbers.

The ability to store and retrieve information quickly and efficiently are two primary reasons to use an online database. Equally important is the ability to print out the information in useful and attractive reports. In this Review & Practice section, you have an opportunity to apply the techniques you learned for creating and enhancing grouped reports.

Scenario

As your reports are circulated throughout the company, staff members begin to realize that you can print the information they need in a format that is attractive and easy to use. More requests for specialized reports arrive on your desk, including one from Lillian Farber, the company president.

Step 1: *Create a Detail Report and Hide Duplicates*

You have been asked to create a report that lists the contact names and phone numbers for the suppliers of ingredients for Sweet Lil's bonbons. The Ingredient Source query contains the information you want.

1   Use the AutoReport: Tabular wizard to create a tabular detail report based on the Ingredient Source query.

2   Format the report with the Bold AutoFormat.

3   Preview the report.

4   In Design view, use the Sorting And Grouping button to sort by Category.

5   To avoid printing duplicate entries, set the Hide Duplicates property of the Category text box (under the Detail section) to Yes.

6   Preview the report again.

7   Save the report with the name **Ingredient Source** and close it.

For more information on	See
Using a Report Wizard	Lesson 15
Hiding duplicate entries	Lesson 15
Previewing a report	Lesson 15

Step 2: *Display the Cost of Bonbons in Each Box*

Lillian Farber, the company president, wants to reduce box costs again. She wants a report that lists the bonbons in each box along with the cost of each bonbon. She also wants to know the total cost of the bonbons in each box.

Use a Report Wizard to make a report that shows the information Lillian wants.

1   Create a new grouped report by using all the fields in the Bonbons By Box query.

2   Group by Box Name, and use Normal grouping.

3   Sort by Bonbon Name.

4   Sum the Cost of Bonbons field, but do not calculate percentages of total.

5   Select the Stepped layout, Portrait orientation, and Corporate style for your report.

6   Name your report **Cost of Boxes**

7   Preview the report.

8   Save and close the report.

For more information on	See
Creating a grouped report	Lesson 16

Step 3: Describe the Group Totals and Change the Sort Order

Make it easier for Lillian to skim the Cost Of Boxes report by adding a descriptive line, reading "Total Cost," next to the total amount for each box. Change the second sort field so that the bonbons within each box are sorted by cost.

1   In Design view, use the Text Box tool to create a text box in the Box Name footer, and place it to the left of the Summary text box.

2   In the text box, type the expression ="**Total Cost for**"&" "&[Box Name]

3   Widen the box, and make the text bold.

4   In the Sorting And Grouping box, change the second field to group by Cost Of Bonbons in descending order.

5   Preview the report, and then save it.

For more information on	See
Using an expression in a report	Lesson 16
Changing the sort order	Lesson 16

Step 4: Print Groups Together and Add Custom Page Numbers

Two more steps make the report more convenient to use: keeping each list of bonbons together on a page, and adding page numbering that includes the report's total page count (but is not displayed on the first page).

1   In the Sorting And Grouping box, select the Box Name expression, and then select Whole Group for the Keep Together property.

2   In the Page footer, delete the text box that now contains the page number expression, and create a new one.

3   In the Page Numbers dialog box, set the page numbers to include total pages and to not be displayed on the first page.

4   Preview the report.

5   Save and close the Cost Of Boxes report.

For more information on	See
Printing groups together	Lesson 16
Adding custom page numbers	Lesson 16

If you want to quit Microsoft Access for now

▶   In the Microsoft Access window, click the Close button. Or, on the File menu, click Exit.

This closes the table and exits Microsoft Access.

Appendix

Using Expressions

No matter what type of work you're doing with Microsoft Access, you'll most likely need to use expressions. For example, you might want to calculate a subtotal on a report or design a query that asks for all products that cost $10. Or, you might want to filter a form so that you see the records for only your sales region. In all these cases, you need to create an expression. This appendix provides guidelines for writing expressions and examples of common expressions.

What Are Expressions?

Expressions are formulas that calculate a value. For example, the following expression multiplies the box price by 1.1 (which is the same as raising the price by 10 percent):
=[Box Price] * 1.1

An expression can include *functions*, *identifiers*, *operators*, *literal values*, and *constants*. The following expression contains most of these elements.

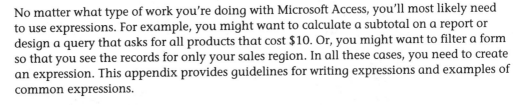

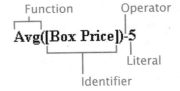

Functions help you perform specialized calculations easily. For example, you can use the **Avg** function to find the average of values in a field or the **Sum** function to find the total of all values in a field.

267

Identifiers refer to a value in your database, such as the value of a field, control, or property. For example, [Order Date] refers to the value in the Order Date field.

Operators specify an action (such as addition) to be performed on one or more elements of an expression. Operators include familiar arithmetic operators such as +, –, *, and /, as well as other operators such as =, <, >, &, **And**, **Or**, and **Like**.

Literal values are values that Microsoft Access uses exactly as you enter them. For example, the number 25 and the text value "San Francisco" are literals.

Constants represent values that don't change. For example, the constant **Null** always means a field that contains no characters or values. A constant might also be **True**, **False**, **Yes**, or **No**.

Guidelines for Entering Expressions

In some cases, when you enter an expression, Microsoft Access inserts characters for you automatically. For example, Microsoft Access might insert brackets, number signs, or quotation marks. The examples in this appendix show you how to type the entire expression, instead of having Microsoft Access supply additional characters.

Follow these general guidelines when you're entering an expression.

Element	How to enter	Example
Identifier	Enclose field names and control names in brackets.	[Order Date]
	Use a period (.) to separate the name of a table from a field in the table.	[Boxes].[Box Price]
	If an expression needs to get values from a different database object, use an exclamation point (!) to separate the type of object (Forms), the name of the form (Boxes), and the name of the control on the form (Boxes ID).	Forms![Boxes]![Boxes ID]
Date	Enclose dates in number signs (#). Number signs automatically appear around a date/time value you type in a validation expression or in a criteria expression for a field whose data type is Date/Time.	#10/10/94# #10-Oct-94#
Text	Enclose text in quotation marks. If the text doesn't contain a space or punctuation, you can type the text without quotation marks. The marks will then appear automatically.	California "British Columbia"
Number	Don't enter a currency symbol ($) or a separating comma.	8934.75 (not $8,934.75 or 8,934.75)

Creating Expressions with the Expression Builder

When you want to create a common expression quickly, or when you want help in creating an expression, you can use the Expression Builder. You can start the Expression Builder from places where you would often write an expression, such as in a property sheet or in a criteria box in the QBE grid.

In a property sheet, first you click the property box where you want an expression, and then you click the Build button next to the box.

In the Query window, you use the right mouse button to click where you want an expression, and then you choose Build from the shortcut menu. If the property box or query box where you start the Expression Builder already contains a value, that value is automatically copied into the Expression box.

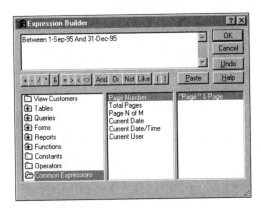

When the Expression Builder appears, you can select types of expressions, field names, and operators, and then paste them into the Expression box. You can also type in any elements you want. To accept the expression you built, choose OK.

Using Expressions in Forms and Reports

You use expressions in forms and reports to get information that you cannot get directly from the tables in a database. For example, you can create expressions that calculate totals, add the values from two fields, or set a default value for a field.

Calculated Control Expression Examples

When you want a form or report to calculate a value, you can create a calculated control that gets its value from an expression. You add the control to your form or report, and then you type an expression directly in the control (frequently a text box) or in the Control Source property box for the control.

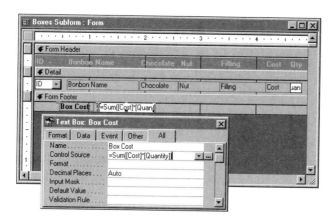

When you type expressions in calculated controls, be sure to include an equal sign (=) to the left of the expression. For example: **=[Salary] * 2**

When you type a long expression in a property box, you might want to press SHIFT+F2 to display the whole expression at once.

The following table shows some common expressions used for calculated controls.

Expression	Microsoft Access displays
=[Quantity]*[Box Price]	The product of the Quantity and Box Price field values.
=[First Name] &" "&[Last Name]	The values of the First Name and Last Name fields, separated by a space.
=[Bonbon Cost]*1.5	The value in the Bonbon Cost field multiplied by 1.5.
=Date( )	Today's date.
=Page	The page number of the current page.
="Page " & Page & " of " & Pages	The page number of the current page followed by the total number of pages.
="Sales for " &[State/Province]	The text "Sales for" followed by the value in the State/Province field.
=[State/Province Total]/[Grand Total]	The value from the State/Province Total control divided by the value from the Grand Total control.
=Sum([Bonbon Cost])	The sum of the values in the Bonbon Cost field.
=[Orders Subform].Form![Order Subtotal]	The value from the Order Subtotal control on the Orders subform. (To see how to use the expression, refer to the Subtotal control on the Orders form.)
=DatePart("yyyy",[Order Date])	Only the year portion of the date. (The comma is used to separate arguments in a function.)

Validation Expression Examples

You can set validation rules for a field on a form to make sure that you enter the right type of data into the field. To specify a rule, you type an expression in the Validation Rule property box for the control.

The following table shows some typical validation expressions.

Expression	When you enter data, it must
>=Date( )	Be a date that's either today's date or some date in the future.
Between 10 And 100	Be a value between 10 and 100, inclusive.
"USA" Or "Canada"	Match USA or Canada.
Like "[A-Z]##"	Include one letter followed by two numbers (for example, B23).

Using Expressions in Queries and Filters

You use expressions in queries and filters to specify criteria. In queries, you can also use expressions to create fields that are based on a calculation. You don't have to include an equal sign to the left of a query or filter expression.

Criteria Expression Examples

When you're designing a query or filter, you use expressions as criteria. These criteria tell Microsoft Access which records you want to see. You enter criteria for a field into the Criteria box for that field. For example, to find people with customer IDs greater than 100, you'd type the expression >**100** in the Criteria box for the Customer ID field.

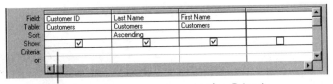

Type query expressions in the Criteria box in the appropriate Field column.

The following examples show some frequently used criteria expressions that you might use in a query based on the Orders table in the Sweet Lil's database.

271

Field	Criteria expression	Query finds orders
Customer ID	89	For the customer whose ID is 89
Customer ID	>=60	For customers with IDs greater than or equal to 60
Ship City	"Seattle" Or "New York"	For Seattle or New York
State/Province Ship	Not "Ontario"	For all states and provinces except Ontario
Ship Last Name	Like "Mc*"	For names beginning with "Mc"
Ship Last Name	Like "J*son"	For names beginning with "J" and ending in "son"
Carrier ID	Null	That have no value in the Carrier ID field
Order Date	Between 1-Dec-94 And 15-Dec-94	Placed during the first 15 days of December 1994
Ship Last Name	Like [C] & "*" *(for parameter queries only)*	For last names starting with "C"

Calculated Field Expression Examples

You can use expressions to create new query fields. You enter the expression into a Field box in the QBE grid.

Type calculated expressions in the Field box in the Criteria grid.

The following examples show some common calculated field expressions.

Name and expression	Microsoft Access displays
Sale Price: [Box Price] * 0.8	The values of the Box Price field multiplied by 0.8 (reduces the values by 20 percent).
Sale Price: CCur([Box Price] * 0.8)	The values of the Box Price field reduced by 20 percent and formatted as currency values (for example, $2,345.50).
Extended Price: [Order Details].[Quantity]*[Boxes].[Box Price]	The product of the Quantity field in the Order Details table and the Box Price field in the Boxes table.

For More Information

Although this appendix shows examples of expressions in forms, reports, queries, and filters, you can also use expressions in tables, macros, and modules. You'll find extensive information on expressions in the Microsoft Access documentation.

For online information about	Use the Answer Wizard to search for
Creating or entering expressions	**expressions**
Entering expressions in forms	**expressions in forms**
Entering expressions in reports	**expressions in reports**
Entering expressions in queries	**expressions in queries**
Entering expressions in filters	**expressions in filters**
Using Expression Builder	**expression builder**

Glossary

This glossary contains definitions of terms used in *Microsoft Access for Windows 95 Step by Step*. For definitions of additional database terms, see the online glossary in Microsoft Access Help. (On the Help menu, click Answer Wizard; then type the word or words, and press ENTER.)

AutoForm Wizard   A tool that automatically creates a form that displays the values of all the fields and records of the selected table or query.

AutoReport Wizard   A tool that automatically creates a report using all the fields in the selected table or query. The report appears in the Print Preview window.

bound control   A control that's tied to a specific field in the underlying table or query so that it can display data from the underlying field. *See also* unbound control.

bound object frame   An object frame that displays objects that are stored in a field in a table. In Form view and in reports, you see a different object in the object frame for each record. *See also* unbound object frame *and* image control.

calculated control   A control on a form or report that is tied to an expression rather than a field. A calculated control can combine text values from fields in the underlying table or query, or it can perform calculations on values from the fields.

calculated field   A field defined in a query that displays the result of an expression rather than stored data. The value is recalculated each time a value in the expression changes.

check box   A control that provides a graphical way to display Yes/No data. When a check box is selected, a check mark appears in the box.

Clipboard   The temporary storage area used by Microsoft Windows to store text, graphics, and other data. You transfer data to the Clipboard by choosing Cut or Copy from the Edit menu. You transfer data from the Clipboard by choosing the Paste command from the Edit menu.

combo box   A control, similar to both a list box and a text box, in which you type a value or select a value from a list.

command button   A control that runs a macro, carries out an event procedure, or calls an Access Basic function. A command button condenses related tasks into a single step. Command buttons are sometimes referred to as push buttons.

Command Button Wizard   A tool that helps you add a command button to a form.

comparison operator   There are six standard comparison (logical) operators that you can use in Microsoft Access expressions, as shown in the following table:

Operator	Meaning
=	Equal to
>	Greater than

Operator	Meaning
<	Less than
>=	Greater than or equal to
<=	Less than or equal to
<>	Not equal to

constant A value that doesn't change. For example, the constant *Null* always means a field that contains no characters or values. Other constants might be *Yes* or *True* or a numerical value that is not the result of an expression or formula.

control An object on a form or report that displays data, performs an action, or decorates the form or report.

criteria A set of limiting conditions, such as "Denmark" or >3000. You can use criteria in creating queries or filters to show a specific set of records.

crosstab query A query that displays summarized values from a single field and rearranges the values by rows and columns.

data The information stored in tables in a database. In Microsoft Access, data can be text, numbers, dates, pictures, or OLE objects.

database Generally, a collection of data related to a particular topic or purpose. A Microsoft Access database file can contain tables, queries, forms, reports, macros, and modules.

database objects Tables, queries, forms, reports, macros, and modules.

database tabs Tabs in the Database window that you can click to display a list of objects of the same type. For example, you click the Forms tab to display a list of all the forms in your database.

database window The window that is displayed when you open a Microsoft Access database. It contains the Tables, Queries, Forms, Reports, Macros, and Modules tabs, which you can click to display a list of all objects of that type in the database.

Database Wizard A tool that helps you create a new database by asking you questions and then creating a database based on your answers.

Datasheet view A view that displays multiple records in a row-and-column format, enabling you to view many records at the same time. Datasheet view is available for tables, queries, and forms.

data type A property of a field that determines what kind of data it can hold.

Design view A view you use to design tables, queries, forms, and reports.

detail section A section of a report or form used to display the records from the underlying table or query.

display format   The format in which data is displayed in a datasheet or a form. The same underlying data may be displayed in different ways depending on the data type of the field. For example, a Yes/No data type can also be displayed as True/False or On/Off.

drag and drop   The ability to drag an object onto another to perform an action. For example, in the Query window, you can drag a field from the field list to the QBE grid to add the field to your query. To drag an object, position the pointer over the object, hold down the mouse button while you move the mouse, and then release the mouse button when the object is positioned where you want it.

dynaset   The set of records that results from running a query or applying a filter.

embed   To insert an object into a form or a report. You can use the Insert Object command to create a new object, or you can insert an existing OLE object using the Copy and Paste commands. After the object is embedded, you can edit it. If the object comes from another file, only the embedded object in your database is changed when you modify it. *See also* link.

expression   A formula that calculates a value. You can use expressions in forms, reports, tables, queries, macros, and modules. For example, in queries you use expressions (such as >100) in criteria to specify which records Microsoft Access should retrieve.

Expression Builder   A tool that can help you create an expression. It is available wherever you want to enter the expression (for example, in many property boxes or in the Field or Criteria rows of a query). The Expression Builder contains a list of common expressions from which you can select.

external table   A table outside the open Microsoft Access database.

field   A category of information, such as Last Name or Address. On a form, a field is an area where you can enter data. A field is represented as a column in a datasheet.

field list   A small window that lists all the fields in the underlying table or query. You use field lists in the Design view of a form, report, or query, and in the Relationships window.

field selector   A small box or bar at the top of a datasheet column that you can click to select an entire column.

filter   A set of criteria you apply to records to show a subset of the records or to sort the records.

floating palette   A palette that can be dragged away from its toolbar. *See also* palette.

foreign key   A field (or fields) in a related table that contains the values that match the values in the primary key field in the primary table.

form   A Microsoft Access database object on which you place controls for entering, displaying, and editing data in fields.

Form view   Typically, a view that displays the data one record at a time in fields on a form. Form view is convenient for entering and modifying information in a database.

Form Wizard   A tool that helps you create a variety of forms by asking you questions and then creating a form based on your answers.

function   A routine that performs a specialized calculation. For example, you can use the Avg function to find the average of values in a field.

group   A collection of similar records in a report.

group footer   Text and/or graphics that appear at the bottom of a group in a report. For example, a group footer can display the total sales for the group.

group header   Text and/or graphics that appear at the top of a group in a report. A group header typically displays the group name.

image control   A control that is not connected to a field or an expression. You can use an image control to display graphics and pictures from other programs. An image control is similar to, but faster than, an unbound object frame.

import   A process by which Microsoft Access copies data from another source into your database.

input mask   A control property that determines display format, controls what values may be entered, and makes data entry faster (for example, a phone number input mask formats a phone number with parentheses and hyphens, but you type only the numbers).

insertion point   A blinking vertical line that shows where typed characters will be inserted.

join   An association between a field in one table and a field with the same data type in another table. *See also* relationship between tables.

join line   A line between fields displayed in field lists in the Relationships window or the Query window that indicates the matching fields in the underlying tables.

junction table   A table that provides a link between two tables that have a many-to-many relationship so that a relationship is created between the two tables.

label   A control that displays text that you use as a title for a form or report or to identify fields on a form or report.

Label Wizard   A tool that automatically creates mailing labels based on your answers to a set of questions.

link   A connection between a source file and a destination file. A link inserts a copy of an object from the source file into the destination file while maintaining the connection between the two. When you make changes to a linked object, the changes are saved in the object's source file, not in your database file. *See also* embed.

linked table   A table stored in a file outside the open database but from which Microsoft Access can access records. You can add, edit, and delete records in a linked table, but you can't modify the structure of the table.

list box   A control that displays a list of values from which you can select.

many-to-many relationship   A relationship between two tables in which one record in either table can have many matching records in the other table. *See also* one-to-many relationship *and* one-to-one relationship.

navigation buttons   The five arrows in the lower-left corner in Datasheet view, Form view, and Print Preview. Use these buttons to move to the first record (or page), the previous record (or page), the next record (or page), the last record (or page), or a new record.

null field   A field containing no characters or values (an empty field).

object frame   A control used to add, edit, or view OLE objects. There are two types of object frames: bound object frames and unbound object frames. *See also* bound object frame *and* unbound object frame.

OLE   A protocol by which an object, such as a graph, in a source program or document can be linked to or embedded in a destination document, such as a form or a report.

OLE object   Any piece of information created within a program for Windows that supports OLE. OLE objects include pictures, graphs, and sounds.

one-to-many relationship   A relationship between tables in which one record in the primary table can have many matching records in the related table. *See also* many-to-many relationship *and* one-to-one relationship."

one-to-one relationship   A relationship between tables in which one record in the primary table can have only one matching record in the related table. *See also* many-to-many relationship *and* one-to-many relationship.

operator   A symbol or word, such as ">" or "And," that indicates an action to be performed on one or more elements of an expression. For example, the arithmetic operators +, -, *, and / indicate addition, subtraction, multiplication, and division, respectively.

option button   A control that you can click to choose a value from an underlying table. An option button allows a Yes/No choice and is mutually exclusive when grouped with other option buttons. Option buttons are sometimes referred to as radio buttons.

option group   A control that groups a set of option buttons so that they will work together to provide related, but mutually exclusive, choices.

page footer   Text and/or graphics that appear at the bottom of every page of a report. A page footer typically displays the page number.

page header   Text and/or graphics that appear at the top of every page of a report. A page header typically displays a heading for each column of data.

palette   A dialog box containing choices for color and other special effects that you use when designing a form or report. A palette appears when you click a toolbar button, such as Border Color. *See also* floating palette.

parameter query   A query that asks you to enter one or more parameters—or criteria—when you run the query. For example, a parameter query might ask you to enter beginning and ending dates or a city name.

primary key   One or more fields whose value or values uniquely identify each record in a table.

Print Preview   A view that shows you how your form or report will look when it is printed.

property   An attribute of a control, field, table, query, form, or report that you can set to define one of the object's characteristics (such as size, color, or position) or an aspect of its behavior (such as whether it is hidden).

property sheet   A window in which you can view and modify the full set of properties for the selected object.

QBE (query by example)   A technique for designing queries. With graphical QBE, which Microsoft Access uses, you create queries visually by dragging the fields you want to include in the query from the upper portion of the Query window to the QBE grid in the lower portion of the window.

query   A Microsoft Access database object that represents the group of records you want to work with. You can think of a query as a request for a particular collection of data. *See also* Select Query.

Query Wizard   A tool that asks you questions and then creates a query based on your answers.

record   A set of information that belongs together, such as all the information on one job program or one magazine subscription card.

record selector   A small box or bar on the left side of a table, query, or form, in Datasheet view or in Form view that you can click to select an entire record.

relational database   A database in which information is stored in tables, allowing efficient and nonredundant data storage and retrieval.

relationship between tables   The association between data in two tables that have fields with matching values. When tables are related, a new query or form can be created using data from both tables. *See also* join.

report   A Microsoft Access database object that presents data formatted and organized according to your specifications.

report footer   Text and/or graphics that appear once at the end of a report and typically contain summaries, such as grand totals.

report header   Text and/or graphics that appear once at the beginning of a report and typically contain the report title, date, and company logo.

Report Wizard   A tool that helps you create a report by asking you questions and then creating different types of reports based on your answers.

row selector   A small box or bar that you can click to select an entire row in a table's Design view.

Select Query   A query that asks a question about the data stored in your tables and returns a dynaset in the form of a datasheet, without changing the data.

shortcut key   A function key (such as F5) or a key combination (such as CTRL+C) that you can press to carry out a menu command.

Shortcut menu   A menu of commands that is displayed when you click the right mouse button while your mouse pointer is on a toolbar, property sheet, control, or other object. The menu of commands depends on the object you click.

sort order   The order in which records are displayed—either ascending (A–Z and 0–9) or descending (Z–A and 9–0).

status bar   A horizontal bar at the bottom of the screen that displays information about commands, toolbar buttons, and other options.

subform   A form contained within another form.

table   A collection of data with the same subject or topic. A table stores data in records (rows) and fields (columns).

Table Wizard   A tool that helps you create a table by asking you questions and then creating a table based on your answers.

tab order   The order in which fields are selected when you press the TAB key to move from field to field in Form view.

text box   A control that displays data from a field. A text box can display text, numbers, or dates, and you can use it to type in new data, or change existing data.

toolbar   A bar at the edge of the Microsoft Access window containing a set of buttons that you can click to carry out common menu commands. The buttons displayed on the toolbar change depending on which window or view is currently selected.

toolbox   A box containing the set of tools you use in Design view to place controls on a form or a report.

unbound control   A control that is not connected to a field or expression. You can use an unbound control to display informational text, such as instructions about using your form, or graphics and pictures from other programs. *See also* bound control.

unbound object frame   A frame that displays an object that's part of the design of the form or report, such as a company logo. *See also* image control.

underlying table or query   The table or query that contains the data you want to display in a form, report, or query.

validation   The process of checking whether entered data meets certain conditions or limitations.

validation rule   A rule that sets limits or conditions on what can be entered in a particular field.

value   An individual piece of data, such as a last name, an address, or an ID number.

wildcard character   You can use wildcard characters, such as the asterisk (*) and the question mark (?), in searches using the Find and Replace commands. Wildcard characters can also be used in query criteria and other expressions to include all records or other items that begin with specific characters or match a certain pattern.

wizards   Microsoft Access tools that help you create a form, report, query, table, or database by asking you questions and then creating the object based on your answers.

Zoom window   An expanded text box that you can use to enter expressions or text instead of using the small input area in a property sheet or in the QBE grid. You open the Zoom window by pressing SHIFT+F2.

Index

Index

Index

detail section, 173, 237, 238, 248, 276
dialog boxes, xxxi–xxxii
dimmed menu commands, xxviii, xxix
display format, defined, 83, 277
Ditto key, 29, 30
division operator (/), 268
dollar sign ($), 268
double-clicking, xxvi
drag and drop, xxvi, 277
drawings. *See* pictures
dynasets, 126, 277

E

Edit menu, overview, xxviii–xxix
ellipsis (...), xxxi
embedding
 defined, 192, 277
 pictures in forms, 193–95
Enter Parameter Value dialog box, 150, 152
equal sign (=) in expressions, 207, 253, 270
equal-to operator (=), 268
error messages, 219, 220
Excel. *See* Microsoft Excel
exclamation point (!), 268
exporting data, 100–101
Expression Builder, 269, 277
expressions
 binding controls to, 208–9
 calculated control examples, 269–70
 in calculated fields, 141, 272
 creating with Expression Builder, 269
 criteria examples, 271–72
 defined, 129, 277
 entering, 53, 129, 130, 141, 208, 253, 268
 in filters, 53, 56, 271–72
 in forms, 269–71
 in group footers, 252–53
 in group headers, 257–58
 list of, 270
 overview, 267–68
 in queries, 129, 130, 134, 141, 271–72
 quotation marks in, 208, 253, 268
 in reports, 251, 252–53, 269–71
 square brackets in, 141, 208, 253, 268
 validation rule examples, 271

external tables
 defined, 277
 importing, 96–97
 linking to, 92–94

F

field lists, 178, 216, 277
field properties
 changing, 97–98, 142
 in linked tables, 94–95
 overview, 85
 Required, 221
 setting, 87–88
 Validation Rule, 219, 220
 Validation Text, 219, 220
fields
 adding to forms, 177–80
 adding to queries, 127, 129, 133, 137, 143, 157
 binding controls to, 177–80, 195–96
 calculated, 140–42, 272, 275
 changing properties, 97–98, 142
 check box, 86, 180–81
 combo box, 26–27, 214–17
 data types, 81, 83, 84, 86, 88
 defined, xli, 7, 277
 deleting from queries, 137, 143
 entering data, 8
 hiding duplicate values, 241–42
 in junction tables, 114–15
 list box, 26, 212, 213
 lookup, 105–7
 matching, 108, 111, 114
 moving on tables, 107
 naming, 83–85
 number, 83
 overview, 78
 renaming in queries, 139–40
 requiring data entry, 220–22
 showing/hiding in queries, 131–32
 text, 83
 validating data, 37–38
field selector, 20, 277
Field Size property, 87, 88
file formats, 92, 96
files. *See also* databases
 importing, 92, 96–97
 importing vs. linking, 92, 96

286

Index

Index

Running Microsoft® Access for Windows® 95

"This easy-to-read book includes extensive diagrams, undocumented tips, and solutions geared to making a more efficient database. Detailed examples on building functions and macros are also included. Each chapter is so well structured that a reader can easily find out how to execute a particular function."

PC Magazine

Here is the book that will appeal to the greatest number of Microsoft Access users-a complete and thorough tutorial on this full-featured relational database management system. This book runs users through the ins and outs of data access; relational database design; techniques for building queries, forms, and reports; and strategies for developing powerful macro-driven applications. A perfect book for ambitious beginning to experienced users of Microsoft Access who want a thorough understanding of and reference to this powerful product. Includes disk with sample database.

ISBN 1-55615-886-6
900 pages
$39.95 ($53.95 Canada)

Microsoft Press® books are available wherever quality books are sold and through CompuServe's Electronic Mall—**GO MSP**.
Call **1-800-MSPRESS** for more information or to place a credit card order.* Please refer to **BBK** when placing your order. Prices subject to change.
*In Canada, contact Macmillan Canada, Attn: Microsoft Press Dept., 164 Commander Blvd., Agincourt, Ontario, Canada M1S 3C7, or call 1-800-667-1115.
Outside the U.S. and Canada, write to International Coordinator, Microsoft Press, One Microsoft Way, Redmond, WA 98052-6399, or fax +1-206-936-7329.

Microsoft Press

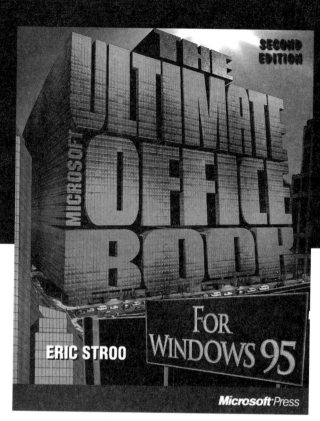

SECOND EDITION

THE ULTIMATE OFFICE BOOK

MICROSOFT

ERIC STROO

FOR WINDOWS 95

Microsoft Press

This is one book
that you'll want
to keep close to
your computer!

ISBN 1-55615-894-7
336 pages
$24.95 ($33.95 Canada)

This colorful,
interesting, fact-
filled guide shows
intermediate users
how to use Office
applications together
to realize the full power and versatility they offer.
With an emphasis on "document-centric" computing,
it focuses on the interoperability, integration, and
consistency of the applications in Microsoft® Office
for Windows® 95. Users will learn how to share data
through linking and embedding objects and how to
choose the right tools from any application to complete
a task intelligently. An updated and revised Question
and Answer section, taken from Microsoft Product
Support's most-asked questions, is included.

Microsoft Press® books are available wherever quality books are sold and through CompuServe's Electronic Mall—**GO MSP**.
Call **1-800-MSPRESS** for more information or to place a credit card order.* Please refer to **BBK** when placing your order. Prices subject to change.
*In Canada, contact Macmillan Canada, Attn: Microsoft Press Dept., 164 Commander Blvd., Agincourt, Ontario, Canada M1S 3C7, or call 1-800-667-1115.
Outside the U.S. and Canada, write to International Coordinator, Microsoft Press, One Microsoft Way, Redmond, WA 98052-6399, or fax +1-206-936-7329.

Microsoft Press

WHO KNOWS MORE
ABOUT WINDOWS® 95
THAN
MICROSOFT PRESS?

ISBN 1-55615-816-5
224 pages
$19.95 ($26.95 Canada)

ISBN 1-55615-683-9
320 pages
$29.95 ($39.95 Canada)

These books are essential if you are a newcomer to Microsoft® Windows® or an upgrader wanting to capitalize on your knowledge of Windows 3.1. Both are written in a straightforward, no-nonsense way, with well-illustrated step-by-step examples, and both include practice files on disk. Learn to use Microsoft's newest operating system quickly and easily with MICROSOFT WINDOWS 95 STEP BY STEP and UPGRADING TO MICROSOFT WINDOWS 95 STEP BY STEP, both from Microsoft Press.

Microsoft Press® books are available wherever quality books are sold and through CompuServe's Electronic Mall—GO MSP.
Call **1-800-MSPRESS** for more information or to place a credit card order.* Please refer to **BBK** when placing your order. Prices subject to change.

*In Canada, contact Macmillan Canada, Attn: Microsoft Press Dept., 164 Commander Blvd., Agincourt, Ontario, Canada M1S 3C7, or call 1-800-667-1115.
Outside the U.S. and Canada, write to International Coordinator, Microsoft Press, One Microsoft Way, Redmond, WA 98052-6399, or fax +1-206-936-7329.

IT'S A JUNGLE OUT THERE!

FIELD GUIDE TO
MICROSOFT®
ACCESS
FOR WINDOWS® 95

QUICK, EASY ANSWERS

STEPHEN L. NELSON

ISBN 1-55615-875-0

FIELD GUIDE TO
MICROSOFT®
EXCEL
FOR WINDOWS® 95

QUICK, EASY ANSWERS

STEPHEN L. NELSON

ISBN 1-55615-839-4

FIELD GUIDE TO
THE INTERNET
WITH WINDOWS® 95

QUICK, EASY ANSWERS

STEPHEN L. NELSON

ISBN 1-55615-822-X

FIELD GUIDE TO
MICROSOFT®
WORD
FOR WINDOWS® 95

QUICK, EASY ANSWERS

STEPHEN L. NELSON

ISBN 1-55615-832-7

FIELD GUIDE TO
MICROSOFT®
POWERPOINT
FOR WINDOWS® 95

QUICK, EASY ANSWERS

STEPHEN L. NELSON

ISBN 1-55615-841-6

ALL FIELD GUIDE TITLES
ONLY $9.95 EACH!
($12.95 CANADA)

Field Guides are perfect for
new users, for experienced
users who want quick
answers to their questions,
and for users of laptop
computers (who already have
enough weight to lug around).
They're small, task-oriented,
illustrated books organized in easy-to-
remember sections, with rich cross-referencing
for quick lookup. Simply put, they're great
books at a great price!

IMPORTANT — READ CAREFULLY BEFORE OPENING SOFTWARE PACKET(S).
By opening the sealed packet(s) containing the software, you indicate your acceptance
of the following Microsoft License Agreement.

Microsoft License Agreement

MICROSOFT LICENSE AGREEMENT
(Single User Products)

This is a legal agreement between you (either an individual or an entity) and Microsoft Corporation. By opening the sealed software packet(s) you are agreeing to be bound by the terms of this agreement. If you do not agree to the terms of this agreement, promptly return the book, including the unopened software packet(s), to the place you obtained it for a full refund.

MICROSOFT SOFTWARE LICENSE

1. GRANT OF LICENSE. Microsoft grants to you the right to use one copy of the Microsoft software program included with this book (the "SOFTWARE") on a single terminal connected to a single computer. The SOFTWARE is in "use" on a computer when it is loaded into temporary memory (i.e., RAM) or installed into permanent memory (e.g., hard disk, CD-ROM, or other storage device) of that computer. You may not network the SOFTWARE or otherwise use it on more than one computer or computer terminal at the same time.

2. COPYRIGHT. The SOFTWARE is owned by Microsoft or its suppliers and is protected by United States copyright laws and international treaty provisions. Therefore, you must treat the SOFTWARE like any other copyrighted material (e.g., a book or musical recording) except that you may either (a) make one copy of the SOFTWARE solely for backup or archival purposes, or (b) transfer the SOFTWARE to a single hard disk provided you keep the original solely for backup or archival purposes. You may not copy the written materials accompanying the SOFTWARE.

3. OTHER RESTRICTIONS. You may not rent or lease the SOFTWARE, but you may transfer the SOFTWARE and accompanying written materials on a permanent basis provided you retain no copies and the recipient agrees to the terms of this Agreement. You may not reverse engineer, decompile, or disassemble the SOFTWARE. If the SOFTWARE is an update or has been updated, any transfer must include the most recent update and all prior versions.

4. DUAL MEDIA SOFTWARE. If the SOFTWARE package contains both 3.5" and 5.25" disks, then you may use only the disks appropriate for your single-user computer. You may not use the other disks on another computer or loan, rent, lease, or transfer them to another user except as part of the permanent transfer (as provided above) of all SOFTWARE and written materials.

5. LANGUAGE SOFTWARE. If the SOFTWARE is a Microsoft language product, then you have a royalty-free right to reproduce and distribute executable files created using the SOFTWARE. If the language product is a Basic or COBOL product, then Microsoft grants you a royalty-free right to reproduce and distribute the run-time modules of the SOFTWARE provided that you: (a) distribute the run-time modules only in conjunction with and as a part of your software product; (b) do not use Microsoft's name, logo, or trademarks to market your software product; (c) include a valid copyright notice on your software product; and (d) agree to indemnify, hold harmless, and defend Microsoft and its suppliers from and against any claims or lawsuits, including attorneys' fees, that arise or result from the use or distribution of your software product. The "run-time modules" are those files in the SOFTWARE that are identified in the accompanying written materials as required during execution of your software program. The run-time modules are limited to run-time files, install files, and ISAM and REBUILD files. If required in the SOFTWARE documentation, you agree to display the designated patent notices on the packaging and in the README file of your software product.

LIMITED WARRANTY

LIMITED WARRANTY. Microsoft warrants that (a) the SOFTWARE will perform substantially in accordance with the accompanying written materials for a period of ninety (90) days from the date of receipt, and (b) any hardware accompanying the SOFTWARE will be free from defects in materials and workmanship under normal use and service for a period of one (1) year from the date of receipt. Any implied warranties on the SOFTWARE and hardware are limited to ninety (90) days and one (1) year, respectively. Some states/countries do not allow limitations on duration of an implied warranty, so the above limitation may not apply to you.

CUSTOMER REMEDIES. Microsoft's and its suppliers' entire liability and your exclusive remedy shall be, at Microsoft's option, either (a) return of the price paid, or (b) repair or replacement of the SOFTWARE or hardware that does not meet Microsoft's Limited Warranty and which is returned to Microsoft with a copy of your receipt. This Limited Warranty is void if failure of the SOFTWARE or hardware has resulted from accident, abuse, or misapplication. Any replacement SOFTWARE or hardware will be warranted for the remainder of the original warranty period or thirty (30) days, whichever is longer. Outside the United States, these remedies are not available without proof of purchase from an authorized non-U.S. source.

NO OTHER WARRANTIES. Microsoft and its suppliers disclaim all other warranties, either express or implied, including, but not limited to implied warranties of merchantability and fitness for a particular purpose, with regard to the SOFTWARE, the accompanying written materials, and any accompanying hardware. This limited warranty gives you specific legal rights. You may have others which vary from state/country to state/country.

NO LIABILITY FOR CONSEQUENTIAL DAMAGES. In no event shall Microsoft or its suppliers be liable for any damages whatsoever (including without limitation, damages for loss of business profits, business interruption, loss of business information, or any other pecuniary loss) arising out of the use of or inability to use this Microsoft product, even if Microsoft has been advised of the possibility of such damages. Because some states/countries do not allow the exclusion or limitation of liability for consequential or incidental damages, the above limitation may not apply to you.

U.S. GOVERNMENT RESTRICTED RIGHTS

The SOFTWARE and documentation are provided with RESTRICTED RIGHTS. Use, duplication, or disclosure by the Government is subject to restrictions as set forth in subparagraph (c)(1)(ii) of The Rights in Technical Data and Computer Software clause at DFARS 252.227-7013 or subparagraphs (c)(1) and (2) of the Commercial Computer Software — Restricted Rights 48 CFR 52.227-19, as applicable. Manufacturer is Microsoft Corporation, One Microsoft Way, Redmond, WA 98052-6399.

This Agreement is governed by the laws of the State of Washington.

Should you have any questions concerning this Agreement, or if you desire to contact Microsoft for any reason, please write: Microsoft Sales and Service, One Microsoft Way, Redmond, WA 98052-6399.

CORPORATE ORDERS

If you're placing a large-volume corporate order for additional copies of this *Step by Step* title, or for any other Microsoft Press book, you may be eligible for our corporate discount.

Call **1-800-888-3303, ext. 62669,** for details.

The
Step by Step
Practice Files Disk

The enclosed 3.5-inch disk contains timesaving, ready-to-use practice files that complement the lessons in this book. To use the practice files, you'll need the Windows 95 operating system.

Each *Step by Step* lesson uses practice files from the disk. Before you begin the *Step by Step* lessons, read the "Getting Ready" section of the book for easy instructions telling how to install the files on your computer's hard disk. As you work through each lesson, be sure to follow the instructions for renaming the practice files so that you can go through a lesson more than once if you need to.

Please take a few moments to read the License Agreement on the previous page before using the enclosed disk.